The
GOURMAN REPORT

A Rating of Graduate and Professional Programs in American and International Universities

SIXTH EDITION
Revised

Dr. Jack Gourman

 National Education Standards

Editorial inquiries concerning this book should be addressed to:
Editor
National Education Standards
One Wilshire Building
Suite 1210
624 South Grand Avenue
Los Angeles, California 90017

International Standard Serial Number (ISSN) 1049-717X

ISBN: 0-918192-15-3

Printed in the United States of America

PREFACE to the sixth edition

As with previous editions, THE GOURMAN REPORT: A RATING OF GRADUATE AND PROFESSIONAL PROGRAMS addresses the need for a qualitative evaluation of higher-level education in the United States, Canada, and International universities. We have tried to organize the data so educators, administrators, corporations, students and others can quickly and efficiently locate the material of interest to them. To this end, several new fields have been added. These new programs reflect the importance of the respective disciplines to our nation's economic and technical development. Excluded from the sixth edition are the Soviet universities because of internal affairs and political instability.

As always, the greatest and most important change is in the ratings themselves. I regret that, in all too many cases, readers will turn to the ranking for their own programs and discover a lower score than in the last book. Let me be blunt: higher education is in ill health today. Years of fiscal malnutrition have taken their toll. Public indifference, irresponsible statements and actions from elected officials and others in a position of authority, and growing cynicism on the part of faculty and administrators combine to compound the symptoms. And, while the "patient" is the institution, those most aggrieved are the students themselves. Perhaps naively, young men and women still look to higher education for the knowledge and understanding they will need in later life. At many of today's schools, their chances of finding what they seek are not good.

Even among established schools, many institutions again scored poorly based on one or more of the following shortcomings:

1. Objectives of the program are ill-defined and misunderstood.

2. The present program is not constituted to meet the needs and problems of students and faculty.

3. Institutional reports are not evaluated and beneficial changes are not recommended.

4. Administrators are reluctant to reveal the weakness of programs.

5. The public relations of the institution provides a false image to cover up deficiencies in programs.

6. Requisite improvements are not made in the quality of administrators, faculty instruction, curriculum, library resources and the physical plant.

7. Graduate training is offered by institutions with inferior undergraduate programs.

8. Students suffer from poor counseling.

9. Funds designation for the improvement of faculty, curriculum, library resources and physical areas are misused.

10. Teacher education programs and training are below average.[1]

11. Graduate schools of education below average.[2]

12. Criminal Justice/Criminology Correction programs are inadequate.[3]

13. Special interest pressure is exerted by administrators, to the detriment of the educators and teaching experience.

14. Student grants and scholarships are inadequate or nonexistent.

15. Faculty salaries are inadequate.

16. Funds for faculty research are inadequate.

17. Computer facility not sufficient to support current research activities for both faculty and students.

18. Insufficient funding for research equipment and infrastructure.

19. Number of teaching and research assistantships inadequate.

20. Major research laboratories inadequate.

I am grateful to many people for their contributions to this text. Paul Gregory Gourman designed the entire evaluation project, on both the state and national level, for the MBA/management school ratings. His energy and meticulous attention to detail was exceptional and greatly appreciated. In particular, I wish to thank Deborah Ann Gourman for her technical assistance. Thanks to my wife Blanka, for her never-ending support since the very first edition of THE GOURMAN REPORT. She read several drafts with great care; and commented on various sections of the manuscript. No set of acknowledgments, however, would be complete without a very special mention of Garen Ohanes Anserlian, a Political Science student of mine at California State University, Northridge for his unfailing energy in assisting me with this report.

Finally, I must express my obligation and appreciation to those college and university faculty members, presidents, administrators and trustees/regents without whom our survey would be impossible. While I cannot recognize these individuals by name, I know all readers of my book will join me in thanking them for their anonymous, and therefore selfless, contribution to the cause of quality in higher education.

Jack Gourman
Northridge, California
January, 1993

---

[1] Credential Note:
A student with a baccalaureate degree or higher (and approved by THE GOURMAN REPORT) with a 3.5 grade point average in the major (excluding education majors) and an overall 3.3 grade point average are eligible for a teaching credential.
In addition, the candidate must submit two letters from faculty who can assess their professional potential.
Prospective candidates would apply directly to the state board of education for a teaching credential.
We strongly recommend credential programs be *discontinued* by the educational institution.

[2] The Graduate Schools of Education are not approved by THE GOURMAN REPORT and should be *discontinued* by the educational institution.

[3] Criminal Justice/Criminology and Correction programs are not approved by THE GOURMAN REPORT and should be *discontinued* by the educational institution.

Preface
Introduction
Table of Contents

The Disciplines – A Rating of Graduate and Professional Programs

Part I

GRADUATE PROGRAMS

Table of Contents

Table of Contents

Table of Contents

Table of Contents

Introduction to the sixth edition

THE GOURMAN REPORT is the only qualitative guide to American and International institutions of higher education which assigns a precise, numerical score in assessing the strengths and shortcomings of each school and program. This methodology vastly simplifies the reader's task in examining the effectiveness of a given educational program, or comparing one program against another; and yet the Gourman rating takes into account a wide variety of empirical data, as detailed below.

This text is intended for use by:

—Individuals wishing to make an informed choice about higher education.

—Educators and administrators desirous of an independent evaluation of their program.

—Prospective employers who want to avoid retraining of inadequately prepared graduates from ineffective institutions.

—Schools wishing to improve graduate and professional programs.

—Foundations involved in fund-giving to colleges and universities.

—Licensing authorities in need of objective educational assessments.

—Individuals interested in identifying, and eliminating, fraudulent and inferior institutions.

—Citizens concerned about the quality of today's higher education.

If each institution did its utmost to insure a superior educational experience, and then frankly informed the public of any unavoidable compromises caused by funding, geography or educational focus, then there might be no need for a book such as this one. However, the facts remain that:

—Institutional policy often dictates decisions about faculty, curriculum and physical plant for reasons which have little to do with education.

—Faculty members and administrators are intimidated, by internal and external political pressures from making critical comments about their own institutions.

—Public relations efforts by institutions tend to exaggerate strong areas, and ignore weak ones.

—Frankly fraudulent institutions exist as profit centers, rather than as promulgators of quality education.

—Accreditation appears to be mainly a finding that an institution is not conspicuously defective in physical and staff resources.

We must remember that the quality of graduate and professional education affects the future not only of individuals, but of the nation and its economy. If the following pages can make a contribution, no matter how minor, toward raising awareness of the need for better educational standards, then the purpose of THE GOURMAN REPORT is well served.

Method of Evaluation

In an age of disinformation, the user of this text should keep in mind that THE GOURMAN REPORT is not a "popularity contest", or an "opinion poll", but an objective evaluation which synthesizes complex data into a deceptively convenient numerical rating.

Obviously, much of the material used in compiling THE GOURMAN REPORT is internal – drawn from educators and administrators at the schools themselves. These individuals are permitted to evaluate *only* their own programs – as they know them from daily interface with the educational experience – and not the programs of other institutions. Unsolicited appraisals are occasionally considered (and weighed accordingly), but the bulk of our contributions are requested from persons chosen for their academic qualifications, their published works, and their interests in improving the quality of higher education. It attests to the dedication of these individuals (and also to the serious problems in higher education today) that over 90% of our requests for contributions are met with a positive response.

In addition, THE GOURMAN REPORT draws on many external resources which are a matter of record – e.g., funding for public universities as authorized by legislative bodies, required filings by schools to meet standards of nondiscrimination, and material provided by the institutions (and independently verified) about faculty makeup and experience, fields of study offered, and physical plant. Such resources, while public, are not always accessible to the individual researcher; and someone wishing to utilize this data for comparing a number of institutions and programs would face a daunting task.

Finally, THE GOURMAN REPORT is fortunate to have among its contributors a number of individuals, associations and agencies whose business it is to make correct projections of the success graduates from given institutions and disciplines will enjoy in the "real world". While the methods employed by these resources are proprietary, their findings have consistently been validated by experience, and they are an important part of our research.

To critics who might question the feasibility of an evaluation which draws from such diverse resources, we offer the comparison to the grading of a college essay examination. What may appear to be a subjective process is in fact a patient sifting of empirical data by analysts who understand both the "subject matter" (the fields of study under examination), and the "students" (the colleges and universities themselves). The fact that there are virtually no "tie" scores indicate the accuracy and effectiveness of this methodology, as does the consistent affirmation of the ratings in THE GOURMAN REPORT from readers in a position to independently evaluate the attributes of specific educational programs.

Criteria

The following criteria are taken into consideration in the evaluation of each educational program and institution. It should be noted that, because different disciplines vary in their educational methodology, the significance given each criterion will vary from the rating of one discipline to the next; however, our evaluation is consistent for all schools listed within each field of study.

1. Auspices, control and organization of the institution;

2. Total educational programs offered and degrees conferred (with additional attention to "subfields" available to students within a particular discipline);

3. Age (experience level) of the institution and of the individual discipline or program and division;

4. Faculty, including qualifications, experience, intellectual interests, attainments, and professional productivity (including research);

5. Students, including quality of scholastic work and records of graduates both in graduate study and in practice;

6. Basis of and requirements for admission of students (overall and by individual discipline);

7. Number of students enrolled (overall and for each discipline);

8. Curriculum and curricular content of the program or discipline and division;

9. Standards and quality of instruction (including teaching loads);

10. Quality of administration, including attitudes and policy toward teaching, research and scholarly production in each discipline, and administration research;

11. Quality and availability of non-departmental areas such as counseling and career placement services;

12. Quality of physical plant devoted to graduate, law, medicine and other professional levels;

13. Finances, including budgets, investments, expenditures and sources of income for both public and private institutions;

14. Library, including number of volumes, appropriateness of materials to individual disciplines, and accessibility of materials;

15. Computer facility sufficient to support current research activities for both faculty and students;

16. Sufficient funding for research equipment and infrastructure;

17. Number of teaching and research assistantships;

18. Major research laboratories.

A guide to using THE GOURMAN REPORT

Because the actual ratings within this text are presented without extraneous commentary the following observations should be helpful in guiding both the first-time reader and the experienced user of THE GOURMAN REPORT.

Part I contains ratings of leading institutions (those with scores between 4.0 and 5.0, in rank order) in 101 individual disciplines, from Aerospace Engineering to Zoology. Scores for institutions not scoring 4.0 or above in these disciplines may be found in Part XV.

Part II includes ratings of leading International Law Schools (those with scores between 4.0 and 5.0, in rank order): U.S. Law Schools from "very strong" (4.0 to 5.0) to "adequate" (2.3 to 2.9), with the additional listings for less qualified, but still acceptable, institutions included in consideration of the competitive admissions environment facing today's prospective law student: A ranking of Canadian Law Schools: and a cross-tabulation of leading institutions in the U.S. and abroad.

Part III rates leading Canadian, U.S. and International medical schools and Canadian and U.S. dental (those with scores between 4.0 and 5.0, in rank order), with additional ratings for U.S. schools down to "acceptable plus" (3.0 to 3.5) included for the student seeking admission to a qualified program in today's competitive environment.

Also in Part III, the reader will find a rating of leading graduate programs (4.0 to 5.0) in Veterinary Medicine; and a cross-tabulation of leading medical schools in the U.S. and abroad.

Part IV includes leading graduate programs in nursing (3.6 to 5.0) and optometry (4.0 to 5.0); leading Canadian pharmacy schools (4.0 to 5.0); leading U.S. pharmacy schools (3.6 to 5.0); and leading graduate programs in public health (scores between 4.0 and 5.0, in rank order).

Part V lists the U.S. institutions whose research libraries are distinguished by a rating between 4.0 and 5.0.

Part VI is a rating of 139 graduate schools of engineering on the Approved List of THE GOURMAN REPORT. Schools not listed here may be found under the appropriate engineering headings in Part I.

Part VII is a rating of EMBA/management schools on the Approved List of THE GOURMAN REPORT.

Part VIII is a rating of MBA/management schools on the Approved List of THE GOURMAN REPORT. Out of 500 institutions surveyed, only 100 schools meet the standards which were applied.

Part IX lists doctoral schools in business and management on the Approved List of THE GOURMAN REPORT. The two principal degree designations offered by these programs are the Ph.D. (Doctor of Philosophy) and the DBA (Doctor of Business Administration). Those schools cited met basic standards of curriculum, faculty qualifications, administration, admissions and facilities.

Part X is a rating of selective doctoral programs in business and management for 88 institutions on the Approved List of THE GOURMAN REPORT. Accounting (found in Part I of previous editions) is evaluated alongside finance, management/organizational behavior and marketing programs for each of the qualifying schools.

Part XI provides a rating of leading International universities, by administration, curriculum, faculty, libraries and overall quality.

Part XII, new for this sixth edition includes the section offering graduate work in *criminal justice* not on the approved list of THE GOURMAN REPORT. Criminal justice programs do not emphasize those areas of study that are consistent with the advancement and enhancement of our nation's social system.

Part XIII is an alphabetical listing of departments of teacher education not on the Approved List of THE GOURMAN REPORT. Teaching degrees bestowed by these schools may not be comparable to degrees in fields where faculty members are required to create new knowledge, preserve existing knowledge, or transmit knowledge to others.

Part XIV includes departments of graduate education not on the Approved List of THE GOURMAN REPORT because they do not meet the standard of graduate training with regard to administration, curriculum, faculty or library resources. These institutions offer advanced degrees in such fields as philosophy and history of education, learning and instruction, comparative and international education, higher education, educational administration, and curriculum. Such degrees should not be taken as equivalent to master's or doctorate degrees in disciplines such as engineering, geoscience, chemistry, romance languages, mathematics, physics, English, history, political science, etc.

Part XV lists the top fifty graduate schools in the United States, in rank order. These institutions have distinguished themselves by their commitment to a leadership position in quality education; it is only appropriate that their achievement be recognized in a separate section.

Part XVI rates all accredited graduate schools in the United States, listed alphabetically. This section is intended primarily for use by readers who desire information about a particular institution. By no means should a school's listing be taken as an endorsement or an indication of quality, as ratings vary from "very strong" (4.51 to 4.99) to "unacceptable" (below 2.01).

Part XVII – APPENDIXES contains tables of the number and types of programs evaluated for this sixth edition, as well as listings of the schools included for 13 selected professional fields.

The GOURMAN REPORT
PART I

GRADUATE PROGRAMS

Aerospace Engineering
African Studies
Agricultural Economics
Agricultural Engineering
Agricultural Sciences
Analytical Chemistry
Anthropology
Applied Mathematics
Applied Physics
Architecture
Art History
Asian Languages
Asian Studies
Astronomy
Biochemistry
Bioengineering/Biomedical Engineering
Botany
Cellular/Molecular Biology
Ceramic Sciences/Engineering
Chemical Engineering
Chemistry
City/Regional Planning
Civil Engineering
Classics
Clinical Psychology
Clothing and Textiles
Communication
Comparative Literature
Computer Science
Consumer Economics
Demography/Population Studies
Developmental Psychology
Drama/Theatre
East European/Soviet Studies
Economics
Electrical Engineering
English
Entomology
Environmental Design
Environmental Engineering
Environmental Policy/Resource Management
Experimental Psychology (General)
Forestry
French
Geochemistry
Geography
Geoscience
German
Graphic Design
History
Industrial Design

Industrial Engineering
Industrial Labor Relations
Industrial/Organizational Psychology
Information Sciences
Inorganic Chemistry
Italian
International Relations
Journalism
Landscape Architecture
Library Science
Linguistics
Mass Communication/Theory
Mass/Organizational Communication
Materials Science
Mathematics
Mechanical Engineering
Metallurgical Engineering
Metallurgy
Meteorology/Atmospheric Sciences
Microbiology
Music
Near/Middle Eastern Languages
Near/Middle Eastern Studies
Nuclear Engineering
Occupational Therapy
Operations Research
Organic Chemistry
Petroleum Engineering
Philosophy
Physical Chemistry
Physical Therapy
Physics
Physiology
Planetary Sciences
Plasma Physics
Political Science
Polymer Sciences/Plastics Engineering
Psychology
Psychology/Neuropsychology
Psychology/Neuroscience
Public Administration
Radio/TV/Film
Russian
Slavic Languages
Social Psychology
Social Welfare/Social Work
Sociology
Spanish
Statistics
Urban Design
Zoology

A RATING OF GRADUATE PROGRAMS IN AEROSPACE ENGINEERING
Leading Institutions

Thirty-two institutions with scores in the 4.0-5.0 range, in rank order

INSTITUTION	Rank	Score
M.I.T.	1	4.94
CAL TECH	2	4.93
MICHIGAN (Ann Arbor)	3	4.92
PRINCETON	4	4.91
STANFORD	5	4.89
CORNELL (N.Y.)	6	4.87
ILLINOIS (Urbana)	7	4.85
PURDUE (Lafayette)	8	4.81
GEORGIA TECH	9	4.78
CINCINNATI	10	4.77
IOWA STATE (Ames)	11	4.71
RENSSELAER (N.Y.)	12	4.68
TEXAS (Austin)	13	4.67
OHIO STATE (Columbus)	14	4.61
MARYLAND (College Park)	15	4.58
MINNESOTA (Minneapolis)	16	4.52
VIRGINIA (Charlottesville)	17	4.48
WASHINGTON (Seattle)	18	4.43
PENN STATE (University Park)	19	4.40
U.S.C. (Los Angeles)	20	4.36
ARIZONA (Tucson)	21	4.32
TEXAS A&M (College Station)	22	4.30
CASE WESTERN RESERVE	23	4.29
COLORADO (Boulder)	24	4.26
UCLA	25	4.23
POLYTECHNIC UNIVERSITY (Brooklyn, N.Y.)	26	4.21
KANSAS (Lawrence)	27	4.18
NOTRE DAME	28	4.17
SUNY (Buffalo)	29	4.16
NORTH CAROLINA STATE (Raleigh)	30	4.11
DELAWARE (Newark)	31	4.06
V.P.I. & STATE U.	32	4.05

A RATING OF GRADUATE PROGRAMS IN AFRICAN STUDIES
Leading Institutions

Six institutions with scores in the 4.0-5.0 range, in rank order

INSTITUTION	Rank	Score
JOHNS HOPKINS (D.C.)	1	4.87
WISCONSIN (Madison)	2	4.84
ILLINOIS (Urbana)	3	4.80
CORNELL (N.Y.)	4	4.76
YALE	5	4.72
HOWARD (D.C.)	6	4.69

A RATING OF GRADUATE PROGRAMS IN AGRICULTURAL ECONOMICS
Leading Institutions

Thirty-four institutions with scores in the 4.0-5.0 range, in rank order

INSTITUTION	Rank	Score
CORNELL (N.Y.)	1	4.93
MICHIGAN STATE	2	4.92
ILLINOIS (Urbana)	3	4.91
MINNESOTA (Minneapolis)	4	4.88
CALIFORNIA, DAVIS	5	4.87
PURDUE (Lafayette)	6	4.85
WISCONSIN (Madison)	7	4.70
CALIFORNIA, BERKELEY	8	4.64
STANFORD	9	4.63
PENN STATE (University Park)	10	4.58
IOWA STATE (Ames)	11	4.47
FLORIDA (Gainesville)	12	4.38
OREGON STATE	13	4.36
MISSOURI (Columbia)	14	4.32
OHIO STATE (Columbus)	15	4.28
TEXAS A&M (College Station)	16	4.26
CONNECTICUT (Storrs)	17	4.22
MARYLAND (College Park)	18	4.20
KANSAS STATE	19	4.17
MASSACHUSETTS (Amherst)	20	4.16
WASHINGTON STATE	21	4.15
NEBRASKA (Lincoln)	22	4.14
KENTUCKY	23	4.13
V.P.I. & STATE U.	24	4.12
NORTH CAROLINA STATE (Raleigh)	25	4.11
AUBURN (Auburn)	26	4.10
LSU (Baton Rouge)	27	4.09
COLORADO STATE	28	4.08
GEORGIA (Athens)	29	4.07
OKLAHOMA STATE	30	4.06
MISSISSIPPI STATE	31	4.04
TENNESSEE (Knoxville)	32	4.03
TEXAS TECH	33	4.02
HAWAII (Manoa)	34	4.01

A RATING OF GRADUATE PROGRAMS IN AGRICULTURAL ENGINEERING
Leading Institutions

Thirty-three institutions with scores in the 4.0-5.0 range, in rank order

INSTITUTION	Rank	Score
CORNELL (N.Y.)	1	4.93
MICHIGAN STATE	2	4.92
IOWA STATE (Ames)	3	4.91
ILLINOIS (Urbana)	4	4.90
PURDUE (Lafayette)	5	4.89
MINNESOTA (Minneapolis)	6	4.86
OHIO STATE (Columbus)	7	4.85
TEXAS A&M (College Station)	8	4.84
PENN STATE (University Park)	9	4.80
WISCONSIN (Madison)	10	4.73
CALIFORNIA, DAVIS	11	4.71
MARYLAND (College Park)	12	4.69
MISSOURI (Columbia)	13	4.64
KANSAS STATE	14	4.58
NORTH CAROLINA STATE (Raleigh)	15	4.55
TENNESSEE (Knoxville)	16	4.50
WASHINGTON STATE	17	4.41
FLORIDA (Gainesville)	18	4.36
COLORADO STATE	19	4.35
CLEMSON	20	4.31
V.P.I. & STATE U.	21	4.27
NEBRASKA (Lincoln)	22	4.23
OKLAHOMA STATE	23	4.22
OREGON STATE	24	4.18
KENTUCKY	25	4.16
WYOMING	26	4.13
UTAH STATE	27	4.11
LSU (Baton Rouge)	28	4.10
AUBURN (Auburn)	29	4.08
TEXAS TECH	30	4.06
IDAHO (Moscow)	31	4.04
NORTH DAKOTA STATE	32	4.03
MAINE (Orono)	33	4.02

A RATING OF GRADUATE PROGRAMS IN AGRICULTURAL SCIENCES
Leading Institutions

Thirty-two institutions with scores in the 4.0-5.0 range, in rank order

INSTITUTION	Rank	Score
CORNELL (N.Y.)	1	4.92
TEXAS A&M (College Station)	2	4.90
ILLINOIS (Urbana)	3	4.88
PURDUE (Lafayette)	4	4.86
IOWA STATE (Ames)	5	4.84
MICHIGAN STATE	6	4.80
CALIFORNIA, DAVIS	7	4.76
WISCONSIN (Madison)	8	4.73
MINNESOTA (Minneapolis)	9	4.70
OHIO STATE (Columbus)	10	4.66
KANSAS STATE	11	4.63
MISSOURI (Columbia)	12	4.61
PENN STATE (University Park)	13	4.58
LSU (Baton Rouge)	14	4.56
MASSACHUSETTS (Amherst)	15	4.52
MARYLAND (College Park)	16	4.51
NORTH CAROLINA STATE (Raleigh)	17	4.48
NEBRASKA (Lincoln)	18	4.44
GEORGIA (Athens)	19	4.41
OREGON STATE	20	4.38
TENNESSEE (Knoxville)	21	4.36
COLORADO STATE	22	4.34
OKLAHOMA STATE	23	4.32
UTAH STATE	24	4.28
ARIZONA (Tucson)	25	4.23
CONNECTICUT (Storrs)	26	4.21
FLORIDA (Gainesville)	27	4.18
AUBURN (Auburn)	28	4.16
CLEMSON	29	4.15
TEXAS TECH	30	4.13
WASHINGTON STATE	31	4.10
MAINE (Orono)	32	4.08

A RATING OF GRADUATE PROGRAMS IN ANALYTICAL CHEMISTRY
Leading Institutions

Ten institutions with scores in the 4.0-5.0 range, in rank order

INSTITUTION	Rank	Score
MINNESOTA (Minneapolis)	1	4.90
OHIO STATE (Columbus)	2	4.87
PURDUE (Lafayette)	3	4.83
MICHIGAN (Ann Arbor)	4	4.79
MARYLAND (College Park)	5	4.74
RUTGERS (New Brunswick)	6	4.70
TEXAS A&M (College Station)	7	4.68
PITTSBURGH (Pittsburgh)	8	4.67
FLORIDA (Gainesville)	9	4.65
MISSOURI (Columbia)	10	4.61

A RATING OF GRADUATE PROGRAMS IN ANTHROPOLOGY
Leading Institutions

Forty-seven institutions with scores in the 4.0-5.0 range, in rank order

INSTITUTION	Rank	Score
MICHIGAN (Ann Arbor)	1	4.94
CALIFORNIA, BERKELEY	2	4.93
CHICAGO	3	4.92
PENNSYLVANIA	4	4.91
ARIZONA (Tucson)	5	4.90
STANFORD	6	4.89
YALE	7	4.86
UCLA	8	4.85
HARVARD	9	4.83
NORTHWESTERN (Illinois)	10	4.81
NEW MEXICO	11	4.80
TEXAS (Austin)	12	4.79
CORNELL (N.Y.)	13	4.77
ILLINOIS (Urbana)	14	4.74
CALIFORNIA, SANTA BARBARA	15	4.73
COLUMBIA (N.Y.)	16	4.72
CUNY (Graduate School)	17	4.70
CALIFORNIA, SAN DIEGO	18	4.69
WASHINGTON (Seattle)	19	4.65
FLORIDA (Gainesville)	20	4.64
WISCONSIN (Madison)	21	4.63
PENN STATE (University Park)	22	4.61
MASSACHUSETTS (Amherst)	23	4.56
DUKE	24	4.54
PITTSBURGH (Pittsburgh)	25	4.51
RUTGERS (New Brunswick)	26	4.49
HAWAII (Manoa)	27	4.47
INDIANA (Bloomington)	28	4.45
NORTH CAROLINA (Chapel Hill)	29	4.41
SUNY (Buffalo)	30	4.38
CALIFORNIA, IRVINE	31	4.37
VIRGINIA (Charlottesville)	32	4.32
ARIZONA STATE (Tempe)	33	4.30
MICHIGAN STATE	34	4.25
BRANDEIS	35	4.20
CALIFORNIA, DAVIS	36	4.19
SUNY (Binghampton)	37	4.16
N.Y.U.	38	4.12
PRINCETON	39	4.10
MINNESOTA (Minneapolis)	40	4.09
COLORADO (Boulder)	41	4.08
TULANE	42	4.07
BRYN MAWR	43	4.06
WASHINGTON (St. Louis)	44	4.05
CALIFORNIA, RIVERSIDE	45	4.04
OREGON (Eugene)	46	4.03
SOUTHERN METHODIST	47	4.02

A RATING OF GRADUATE PROGRAMS IN APPLIED MATHEMATICS
Leading Institutions

Twenty-four institutions with scores in the 4.0-5.0 range, in rank order

INSTITUTION	Rank	Score
HARVARD	1	4.90
PRINCETON	2	4.85
CHICAGO	3	4.83
M.I.T.	4	4.81
YALE	5	4.78
WISCONSIN (Madison)	6	4.74
COLUMBIA (N.Y.)	7	4.71
BROWN	8	4.69
CORNELL (N.Y.)	9	4.65
CAL TECH	10	4.63
MARYLAND (College Park)	11	4.58
WASHINGTON (Seattle)	12	4.54
NORTHWESTERN (Illinois)	13	4.52
RICE	14	4.49
PURDUE (Lafayette)	15	4.42
JOHNS HOPKINS	16	4.35
INDIANA (Bloomington)	17	4.30
VIRGINIA (Charlottesville)	18	4.26
PENN STATE (University Park)	19	4.22
COLORADO (Boulder)	20	4.19
MICHIGAN STATE	21	4.17
IOWA (Iowa City)	22	4.15
FLORIDA (Gainesville)	23	4.12
KANSAS (Lawrence)	24	4.10

A RATING OF GRADUATE PROGRAMS IN APPLIED PHYSICS
Leading Institutions

Eleven institutions with scores in the 4.0-5.0 range, in rank order

INSTITUTION	Rank	Score
CAL TECH	1	4.90
HARVARD	2	4.88
PRINCETON	3	4.86
CORNELL (N.Y.)	4	4.84
STANFORD	5	4.81
MICHIGAN (Ann Arbor)	6	4.79
COLUMBIA (N.Y.)	7	4.74
YALE	8	4.70
RENSSELAER (N.Y.)	9	4.66
CARNEGIE-MELLON	10	4.62
COLORADO (Boulder)	11	4.59

A RATING OF GRADUATE PROGRAMS IN ARCHITECTURE
Leading Institutions

Thirty institutions with scores in the 4.0-5.0 range, in rank order

INSTITUTION	Rank	Score
HARVARD	1	4.93
M.I.T.	2	4.92
PRINCETON	3	4.90
CALIFORNIA, BERKELEY	4	4.87
PENNSYLVANIA	5	4.84
CARNEGIE-MELLON	6	4.81
MICHIGAN (Ann Arbor)	7	4.76
GEORGIA TECH	8	4.74
RICE	9	4.71
COLUMBIA (N.Y.)	10	4.68
TEXAS (Austin)	11	4.63
YALE	12	4.61
WASHINGTON (Seattle)	13	4.55
UCLA	14	4.53
TEXAS A&M (College Station)	15	4.49
OHIO STATE (Columbus)	16	4.48
ILLINOIS (Urbana)	17	4.44
V.P.I. & STATE U.	18	4.42
OREGON (Eugene)	19	4.36
ARIZONA STATE	20	4.33
WASHINGTON (St. Louis)	21	4.27
HAWAII (Manoa)	22	4.26
FLORIDA (Gainesville)	23	4.22
RENSSELAER (N.Y.)	24	4.21
NEW MEXICO	25	4.19
HOUSTON (University Park)	26	4.16
VIRGINIA (Charlottesville)	27	4.15
MINNESOTA (Minneapolis)	28	4.14
OKLAHOMA (Norman)	29	4.09
WISCONSIN (Milwaukee)	30	4.08

A RATING OF GRADUATE PROGRAMS IN ART HISTORY
Leading Institutions

Thirty institutions with scores in the 4.0-5.0 range, in rank order

INSTITUTION	Rank	Score
N.Y.U.	1	4.91
HARVARD	2	4.89
YALE	3	4.86
COLUMBIA (N.Y.)	4	4.82
PRINCETON	5	4.78
CALIFORNIA, BERKELEY	6	4.74
STANFORD	7	4.69
MICHIGAN (Ann Arbor)	8	4.64
BRYN MAWR	9	4.56
JOHNS HOPKINS	10	4.50
PENNSYLVANIA	11	4.49
BROWN	12	4.44
UCLA	13	4.42
CHICAGO	14	4.38
NORTH CAROLINA (Chapel Hill)	15	4.36
CORNELL (N.Y.)	16	4.32
PITTSBURGH (Pittsburgh)	17	4.30
INDIANA (Bloomington)	18	4.25
VIRGINIA (Charlottesville)	19	4.22
KANSAS (Lawrence)	20	4.19
BOSTON U.	21	4.16
NORTHWESTERN (Evanston)	22	4.14
MARYLAND (College Park)	23	4.13
RUTGERS (New Brunswick)	24	4.12
MINNESOTA (Minneapolis)	25	4.11
PENN STATE (University Park)	26	4.10
IOWA (Iowa City)	27	4.08
TEXAS (Austin)	28	4.07
WASHINGTON (St. Louis)	29	4.05
WISCONSIN (Madison)	30	4.04

A RATING OF GRADUATE PROGRAMS IN ASIAN LANGUAGES
Leading Institutions

Ten institutions with scores in the 4.0-5.0 range, in rank order

INSTITUTION	Rank	Score
HARVARD	1	4.87
CALIFORNIA, BERKELEY	2	4.83
COLUMBIA (N.Y.)	3	4.80
CHICAGO	4	4.77
MICHIGAN (Ann Arbor)	5	4.74
UCLA	6	4.71
WISCONSIN (Madison)	7	4.68
CORNELL (N.Y.)	8	4.62
INDIANA (Bloomington)	9	4.58
STANFORD	10	4.55

A RATING OF GRADUATE PROGRAMS IN ASIAN STUDIES
Leading Institutions

Eleven institutions with scores in the 4.0-5.0 range, in rank order

INSTITUTION	Rank	Score
CHICAGO	1	4.86
COLUMBIA (N.Y.)	2	4.84
HARVARD	3	4.80
PRINCETON	4	4.78
CALIFORNIA, BERKELEY	5	4.77
PENNSYLVANIA	6	4.75
WASHINGTON (Seattle)	7	4.73
WISCONSIN (Madison)	8	4.72
MICHIGAN (Ann Arbor)	9	4.71
UCLA	10	4.70
INDIANA (Bloomington)	11	4.67

A RATING OF GRADUATE PROGRAMS IN ASTRONOMY
Leading Institutions

Thirty-three institutions with scores in the 4.0-5.0 range, in rank order

INSTITUTION	Rank	Score
CAL TECH	1	4.94
CORNELL (N.Y.)	2	4.93
CALIFORNIA, BERKELEY	3	4.92
HARVARD	4	4.91
PRINCETON	5	4.90
M.I.T.	6	4.86
CHICAGO	7	4.83
ARIZONA	8	4.82
WISCONSIN (Madison)	9	4.76
MICHIGAN (Ann Arbor)	10	4.73
YALE	11	4.70
MARYLAND (College Park)	12	4.66
UCLA	13	4.64
CASE WESTERN RESERVE	14	4.63
TEXAS (Austin)	15	4.61
VIRGINIA (Charlottesville)	16	4.59
ILLINOIS (Urbana)	17	4.54
COLUMBIA (N.Y.)	18	4.51
WASHINGTON (Seattle)	19	4.49
CALIFORNIA, SANTA CRUZ	20	4.47
INDIANA (Bloomington)	21	4.40
NORTHWESTERN (Illinois)	22	4.38
KANSAS (Lawrence)	23	4.36
PENNSYLVANIA	24	4.35
OHIO STATE (Columbus)	25	4.30
NORTH CAROLINA (Chapel Hill)	26	4.26
FLORIDA (Gainesville)	27	4.24
RICE	28	4.22
SUNY (Stony Brook)	29	4.16
PENN STATE (University Park)	30	4.14
MASSACHUSETTS (Amherst)	31	4.10
MINNESOTA (Minneapolis)	32	4.08
BOSTON U.	33	4.05

A RATING OF GRADUATE PROGRAMS IN BIOCHEMISTRY
Leading Institutions

Fifty-one institutions with scores in the 4.0-5.0 range, in rank order

INSTITUTION	Rank	Score
M.I.T.	1	4.97
STANFORD	2	4.96
HARVARD	3	4.95
CALIFORNIA, BERKELEY	4	4.94
WISCONSIN (Madison)	5	4.93
YALE	6	4.92
CALIFORNIA, SAN FRANCISCO	7	4.91
ROCKEFELLER (N.Y.)	8	4.89
CORNELL (N.Y.)	9	4.88
UCLA	10	4.87
CHICAGO	11	4.86
CALIFORNIA, SAN DIEGO	12	4.85
DUKE	13	4.83
PENNSYLVANIA	14	4.82
ILLINOIS (Urbana)	15	4.79
MICHIGAN (Ann Arbor)	16	4.76
CORNELL (Medical Center, N.Y.)	17	4.75
CALIFORNIA, DAVIS	18	4.72
COLUMBIA (N.Y.)	19	4.70
NOTRE DAME	20	4.65
JOHNS HOPKINS	21	4.64
NORTHWESTERN (Illinois)	22	4.63
PRINCETON	23	4.60
MICHIGAN STATE	24	4.59
IOWA (Iowa City)	25	4.52
BRANDEIS	26	4.43
CASE WESTERN RESERVE	27	4.42
PURDUE (Lafayette)	28	4.38
NORTH CAROLINA (Chapel Hill)	29	4.36
RICE	30	4.34
VANDERBILT	31	4.30
N.Y.U.	32	4.28
OREGON (Eugene)	33	4.26
RUTGERS (New Brunswick)	34	4.23
SUNY (Stony Brook)	35	4.21
TEXAS (Austin)	36	4.20
VIRGINIA (Charlottesville)	37	4.18
ALBERT EINSTEIN (College of Medicine)	38	4.17
CALIFORNIA, IRVINE	39	4.16
IOWA STATE (Ames)	40	4.14
TEXAS U. HEALTH SCI. CTR. (Houston)	41	4.12
U.S.C. (Los Angeles)	42	4.11
PENN STATE (University Park)	43	4.10
CALIFORNIA, RIVERSIDE	44	4.09
PITTSBURGH (Pittsburgh)	45	4.08
UTAH	46	4.06
BAYLOR COLLEGE OF MEDICINE	47	4.05
SAINT LOUIS U.	48	4.04
COLORADO (Boulder)	49	4.03
CUNY (Graduate School)	50	4.02
OREGON STATE	51	4.01

A RATING OF GRADUATE PROGRAMS IN
BIOENGINEERING/BIOMEDICAL ENGINEERING
Leading Institutions

Twenty-four institutions with scores in the 4.0-5.0 range, in rank order

INSTITUTION	Rank	Score
JOHNS HOPKINS	1	4.91
CALIFORNIA, BERKELEY/SAN FRANCISCO	2	4.89
M.I.T.	3	4.86
HARVARD	4	4.83
PENNSYLVANIA	5	4.82
DUKE	6	4.78
CARNEGIE-MELLON	7	4.75
COLUMBIA (N.Y.)	8	4.72
NORTHWESTERN (Illinois)	9	4.68
CASE WESTERN RESERVE	10	4.63
WASHINGTON (Seattle)	11	4.60
RENSSELAER (N.Y.)	12	4.54
CALIFORNIA, SAN DIEGO	13	4.52
CORNELL (N.Y.)	14	4.49
TEXAS (Austin)	15	4.46
MICHIGAN (Ann Arbor)	16	4.39
BROWN	17	4.38
UTAH	18	4.32
OHIO STATE (Columbus)	19	4.25
MARQUETTE	20	4.23
VIRGINIA (Charlottesville)	21	4.20
PENNSYLVANIA STATE (University Park)	22	4.17
U.S.C. (Los Angeles)	23	4.15
DREXEL	24	4.12

A RATING OF GRADUATE PROGRAMS IN BOTANY
Leading Institutions

Forty institutions with scores in the 4.0-5.0 range, in rank order

INSTITUTION	Rank	Score
CALIFORNIA, DAVIS	1	4.95
TEXAS (Austin)	2	4.93
CALIFORNIA, BERKELEY	3	4.90
WISCONSIN (Madison)	4	4.88
CORNELL (N.Y.)	5	4.87
MICHIGAN (Ann Arbor)	6	4.83
DUKE	7	4.82
YALE	8	4.75
ILLINOIS (Urbana)	9	4.74
CALIFORNIA, RIVERSIDE	10	4.72
MICHIGAN STATE	11	4.71
NORTH CAROLINA STATE (Raleigh)	12	4.70
UCLA	13	4.67
PENN STATE (University Park)	14	4.66
INDIANA (Bloomington)	15	4.64
MINNESOTA (Minneapolis)	16	4.60
NORTH CAROLINA (Chapel Hill)	17	4.58
GEORGIA (Athens)	18	4.56
WASHINGTON (St. Louis)	19	4.52
WASHINGTON (Seattle)	20	4.50
OREGON STATE	21	4.48
PURDUE (Lafayette)	22	4.45
OHIO STATE (Columbus)	23	4.43
KENTUCKY	24	4.41
IOWA STATE (Ames)	25	4.39
MASSACHUSETTS (Amherst)	26	4.36
FLORIDA (Gainesville)	27	4.34
CLAREMONT GRADUATE SCHOOL	28	4.30
NEBRASKA (Lincoln)	29	4.28
SUNY (C. Environ., Sci. & Forestry	30	4.26
OKLAHOMA (Norman)	31	4.22
CALIFORNIA, IRVINE	32	4.19
RUTGERS (New Brunswick)	33	4.18
WASHINGTON STATE	34	4.14
CHICAGO	35	4.13
COLORADO STATE	36	4.12
HAWAII (Manoa)	37	4.11
MARYLAND (College Park)	38	4.09
MISSOURI (Columbia)	39	4.07
IOWA (Iowa City)	40	4.06

A RATING OF GRADUATE PROGRAMS IN CELLULAR/MOLECULAR BIOLOGY
Leading Institutions

Forty-two institutions with scores in the 4.0-5.0 range, in rank order

INSTITUTION	Rank	Score
M.I.T.	1	4.95
CAL TECH	2	4.93
YALE	3	4.90
ROCKEFELLER (N.Y.)	4	4.86
WISCONSIN (Madison)	5	4.84
HARVARD	6	4.83
CALIFORNIA, SAN DIEGO	7	4.80
CALIFORNIA, BERKELEY	8	4.79
COLUMBIA	9	4.74
WASHINGTON (Seattle)	10	4.71
COLORADO (Boulder)	11	4.68
STANFORD	12	4.66
CHICAGO	13	4.63
UCLA	14	4.61
WASHINGTON (St. Louis)	15	4.60
DUKE	16	4.59
BRANDEIS	17	4.56
OREGON (Eugene)	18	4.55
BAYLOR (College of Medicine)	19	4.53
PENNSYLVANIA	20	4.50
PURDUE (Lafayette)	21	4.46
ALBERT EINSTEIN (College of Medicine)	22	4.43
INDIANA (Bloomington)	23	4.41
NORTH CAROLINA (Chapel Hill)	24	4.39
JOHNS HOPKINS	25	4.38
UTAH	26	4.37
NORTHWESTERN (Illinois)	27	4.36
PRINCETON	28	4.34
CALIFORNIA, IRVINE	29	4.33
BROWN	30	4.30
VIRGINIA (Charlottesville)	31	4.28
CALIFORNIA, SANTA BARBARA	32	4.27
CORNELL (Medical Center, N.Y.)	33	4.26
ROCHESTER	34	4.24
ILLINOIS (Urbana)	35	4.23
MICHIGAN (Ann Arbor)	36	4.20
FLORIDA STATE	37	4.18
PITTSBURGH (Pittsburgh)	38	4.17
SUNY (Stony Brook)	39	4.15
TUFTS	40	4.13
MINNESOTA (Minneapolis)	41	4.11
TEXAS (Austin)	42	4.08

A RATING OF GRADUATE PROGRAMS IN CERAMIC SCIENCES AND ENGINEERING
Leading Institutions

Nine institutions with scores in the 4.0-5.0 range, in rank order

INSTITUTION	Rank	Score
ALFRED (SUNY)	1	4.92
ILLINOIS (Urbana)	2	4.90
OHIO STATE (Columbus)	3	4.85
RUTGERS (New Brunswick)	4	4.81
PENN STATE (University Park)	5	4.77
GEORGIA TECH	6	4.71
WASHINGTON (Seattle)	7	4.62
MISSOURI (Rolla)	8	4.59
IOWA STATE (Ames)	9	4.51

A RATING OF GRADUATE PROGRAMS IN CHEMICAL ENGINEERING
Leading Institutions

Fifty institutions with scores in the 4.0-5.0 range, in rank order

INSTITUTION	Rank	Score
MINNESOTA (Minneapolis)	1	4.95
WISCONSIN (Madison)	2	4.92
CAL TECH	3	4.91
CALIFORNIA, BERKELEY	4	4.90
STANFORD	5	4.87
DELAWARE	6	4.86
M.I.T.	7	4.85
ILLINOIS (Urbana)	8	4.84
PRINCETON	9	4.82
HOUSTON (Houston)	10	4.81
NORTHWESTERN (Illinois)	11	4.78
PENNSYLVANIA	12	4.76
TEXAS (Austin)	13	4.75
CARNEGIE-MELLON	14	4.74
PURDUE (Lafayette)	15	4.73
MICHIGAN (Ann Arbor)	16	4.71
WASHINGTON (Seattle)	17	4.69
CORNELL (N.Y.)	18	4.68
NOTRE DAME	19	4.66
RICE	20	4.64
MASSACHUSETTS (Amherst)	21	4.63
IOWA STATE (Ames)	22	4.59
FLORIDA (Gainesville)	23	4.56
ROCHESTER (N.Y.)	24	4.53
SUNY (Buffalo)	25	4.52
COLORADO (Boulder)	26	4.50
PENN STATE (University Park)	27	4.47
WASHINGTON (St. Louis)	28	4.45
CASE WESTERN RESERVE	29	4.44
LEHIGH	30	4.43
OREGON STATE	31	4.37
GEORGIA TECH	32	4.36
NORTH CAROLINA STATE (Raleigh)	33	4.32
OHIO STATE (Columbus)	34	4.29
CUNY (Graduate School)	35	4.28
YALE	36	4.26
RENSSELAER (N.Y.)	37	4.23
TENNESSEE (Knoxville)	38	4.22
VIRGINIA (Charlottesville)	39	4.21
UCLA	40	4.20
UTAH	41	4.18
COLUMBIA (N.Y.)	42	4.16
OKLAHOMA (Norman)	43	4.15
CLARKSON (N.Y.)	44	4.14
CONNECTICUT (Storrs)	45	4.13
MARYLAND (College Park)	46	4.12
TEXAS A&M (College Station)	47	4.11
WEST VIRGINIA	48	4.10
PITTSBURGH (Pittsburgh)	49	4.09
LSU (Baton Rouge)	50	4.08

A RATING OF GRADUATE PROGRAMS IN CHEMISTRY
Leading Institutions

Fifty-two institutions with scores in the 4.0-5.0 range, in rank order

INSTITUTION	Rank	Score
HARVARD	1	4.95
CALIFORNIA, BERKELEY	2	4.94
CAL TECH	3	4.93
M.I.T.	4	4.91
COLUMBIA (N.Y.)	5	4.89
STANFORD	6	4.87
ILLINOIS (Urbana)	7	4.86
UCLA	8	4.85
CHICAGO	9	4.83
CORNELL (N.Y.)	10	4.81
WISCONSIN (Madison)	11	4.79
NORTHWESTERN (Illinois)	12	4.78
PRINCETON	13	4.76
YALE	14	4.73
PURDUE (Lafayette)	15	4.71
NORTH CAROLINA (Chapel Hill)	16	4.70
OHIO STATE (Columbus)	17	4.68
TEXAS (Austin)	18	4.65
CALIFORNIA, SAN DIEGO	19	4.62
INDIANA (Bloomington)	20	4.61
IOWA STATE (Ames)	21	4.60
UTAH	22	4.58
MINNESOTA (Minneapolis)	23	4.57
PENN STATE (University Park)	24	4.53
MICHIGAN (Ann Arbor)	25	4.51
ROCHESTER (N.Y.)	26	4.49
CARNEGIE-MELLON	27	4.47
PENNSYLVANIA	28	4.45
RICE	29	4.44
MICHIGAN STATE	30	4.43
WASHINGTON (Seattle)	31	4.40
NOTRE DAME	32	4.39
PITTSBURGH (Pittsburgh)	33	4.37
U.S.C. (Los Angeles)	34	4.34
FLORIDA (Gainesville)	35	4.31
COLORADO (Boulder)	36	4.28
CALIFORNIA, IRVINE	37	4.27
CALIFORNIA, RIVERSIDE	38	4.24
CALIFORNIA, SANTA BARBARA	39	4.23
JOHNS HOPKINS	40	4.22
FLORIDA STATE	41	4.21
CALIFORNIA, DAVIS	42	4.19
COLORADO STATE	43	4.17
ARIZONA (Tucson)	44	4.16
OREGON (Eugene)	45	4.14
GEORGIA TECH	46	4.13
SUNY (Buffalo)	47	4.10
DUKE	48	4.09
BROWN	49	4.08
SUNY (Stony Brook)	50	4.07
MARYLAND (College Park)	51	4.05
BRANDEIS	52	4.04

A RATING OF GRADUATE PROGRAMS IN CITY/REGIONAL PLANNING
Leading Institutions

Sixteen institutions with scores in the 4.0-5.0 range, in rank order

INSTITUTION	Rank	Score
CALIFORNIA, BERKELEY	1	4.91
M.I.T.	2	4.90
CORNELL (N.Y.)	3	4.88
NORTHWESTERN (Illinois)	4	4.85
PRINCETON	5	4.82
ILLINOIS (Urbana)	6	4.80
UCLA	7	4.79
MICHIGAN (Ann Arbor)	8	4.77
PENNSYLVANIA	9	4.75
COLUMBIA (N.Y.)	10	4.71
WISCONSIN (Madison)	11	4.69
HARVARD	12	4.68
INDIANA (Bloomington)	13	4.66
TEXAS A&M (College Station)	14	4.64
ARIZONA (Tucson)	15	4.62
OHIO STATE (Columbus)	16	4.59

A RATING OF GRADUATE PROGRAMS IN CIVIL ENGINEERING
Leading Institutions

Fifty institutions with scores in the 4.0-5.0 range, in rank order

INSTITUTION	Rank	Score
CALIFORNIA, BERKELEY	1	4.95
M.I.T.	2	4.94
ILLINOIS (Urbana)	3	4.93
CAL TECH	4	4.92
STANFORD	5	4.91
TEXAS (Austin)	6	4.90
CORNELL (N.Y.)	7	4.89
NORTHWESTERN (Illinois)	8	4.87
PURDUE (Lafayette)	9	4.86
MICHIGAN (Ann Arbor)	10	4.85
PRINCETON	11	4.82
COLORADO STATE	12	4.80
WASHINGTON (Seattle)	13	4.78
WISCONSIN (Madison)	14	4.75
BROWN	15	4.72
COLUMBIA (N.Y.)	16	4.71
UCLA	17	4.70
LEHIGH	18	4.67
GEORGIA TECH	19	4.66
CARNEGIE-MELLON	20	4.65
TEXAS A&M (College Station)	21	4.64
CALIFORNIA, DAVIS	22	4.60
COLORADO (Boulder)	23	4.58
NORTH CAROLINA STATE (Raleigh)	24	4.56
OHIO STATE (Columbus)	25	4.53
UTAH STATE	26	4.51
IOWA STATE (Ames)	27	4.49
IOWA (Iowa City)	28	4.45
PENN STATE (University Park)	29	4.41
MASSACHUSETTS (Amherst)	30	4.38
MINNESOTA (Minneapolis)	31	4.31
RICE	32	4.28
RENSSELAER (N.Y.)	33	4.26
WASHINGTON (St. Louis)	34	4.23
DUKE	35	4.20
KANSAS	36	4.19
U.S.C. (Los Angeles)	37	4.15
V.P.I. & STATE U.	38	4.14
OREGON STATE	39	4.13
MICHIGAN STATE	40	4.12
VANDERBILT	41	4.11
MISSOURI (Rolla)	42	4.10
MARYLAND (College Park)	43	4.09
PENNSYLVANIA	44	4.08
FLORIDA (Gainesville)	45	4.07
MISSOURI (Columbia)	46	4.06
SUNY (Buffalo)	47	4.05
PITTSBURGH (Pittsburgh)	48	4.04
OKLAHOMA (Norman)	49	4.03
OKLAHOMA STATE	50	4.02

A RATING OF GRADUATE PROGRAMS IN CLASSICS
Leading Institutions

Thirty institutions with scores in the 4.0-5.0 range, in rank order

INSTITUTION	Rank	Score
HARVARD	1	4.91
CALIFORNIA, BERKELEY	2	4.89
PRINCETON	3	4.87
YALE	4	4.83
MICHIGAN (Ann Arbor)	5	4.80
NORTH CAROLINA (Chapel Hill)	6	4.76
BRYN MAWR	7	4.75
BROWN	8	4.71
TEXAS (Austin)	9	4.68
COLUMBIA (N.Y.)	10	4.65
CORNELL (N.Y.)	11	4.62
PENNSYLVANIA	12	4.58
STANFORD	13	4.55
CHICAGO	14	4.50
ILLINOIS (Urbana)	15	4.46
DUKE	16	4.42
UCLA	17	4.37
INDIANA (Bloomington)	18	4.33
JOHNS HOPKINS	19	4.27
OHIO STATE (Columbus)	20	4.24
WISCONSIN (Madison)	21	4.19
SUNY (Buffalo)	22	4.17
MINNESOTA (Minneapolis)	23	4.16
CINCINNATI	24	4.14
WASHINGTON (Seattle)	25	4.13
BOSTON U.	26	4.12
IOWA (Iowa City)	27	4.09
N.Y.U.	28	4.08
VIRGINIA (Charlottesville)	29	4.07
RUTGERS (New Brunswick)	30	4.05

A RATING OF GRADUATE PROGRAMS IN CLINICAL PSYCHOLOGY
Leading Institutions

Thirty institutions with scores in the 4.0-5.0 range, in rank order

INSTITUTION	Rank	Score
YALE	1	4.71
PENNSYLVANIA	2	4.66
MICHIGAN (Ann Arbor)	3	4.62
MINNESOTA (Minneapolis)	4	4.59
CALIFORNIA, BERKELEY	5	4.58
ILLINOIS (Urbana)	6	4.57
UCLA	7	4.56
INDIANA (Bloomington)	8	4.55
OREGON (Eugene)	9	4.52
COLORADO (Boulder)	10	4.50
WASHINGTON (Seattle)	11	4.46
TEXAS (Austin)	12	4.45
NORTH CAROLINA (Chapel Hill)	13	4.44
NORTHWESTERN (Illinois)	14	4.43
SUNY (Stony Brook)	15	4.40
PENN STATE (University Park)	16	4.39
DUKE	17	4.38
CUNY (Graduate School)	18	4.36
PITTSBURGH (Pittsburgh)	19	4.33
RUTGERS (New Brunswick)	20	4.28
IOWA (Iowa City)	21	4.26
OHIO STATE (Columbus)	22	4.23
WASHINGTON (St. Louis)	23	4.22
PURDUE (Lafayette)	24	4.19
N.Y.U.	25	4.16
U.S.C. (Los Angeles)	26	4.12
CONNECTICUT (Storrs)	27	4.10
UTAH	28	4.08
VANDERBILT	29	4.06
KANSAS (Lawrence)	30	4.03

A RATING OF GRADUATE PROGRAMS IN CLOTHING/TEXTILES
Leading Institutions

Twelve institutions with scores in the 4.0-5.0 range, in rank order

INSTITUTION	Rank	Score
CORNELL (N.Y.)	1	4.83
IOWA STATE (Ames)	2	4.79
MICHIGAN STATE	3	4.74
TEXAS TECH	4	4.71
MARYLAND (College Park)	5	4.70
FLORIDA STATE	6	4.69
LSU (Baton Rouge)	7	4.65
OKLAHOMA STATE	8	4.62
OREGON STATE	9	4.58
GEORGIA (Athens)	10	4.51
TENNESSEE (Knoxville)	11	4.48
TEXAS WOMANS U.	12	4.47

A RATING OF GRADUATE PROGRAMS IN COMMUNICATION
Leading Institutions

Twelve institutions with scores in the 4.0-5.0 range, in rank order

INSTITUTION	Rank	Score
PENNSYLVANIA	1	4.90
SYRACUSE	2	4.89
STANFORD	3	4.84
NORTHWESTERN (Illinois)	4	4.81
U.S.C. (Los Angeles)	5	4.80
MICHIGAN (Ann Arbor)	6	4.75
MICHIGAN STATE	7	4.73
N.Y.U.	8	4.71
FLORIDA STATE	9	4.70
MARYLAND (College Park)	10	4.69
WISCONSIN (Madison)	11	4.68
OHIO STATE (Columbus)	12	4.62

A RATING OF GRADUATE PROGRAMS IN COMPARATIVE LITERATURE
Leading Institutions

Twenty-five institutions with scores in the 4.0-5.0 range, in rank order

INSTITUTION	Rank	Score
COLUMBIA (N.Y.)	1	4.83
CALIFORNIA, BERKELEY	2	4.75
HARVARD	3	4.73
YALE	4	4.66
MICHIGAN (Ann Arbor)	5	4.63
PRINCETON	6	4.58
ILLINOIS (Urbana)	7	4.57
CALIFORNIA, IRVINE	8	4.51
NORTH CAROLINA (Chapel Hill)	9	4.46
BROWN	10	4.41
CORNELL (N.Y.)	11	4.38
N.Y.U.	12	4.35
CHICAGO	13	4.30
IOWA (Iowa City)	14	4.25
PENNSYLVANIA	15	4.22
INDIANA (Bloomington)	16	4.20
WASHINGTON (Seattle)	17	4.15
DUKE	18	4.14
JOHNS HOPKINS	19	4.12
CALIFORNIA, SAN DIEGO	20	4.11
WISCONSIN (Madison)	21	4.08
SUNY (Buffalo)	22	4.06
NORTHWESTERN (Illinois)	23	4.04
CUNY (Graduate School)	24	4.03
UCLA	25	4.02

A RATING OF GRADUATE PROGRAMS IN COMPUTER SCIENCE
Leading Institutions

Forty institutions with scores in the 4.0-5.0 range, in rank order

INSTITUTION	Rank	Score
M.I.T.	1	4.93
STANFORD	2	4.92
CARNEGIE-MELLON	3	4.91
CALIFORNIA, BERKELEY	4	4.90
CORNELL (N.Y.)	5	4.89
UCLA	6	4.87
ILLINOIS (Urbana)	7	4.83
YALE	8	4.79
WASHINGTON (Seattle)	9	4.78
TEXAS (Austin)	10	4.77
WISCONSIN (Madison)	11	4.71
MARYLAND (College Park)	12	4.70
PRINCETON	13	4.68
CAL TECH	14	4.66
UTAH	15	4.63
SUNY (Stony Brook)	16	4.61
BROWN	17	4.58
N.Y.U.	18	4.55
NORTH CAROLINA (Chapel Hill)	19	4.50
PENNSYLVANIA	20	4.46
ROCHESTER (N.Y.)	21	4.43
MINNESOTA (Minneapolis)	22	4.40
MASSACHUSETTS (Amherst)	23	4.38
GEORGIA TECH	24	4.36
U.S.C. (Los Angeles)	25	4.34
OHIO STATE (Columbus)	26	4.29
RICE	27	4.25
DUKE	28	4.20
NORTHWESTERN (Illinois)	29	4.19
SUNY (Buffalo)	30	4.18
SYRACUSE	31	4.17
ARIZONA (Tucson)	32	4.15
CALIFORNIA, SAN DIEGO	33	4.14
RUTGERS (New Brunswick)	34	4.12
COLUMBIA (N.Y.)	35	4.11
CALIFORNIA, IRVINE	36	4.10
INDIANA (Bloomington)	37	4.09
PENN STATE (University Park)	38	4.08
CALIFORNIA, SANTA BARBARA	39	4.07
PITTSBURGH (Pittsburgh)	40	4.06

A RATING OF GRADUATE PROGRAMS IN CONSUMER ECONOMICS
Leading Institutions

Eleven institutions with scores in the 4.0-5.0 range, in rank order

INSTITUTION	Rank	Score
CORNELL (N.Y.)	1	4.84
PURDUE (Lafayette)	2	4.80
MARYLAND (College Park)	3	4.75
MICHIGAN STATE	4	4.72
OHIO STATE (Columbus)	5	4.67
ARIZONA (Tucson)	6	4.64
ILLINOIS (Urbana)	7	4.60
FLORIDA STATE	8	4.57
OREGON STATE	9	4.51
OKLAHOMA STATE	10	4.48
TEXAS WOMANS U.	11	4.43

A RATING OF GRADUATE PROGRAMS IN DEMOGRAPHY/POPULATION STUDIES
Leading Institutions

Ten institutions with scores in the 4.0-5.0 range, in rank order

INSTITUTION	Rank	Score
HARVARD	1	4.84
JOHNS HOPKINS	2	4.80
MICHIGAN (Ann Arbor)	3	4.78
CORNELL (N.Y.)	4	4.77
DUKE	5	4.73
PRINCETON	6	4.71
ILLINOIS (Urbana)	7	4.70
CALIFORNIA, BERKELEY	8	4.69
WASHINGTON (Seattle)	9	4.66
PENNSYLVANIA	10	4.64

A RATING OF GRADUATE PROGRAMS IN DEVELOPMENTAL PSYCHOLOGY
Leading Institutions

Eleven institutions with scores in the 4.0-5.0 range, in rank order

INSTITUTION	Rank	Score
CORNELL (N.Y.)	1	4.59
MICHIGAN (Ann Arbor)	2	4.53
WAYNE STATE (Michigan)	3	4.48
HARVARD	4	4.46
DUKE	5	4.41
RUTGERS (New Brunswick)	6	4.38
NORTH CAROLINA (Chapel Hill)	7	4.36
TEMPLE (Philadelphia)	8	4.32
SUNY (Stony Brook)	9	4.28
TUFTS	10	4.25
OREGON (Eugene)	11	4.22

A RATING OF GRADUATE PROGRAMS IN DRAMA/THEATRE
Leading Institutions

Thirty-two institutions with scores in the 4.0-5.0 range, in rank order

INSTITUTION	Rank	Score
YALE	1	4.91
UCLA	2	4.90
NORTHWESTERN (Illinois)	3	4.89
STANFORD	4	4.86
IOWA (Iowa City)	5	4.83
MINNESOTA (Minneapolis)	6	4.75
INDIANA (Bloomington)	7	4.74
N.Y.U.	8	4.73
U.S.C. (Los Angeles)	9	4.72
CALIFORNIA, BERKELEY	10	4.64
MICHIGAN STATE	11	4.63
WISCONSIN (Madison)	12	4.60
WASHINGTON (Seattle)	13	4.55
CARNEGIE-MELLON	14	4.52
CORNELL (N.Y.)	15	4.49
ILLINOIS (Urbana)	16	4.47
OHIO STATE (Columbus)	17	4.38
CALIFORNIA, SANTA BARBARA	18	4.37
TEXAS (Austin)	19	4.34
NORTH CAROLINA (Chapel Hill)	20	4.29
MICHIGAN (Ann Arbor)	21	4.23
COLUMBIA (N.Y.)	22	4.19
CASE WESTERN RESERVE	23	4.14
WAYNE STATE (Michigan)	24	4.13
OREGON (Eugene)	25	4.09
MARYLAND (College Park)	26	4.07
TULANE	27	4.06
CATHOLIC U. (D.C.)	28	4.05
FLORIDA STATE	29	4.04
TUFTS	30	4.03
KANSAS (Lawrence)	31	4.02
PITTSBURGH (Pittsburgh)	32	4.01

A RATING OF GRADUATE PROGRAMS IN EAST EUROPEAN/SOVIET STUDIES
Leading Institutions

Eight institutions with scores in the 4.0-5.0 range, in rank order

INSTITUTION	Rank	Score
HARVARD	1	4.85
PRINCETON	2	4.81
STANFORD	3	4.79
MICHIGAN (Ann Arbor)	4	4.74
WASHINGTON (Seattle)	5	4.69
YALE	6	4.66
GEORGETOWN (D.C.)	7	4.62
INDIANA (Bloomington)	8	4.57

A RATING OF GRADUATE PROGRAMS IN ECONOMICS
Leading Institutions

Forty-five institutions with scores in the 4.0-5.0 range, in rank order

INSTITUTION	Rank	Score
M.I.T.	1	4.95
CHICAGO	2	4.93
STANFORD	3	4.92
PRINCETON	4	4.91
HARVARD	5	4.90
YALE	6	4.87
MINNESOTA (Minneapolis)	7	4.86
PENNSYLVANIA	8	4.85
CALIFORNIA, BERKELEY	9	4.81
WISCONSIN (Madison)	10	4.80
NORTHWESTERN (Illinois)	11	4.78
COLUMBIA (N.Y.)	12	4.75
UCLA	13	4.69
MICHIGAN (Ann Arbor)	14	4.67
ROCHESTER (N.Y.)	15	4.64
BROWN	16	4.61
CARNEGIE-MELLON	17	4.60
JOHNS HOPKINS	18	4.56
CALIFORNIA, SAN DIEGO	19	4.54
CORNELL (N.Y.)	20	4.53
DUKE	21	4.51
ILLINOIS (Urbana)	22	4.45
N.Y.U.	23	4.43
CALIFORNIA, DAVIS	24	4.42
VIRGINIA (Charlottesville)	25	4.40
MARYLAND (College Park)	26	4.37
WASHINGTON (Seattle)	27	4.35
MICHIGAN STATE	28	4.33
NORTH CAROLINA (Chapel Hill)	29	4.30
IOWA (Iowa City)	30	4.28
PITTSBURGH (Pittsburgh)	31	4.25
IOWA STATE (Ames)	32	4.23
WASHINGTON (St. Louis)	33	4.22
PURDUE (Lafayette)	34	4.21
U.S.C. (Los Angeles)	35	4.18
TEXAS A&M (College Station)	36	4.17
CALIFORNIA, SANTA BARBARA	37	4.16
OHIO STATE (Columbus)	38	4.14
VANDERBILT	39	4.13
BOSTON U.	40	4.10
CAL TECH	41	4.09
SUNY (Stony Brook)	42	4.08
V.P.I. & STATE U.	43	4.07
MASSACHUSETTS (Amherst)	44	4.06
CLAREMONT GRADUATE SCHOOL	45	4.05

A RATING OF GRADUATE PROGRAMS IN ELECTRICAL ENGINEERING
Leading Institutions

Fifty institutions with scores in the 4.0-5.0 range, in rank order

INSTITUTION	Rank	Score
M.I.T.	1	4.93
CALIFORNIA, BERKELEY	2	4.92
STANFORD	3	4.91
ILLINOIS (Urbana)	4	4.90
CAL TECH	5	4.89
CORNELL	6	4.88
U.S.C. (Los Angeles)	7	4.87
PURDUE (Lafayette)	8	4.86
UCLA	9	4.85
PRINCETON	10	4.84
MICHIGAN (Ann Arbor)	11	4.83
CARNEGIE-MELLON	12	4.80
POLYTECHNIC UNIVERSITY (Brooklyn, N.Y.)	13	4.79
TEXAS (Austin)	14	4.78
COLUMBIA (N.Y.)	15	4.76
MARYLAND (College Park)	16	4.73
OHIO STATE (Columbus)	17	4.71
GEORGIA TECH	18	4.65
CALIFORNIA, SANTA BARBARA	19	4.62
MINNESOTA (Minneapolis)	20	4.61
NORTHWESTERN (Illinois)	21	4.60
JOHNS HOPKINS	22	4.55
RENSSELAER (N.Y.)	23	4.53
RICE	24	4.51
WISCONSIN (Madison)	25	4.48
CALIFORNIA, SAN DIEGO	26	4.46
PENNSYLVANIA	27	4.45
FLORIDA (Gainesville)	28	4.43
BROWN	29	4.41
COLORADO (Boulder)	30	4.40
WASHINGTON (Seattle)	31	4.37
ARIZONA (Tucson)	32	4.35
YALE	33	4.28
CASE WESTERN RESERVE	34	4.27
PENN STATE (University Park)	35	4.25
HAWAII (Manoa)	36	4.24
MICHIGAN STATE	37	4.23
MISSOURI (Rolla)	38	4.22
MASSACHUSETTS (Amherst)	39	4.20
NOTRE DAME	40	4.18
PITTSBURGH (Pittsburgh)	41	4.17
V.P.I. & STATE U.	42	4.15
SYRACUSE	43	4.14
NORTH CAROLINA (Raleigh)	44	4.13
WASHINGTON (St. Louis)	45	4.12
IOWA STATE (Ames)	46	4.11
CALIFORNIA, DAVIS	47	4.10
DUKE	48	4.06
KANSAS (Lawrence)	49	4.03
TEXAS TECH	50	4.02

A RATING OF GRADUATE PROGRAMS IN ENGLISH
Leading Institutions

Fifty-three institutions with scores in the 4.0-5.0 range, in rank order

INSTITUTION	Rank	Score
HARVARD	1	4.95
CALIFORNIA, BERKELEY	2	4.94
YALE	3	4.93
STANFORD	4	4.92
PRINCETON	5	4.91
CORNELL (N.Y.)	6	4.90
CHICAGO	7	4.89
JOHNS HOPKINS	8	4.87
VIRGINIA (Charlottesville)	9	4.85
COLUMBIA	10	4.84
PENNSYLVANIA	11	4.82
UCLA	12	4.81
BROWN	13	4.79
MICHIGAN (Ann Arbor)	14	4.78
INDIANA (Bloomington)	15	4.75
CALIFORNIA, IRVINE	16	4.72
WISCONSIN (Madison)	17	4.71
NORTHWESTERN (Illinois)	18	4.70
NORTH CAROLINA (Chapel Hill)	19	4.67
CUNY (Graduate School)	20	4.65
TEXAS (Austin)	21	4.64
IOWA (Iowa City)	22	4.62
N.Y.U.	23	4.59
ILLINOIS (Urbana)	24	4.55
DUKE	25	4.54
WASHINGTON (Seattle)	26	4.51
NOTRE DAME	27	4.49
SUNY (Stony Brook)	28	4.46
SUNY (Buffalo)	29	4.44
CALIFORNIA, SAN DIEGO	30	4.42
MARYLAND (College Park)	31	4.40
ROCHESTER (N.Y.)	32	4.38
U.S.C. (Los Angeles)	33	4.36
EMORY	34	4.35
OHIO STATE (Columbus)	35	4.34
MICHIGAN STATE	36	4.33
PENN STATE (University Park)	37	4.30
MASSACHUSETTS (Amherst)	38	4.26
MINNESOTA (Minneapolis)	39	4.25
CLAREMONT GRADUATE SCHOOL	40	4.22
WASHINGTON (St. Louis)	41	4.21
VANDERBILT	42	4.19
COLORADO (Boulder)	43	4.16
RICE	44	4.14
BRANDEIS	45	4.13
BOSTON U.	46	4.11
TUFTS	47	4.09
CALIFORNIA, DAVIS	48	4.06
RUTGERS (New Brunswick)	49	4.05
WISCONSIN (Milwaukee)	50	4.04
CALIFORNIA, SANTA BARBARA	51	4.03
SUNY (Binghampton)	52	4.02
SOUTH CAROLINA (Columbia)	53	4.01

A RATING OF GRADUATE PROGRAMS IN ENTOMOLOGY
Leading Institutions

Thirty-one institutions with scores in the 4.0-5.0 range, in rank order

INSTITUTION	Rank	Score
CALIFORNIA, BERKELEY	1	4.94
CORNELL (N.Y.)	2	4.93
ILLINOIS (Urbana)	3	4.92
CALIFORNIA, DAVIS	4	4.91
MINNESOTA (Minneapolis)	5	4.90
MICHIGAN STATE	6	4.84
WISCONSIN (Madison)	7	4.80
PURDUE (Lafayette)	8	4.79
KANSAS (Lawrence)	9	4.78
OHIO STATE (Columbus)	10	4.76
IOWA STATE (Ames)	11	4.72
CALIFORNIA, RIVERSIDE	12	4.68
OREGON STATE	13	4.62
KANSAS STATE	14	4.56
NORTH CAROLINA STATE (Raleigh)	15	4.51
TEXAS A&M (College Station)	16	4.49
RUTGERS (New Brunswick)	17	4.44
LSU (Baton Rouge)	18	4.28
FLORIDA (Gainesville)	19	4.25
PENN STATE (University Park)	20	4.23
MASSACHUSETTS (Amherst)	21	4.21
MISSOURI (Columbia)	22	4.17
ARIZONA (Tucson)	23	4.13
WASHINGTON STATE	24	4.12
MARYLAND (College Park)	25	4.11
COLORADO STATE	26	4.09
AUBURN (Auburn)	27	4.08
NEBRASKA (Lincoln)	28	4.06
GEORGIA (Athens)	29	4.05
OKLAHOMA STATE	30	4.04
V.P.I. & STATE U.	31	4.02

A RATING OF GRADUATE PROGRAMS IN ENVIRONMENTAL DESIGN
Leading Institutions

Five institutions with scores in the 4.0-5.0 range, in rank order

INSTITUTION	Rank	Score
M.I.T.	1	4.88
CALIFORNIA, BERKELEY	2	4.86
CORNELL (N.Y.)	3	4.81
TEXAS A&M (College Station)	4	4.78
YALE	5	4.73

A RATING OF GRADUATE PROGRAMS IN ENVIRONMENTAL ENGINEERING
Leading Institutions

Ten institutions with scores in the 4.0-5.0 range, in rank order

INSTITUTION	Rank	Score
CAL TECH	1	4.87
CINCINNATI	2	4.83
TEXAS (Austin)	3	4.80
GEORGIA TECH	4	4.76
V.P.I. & STATE U.	5	4.73
NORTH CAROLINA (Chapel Hill)	6	4.69
FLORIDA (Gainesville)	7	4.65
MASSACHUSETTS (Amherst)	8	4.60
COLORADO STATE	9	4.53
CLEMSON	10	4.51

A RATING OF GRADUATE PROGRAMS IN ENVIRONMENTAL POLICY/RESOURCE MANAGEMENT
Leading Institutions

Fifteen institutions with scores in the 4.0-5.0 range, in rank order

INSTITUTION	Rank	Score
CALIFORNIA, BERKELEY	1	4.85
INDIANA (Bloomington)	2	4.83
PRINCETON	3	4.80
DUKE	4	4.76
PENNSYLVANIA STATE (University Park)	5	4.71
MARYLAND (College Park)	6	4.69
PENNSYLVANIA	7	4.68
MICHIGAN STATE	8	4.67
UCLA	9	4.66
MICHIGAN (Ann Arbor)	10	4.62
WISCONSIN (Madison)	11	4.60
SUNY (College of Environmental Science and Forestry)	12	4.58
RENSSELAER (N.Y.)	13	4.56
CALIFORNIA, RIVERSIDE	14	4.55
MINNESOTA (Minneapolis)	15	4.53

A RATING OF GRADUATE PROGRAMS IN EXPERIMENTAL PSYCHOLOGY (GENERAL)
Leading Institutions

Nineteen institutions with scores in the 4.0-5.0 range, in rank order

INSTITUTION	Rank	Score
PENNSYLVANIA	1	4.70
MICHIGAN (Ann Arbor)	2	4.66
MINNESOTA (Minneapolis)	3	4.62
ILLINOIS (Urbana)	4	4.59
CALIFORNIA, SAN DIEGO	5	4.58
COLUMBIA (N.Y.)	6	4.52
YALE	7	4.49
CORNELL (N.Y.)	8	4.43
COLORADO (Boulder)	9	4.41
BROWN	10	4.40
NORTH CAROLINA (Chapel Hill)	11	4.38
OREGON (Eugene)	12	4.36
PENN STATE (University Park)	13	4.33
DUKE	14	4.30
IOWA (Iowa City)	15	4.27
KANSAS (Lawrence)	16	4.25
N.Y.U.	17	4.20
U.S.C. (Los Angeles)	18	4.13
CUNY (Graduate School and University Center)	19	4.09

A RATING OF GRADUATE PROGRAMS IN FORESTRY
Leading Institutions

Thirty-three institutions with scores in the 4.0-5.0 range, in rank order

INSTITUTION	Rank	Score
CALIFORNIA, BERKELEY	1	4.92
MINNESOTA (Minneapolis)	2	4.91
MICHIGAN (Ann Arbor)	3	4.90
SUNY (College of Environmental Science and Forestry, Syracuse)	4	4.89
DUKE	5	4.88
WISCONSIN (Madison)	6	4.87
YALE	7	4.85
PENN STATE (University Park)	8	4.84
PURDUE (Lafayette)	9	4.83
OREGON STATE	10	4.79
WASHINGTON (Seattle)	11	4.78
MISSOURI (Columbia)	12	4.76
IOWA STATE (Ames)	13	4.73
COLORADO STATE	14	4.71
NORTH CAROLINA STATE (Raleigh)	15	4.69
MONTANA (Missoula)	16	4.64
GEORGIA (Athens)	17	4.63
MICHIGAN STATE	18	4.61
IDAHO	19	4.57
UTAH STATE	20	4.54
MAINE (Orono)	21	4.51
TEXAS A&M (College Station)	22	4.48
V.P.I. & STATE U.	23	4.47
AUBURN (Auburn)	24	4.45
WEST VIRGINIA	25	4.40
FLORIDA (Gainesville)	26	4.39
MASSACHUSETTS (Amherst)	27	4.36
MISSISSIPPI STATE	28	4.32
LSU (Baton Rouge)	29	4.25
CLEMSON	30	4.20
STEPHEN F. AUSTIN STATE U.	31	4.15
OHIO STATE (Columbus)	32	4.12
ARIZONA (Tucson)	33	4.09

A RATING OF GRADUATE PROGRAMS IN FRENCH
Leading Institutions

Thirty-six institutions with scores in the 4.0-5.0 range, in rank order

INSTITUTION	Rank	Score
YALE	1	4.95
PRINCETON	2	4.93
COLUMBIA (N.Y.)	3	4.92
N.Y.U.	4	4.91
CORNELL (N.Y.)	5	4.89
INDIANA (Bloomington)	6	4.88
MICHIGAN (Ann Arbor)	7	4.87
PENNSYLVANIA	8	4.84
CALIFORNIA, BERKELEY	9	4.80
STANFORD	10	4.79
ILLINOIS (Urbana)	11	4.76
HARVARD	12	4.74
VIRGINIA (Charlottesville)	13	4.72
WISCONSIN (Madison)	14	4.69
CHICAGO	15	4.67
DUKE	16	4.65
CUNY (Graduate School)	17	4.63
TEXAS (Austin)	18	4.60
BROWN	19	4.58
NORTH CAROLINA (Chapel Hill)	20	4.57
CALIFORNIA, IRVINE	21	4.55
SUNY (Buffalo)	22	4.53
CALIFORNIA, SANTA BARBARA	23	4.49
PENN STATE (University Park)	24	4.47
CALIFORNIA, DAVIS	25	4.45
VANDERBILT	26	4.41
JOHNS HOPKINS	27	4.40
OHIO STATE (Columbus)	28	4.33
UCLA	29	4.27
RICE	30	4.26
WASHINGTON (Seattle)	31	4.22
BRYN MAWR	32	4.19
RUTGERS (New Brunswick)	33	4.17
WASHINGTON (St. Louis)	34	4.16
MINNESOTA (Minneapolis)	35	4.14
NORTHWESTERN (Illinois)	36	4.11

A RATING OF GRADUATE PROGRAMS IN GEOCHEMISTRY
Leading Institutions

Twelve institutions with scores in the 4.0-5.0 range, in rank order

INSTITUTION	Rank	Score
CAL TECH	1	4.92
COLUMBIA (N.Y.)	2	4.88
ILLINOIS (Urbana)	3	4.85
MICHIGAN (Ann Arbor)	4	4.82
JOHNS HOPKINS	5	4.79
INDIANA (Bloomington)	6	4.76
COLORADO SCHOOL OF MINES	7	4.75
RICE	8	4.72
PENNSYLVANIA STATE (University Park)	9	4.69
OHIO STATE (Columbus)	10	4.66
WASHINGTON (St. Louis)	11	4.64
YALE	12	4.60

A RATING OF GRADUATE PROGRAMS IN GEOGRAPHY
Leading Institutions

Twenty-nine institutions with scores in the 4.0-5.0 range, in rank order

INSTITUTION	Rank	Score
MINNESOTA (Minneapolis)	1	4.95
PENN STATE (University Park)	2	4.93
CALIFORNIA, BERKELEY	3	4.90
WISCONSIN (Madison)	4	4.88
CHICAGO	5	4.86
OHIO STATE (Columbus)	6	4.84
UCLA	7	4.79
CLARK (Massachusetts)	8	4.73
WASHINGTON (Seattle)	9	4.67
ILLINOIS (Urbana)	10	4.62
SYRACUSE	11	4.54
IOWA (Iowa City)	12	4.47
JOHNS HOPKINS	13	4.41
KANSAS (Lawrence)	14	4.33
LSU (Baton Rouge)	15	4.30
GEORGIA (Athens)	16	4.26
COLORADO (Boulder)	17	4.25
SUNY (Buffalo)	18	4.20
HAWAII (Manoa)	19	4.16
MICHIGAN (Ann Arbor)	20	4.15
WISCONSIN (Milwaukee)	21	4.11
MICHIGAN STATE	22	4.10
RUTGERS (New Brunswick)	23	4.09
NEBRASKA (Lincoln)	24	4.08
NORTH CAROLINA (Chapel Hill)	25	4.07
BOSTON U.	26	4.06
TEXAS (Austin)	27	4.05
MARYLAND (College Park)	28	4.04
ARIZONA (Tucson)	29	4.03

A RATING OF GRADUATE PROGRAMS IN GEOSCIENCE
Leading Institutions

Forty-one institutions with scores in the 4.0-5.0 range, in rank order

INSTITUTION	Rank	Score
CAL TECH	1	4.94
M.I.T.	2	4.93
UCLA	3	4.92
STANFORD	4	4.91
COLUMBIA (N.Y.)	5	4.90
HARVARD	6	4.88
CHICAGO	7	4.86
PRINCETON	8	4.84
YALE	9	4.82
CALIFORNIA, BERKELEY	10	4.81
CORNELL (N.Y.)	11	4.79
WISCONSIN (Madison)	12	4.77
PENN STATE (University Park)	13	4.75
TEXAS (Austin)	14	4.74
ARIZONA (Tucson)	15	4.72
BROWN	16	4.70
MICHIGAN (Ann Arbor)	17	4.69
JOHNS HOPKINS	18	4.66
CALIFORNIA, SANTA BARBARA	19	4.65
SUNY (Stony Brook)	20	4.63
NORTHWESTERN (Illinois)	21	4.61
WASHINGTON (Seattle)	22	4.55
INDIANA (Bloomington)	23	4.53
MINNESOTA (Minneapolis)	24	4.48
COLORADO (Boulder)	25	4.47
ILLINOIS (Urbana)	26	4.43
U.S.C. (Los Angeles)	27	4.40
CALIFORNIA, SANTA CRUZ	28	4.39
UTAH	29	4.37
ARIZONA STATE (Tempe)	30	4.36
SUNY (Albany)	31	4.35
MASSACHUSETTS (Amherst)	32	4.32
NORTH CAROLINA (Chapel Hill)	33	4.30
MIAMI (Florida)	34	4.26
TEXAS A&M (College Station)	35	4.21
CALIFORNIA, DAVIS	36	4.19
OHIO STATE (Columbus)	37	4.17
PURDUE (Lafayette)	38	4.15
V.P.I. & STATE U.	39	4.13
KANSAS (Lawrence)	40	4.11
WASHINGTON (St. Louis)	41	4.10

A RATING OF GRADUATE PROGRAMS IN GERMAN
Leading Institutions

Thirty-five institutions with scores in the 4.0-5.0 range, in rank order

INSTITUTION	Rank	Score
YALE	1	4.94
PRINCETON	2	4.93
WISCONSIN (Madison)	3	4.90
INDIANA (Bloomington)	4	4.89
CALIFORNIA, BERKELEY	5	4.87
TEXAS (Austin)	6	4.86
STANFORD	7	4.82
CORNELL (N.Y.)	8	4.79
HARVARD	9	4.76
ILLINOIS (Urbana)	10	4.74
VIRGINIA (Charlottesville)	11	4.70
UCLA	12	4.67
WASHINGTON (Seattle)	13	4.66
MICHIGAN (Ann Arbor)	14	4.64
MASSACHUSETTS (Amherst)	15	4.61
PENNSYLVANIA	16	4.58
WASHINGTON (St. Louis)	17	4.55
OHIO STATE (Columbus)	18	4.50
NORTH CAROLINA (Chapel Hill)	19	4.46
MINNESOTA (Minneapolis)	20	4.45
NORTHWESTERN (Illinois)	21	4.40
CALIFORNIA, SANTA BARBARA	22	4.39
BROWN	23	4.35
JOHNS HOPKINS	24	4.31
CALIFORNIA, IRVINE	25	4.25
CHICAGO	26	4.21
N.Y.U.	27	4.17
SUNY (Buffalo)	28	4.15
CALIFORNIA, DAVIS	29	4.09
CONNECTICUT (Storrs)	30	4.08
PENN STATE (University Park)	31	4.07
CUNY (Graduate School)	32	4.06
KANSAS (Lawrence)	33	4.05
PITTSBURGH (Pittsburgh)	34	4.04
RICE	35	4.03

A RATING OF GRADUATE PROGRAMS IN GRAPHIC DESIGN
Leading Institutions

Eleven institutions with scores in the 4.0-5.0 range, in rank order

INSTITUTION	Rank	Score
CORNELL (N.Y.)	1	4.82
INDIANA (Bloomington)	2	4.79
IOWA STATE (Ames)	3	4.75
KANSAS (Lawrence)	4	4.70
OHIO STATE (Columbus)	5	4.66
PENNSYLVANIA STATE (University Park)	6	4.65
ILLINOIS (Urbana)	7	4.64
CINCINNATI	8	4.60
MICHIGAN (Ann Arbor)	9	4.55
HOUSTON (Houston)	10	4.51
NORTH CAROLINA STATE (Raleigh)	11	4.49

A RATING OF GRADUATE PROGRAMS IN HISTORY
Leading Institutions

Forty-four institutions with scores in the 4.0-5.0 range, in rank order

INSTITUTION	Rank	Score
YALE	1	4.95
CALIFORNIA, BERKELEY	2	4.94
PRINCETON	3	4.93
HARVARD	4	4.92
MICHIGAN (Ann Arbor)	5	4.91
STANFORD	6	4.90
COLUMBIA (N.Y.)	7	4.89
CHICAGO	8	4.88
JOHNS HOPKINS	9	4.87
WISCONSIN (Madison)	10	4.86
UCLA	11	4.84
INDIANA (Bloomington)	12	4.83
CORNELL (N.Y.)	13	4.81
BROWN	14	4.80
PENNSYLVANIA	15	4.77
NORTH CAROLINA (Chapel Hill)	16	4.75
NORTHWESTERN (Illinois)	17	4.72
ROCHESTER (N.Y.)	18	4.69
BRANDEIS	19	4.68
VIRGINIA (Charlottesville)	20	4.65
DUKE	21	4.61
CUNY (Graduate School)	22	4.57
TEXAS (Austin)	23	4.55
WASHINGTON (Seattle)	24	4.54
MINNESOTA (Minneapolis)	25	4.51
IOWA (Iowa City)	26	4.48
CALIFORNIA, SANTA BARBARA	27	4.47
RUTGERS (New Brunswick)	28	4.42
ILLINOIS (Urbana)	29	4.41
CALIFORNIA, SAN DIEGO	30	4.38
N.Y.U.	31	4.36
NOTRE DAME	32	4.33
CALIFORNIA, DAVIS	33	4.28
VANDERBILT	34	4.27
MARYLAND (College Park)	35	4.20
OHIO STATE (Columbus)	36	4.17
PITTSBURGH (Pittsburgh)	37	4.16
RICE	38	4.14
MISSOURI (Columbia)	39	4.13
WASHINGTON (St. Louis)	40	4.10
KANSAS (Lawrence)	41	4.09
BOSTON U.	42	4.06
MICHIGAN STATE	43	4.05
EMORY	44	4.04

A RATING OF GRADUATE PROGRAMS IN INDUSTRIAL DESIGN
Leading Institutions

Ten institutions with scores in the 4.0-5.0 range, in rank order

INSTITUTION	Rank	Score
ILLINOIS (Urbana)	1	4.84
CINCINNATI	2	4.80
OHIO STATE (Columbus)	3	4.78
NORTH CAROLINA STATE (Raleigh)	4	4.75
ILLINOIS INSTITUTE OF TECHNOLOGY	5	4.71
HOUSTON (Houston)	6	4.66
KANSAS (Lawrence)	7	4.62
MICHIGAN (Ann Arbor)	8	4.58
TEXAS A&M (College Station)	9	4.53
SYRACUSE	10	4.49

A RATING OF GRADUATE PROGRAMS IN INDUSTRIAL ENGINEERING
Leading Institutions

Thirty-nine institutions with scores in the 4.0-5.0 range, in rank order

INSTITUTION	Rank	Score
MICHIGAN (Ann Arbor)	1	4.94
CALIFORNIA, BERKELEY	2	4.93
STANFORD	3	4.91
PURDUE (Lafayette)	4	4.90
WISCONSIN (Madison)	5	4.88
CORNELL (N.Y.)	6	4.86
GEORGIA TECH	7	4.83
NORTHWESTERN (Illinois)	8	4.77
TEXAS A&M (College Station)	9	4.74
OHIO STATE (Columbus)	10	4.72
ILLINOIS (Urbana)	11	4.71
IOWA STATE (Ames)	12	4.68
PITTSBURGH (Pittsburgh)	13	4.63
COLUMBIA (N.Y.)	14	4.60
PENN STATE (University Park)	15	4.54
MISSOURI (Columbia)	16	4.51
OKLAHOMA (Norman)	17	4.47
IOWA (Iowa City)	18	4.46
OKLAHOMA STATE	19	4.43
LEHIGH	20	4.39
KANSAS STATE	21	4.38
V.P.I. & STATE U.	22	4.36
ARIZONA STATE (Tempe)	23	4.35
POLYTECHNIC UNIVERSITY (Brooklyn, N.Y.)	24	4.33
SUNY (Buffalo)	25	4.32
U.S.C. (Los Angeles)	26	4.31
MASSACHUSETTS (Amherst)	27	4.29
CINCINNATI	28	4.28
NORTH CAROLINA STATE (Raleigh)	29	4.26
MINNESOTA (Minneapolis)	30	4.22
HOUSTON (Houston)	31	4.21
TEXAS (Austin)	32	4.19
TEXAS TECH	33	4.17
AUBURN (Auburn)	34	4.16
FLORIDA (Gainesville)	35	4.15
OREGON STATE	36	4.12
WEST VIRGINIA	37	4.11
NEBRASKA (Lincoln)	38	4.09
CLEMSON	39	4.07

A RATING OF GRADUATE PROGRAMS IN INDUSTRIAL LABOR RELATIONS
Leading Institutions

Six institutions with scores in the 4.0-5.0 range, in rank order

INSTITUTION	Rank	Score
CORNELL (N.Y.)	1	4.87
MINNESOTA (Minneapolis)	2	4.83
ILLINOIS (Urbana)	3	4.80
WISCONSIN (Madison)	4	4.76
OHIO STATE (Columbus)	5	4.74
RUTGERS (New Brunswick)	6	4.71

A RATING OF GRADUATE PROGRAMS IN
INDUSTRIAL/ORGANIZATIONAL PSYCHOLOGY
Leading Institutions

Twenty-three institutions with scores in the 4.0-5.0 range, in rank order

INSTITUTION	Rank	Score
MICHIGAN (Ann Arbor)	1	4.76
ILLINOIS (Urbana)	2	4.73
STANFORD	3	4.70
OHIO STATE (Columbus)	4	4.66
PURDUE (Lafayette)	5	4.65
CARNEGIE-MELLON	6	4.64
COLUMBIA (N.Y.)	7	4.60
MINNESOTA (Minneapolis)	8	4.58
WASHINGTON (St. Louis)	9	4.55
TEXAS (Austin)	10	4.54
SUNY (Buffalo)	11	4.51
GEORGE WASHINGTON (D.C.)	12	4.50
CUNY GRADUATE SCHOOL	13	4.47
MICHIGAN STATE	14	4.46
TEXAS A&M (College Station)	15	4.42
N.Y.U.	16	4.39
WAYNE STATE (Michigan)	17	4.36
MARYLAND (College Park)	18	4.30
ILLINOIS INSTITUTE OF TECHNOLOGY	19	4.28
MISSOURI (Saint Louis)	20	4.25
CALIFORNIA, IRVINE	21	4.21
CONNECTICUT (Storrs)	22	4.16
PENN STATE (University Park)	23	4.10

A RATING OF GRADUATE PROGRAMS IN INFORMATION SCIENCES
Leading Institutions

Fourteen institutions with scores in the 4.0-5.0 range, in rank order

INSTITUTION	Rank	Score
CARNEGIE-MELLON	1	4.90
GEORGIA TECH	2	4.86
OHIO STATE (Columbus)	3	4.83
CALIFORNIA, IRVINE	4	4.80
STANFORD	5	4.78
MINNESOTA (Minneapolis)	6	4.76
PENNSYLVANIA	7	4.73
ILLINOIS (Urbana)	8	4.72
MARYLAND (College Park)	9	4.71
WISCONSIN (Madison)	10	4.69
TEXAS (Austin)	11	4.67
FLORIDA (Gainesville)	12	4.64
UCLA	13	4.60
N.Y.U.	14	4.59

A RATING OF GRADUATE PROGRAMS IN INORGANIC CHEMISTRY
Leading Institutions

Sixteen institutions with scores in the 4.0-5.0 range, in rank order

INSTITUTION	Rank	Score
MINNESOTA (Minneapolis)	1	4.91
M.I.T.	2	4.88
OHIO STATE (Columbus)	3	4.85
PURDUE (Lafayette)	4	4.82
HARVARD	5	4.80
COLUMBIA (N.Y.)	6	4.77
MICHIGAN (Ann Arbor)	7	4.74
RUTGERS (New Brunswick)	8	4.71
TEXAS A&M (College Station)	9	4.67
MARYLAND (College Park)	10	4.63
FLORIDA (Gainesville)	11	4.60
PITTSBURGH (Pittsburgh)	12	4.56
MISSOURI (Columbia)	13	4.55
YALE	14	4.51
NOTRE DAME	15	4.47
RENSSELAER (N.Y.)	16	4.43

A RATING OF GRADUATE PROGRAMS IN ITALIAN
Leading Institutions

Twelve institutions with scores in the 4.0-5.0 range, in rank order

INSTITUTION	Rank	Score
HARVARD	1	4.86
COLUMBIA (N.Y.)	2	4.81
N.Y.U.	3	4.79
NORTHWESTERN (Illinois)	4	4.72
CALIFORNIA, BERKELEY	5	4.70
CHICAGO	6	4.66
ILLINOIS (Urbana)	7	4.65
MICHIGAN (Ann Arbor)	8	4.60
PENNSYLVANIA	9	4.58
WISCONSIN (Madison)	10	4.57
YALE	11	4.54
NORTH CAROLINA (Chapel Hill)	12	4.51

A RATING OF GRADUATE PROGRAMS IN INTERNATIONAL RELATIONS
Leading Institutions

Eight institutions with scores in the 4.0-5.0 range, in rank order

INSTITUTION	Rank	Score
HARVARD	1	4.86
PRINCETON	2	4.83
TUFTS	3	4.80
JOHNS HOPKINS (D.C.)	4	4.76
GEORGETOWN (D.C.)	5	4.70
COLUMBIA (N.Y.)	6	4.68
YALE	7	4.64
CHICAGO	8	4.61

A RATING OF GRADUATE PROGRAMS IN JOURNALISM
Leading Institutions

Twenty-two institutions with scores in the 4.0-5.0 range, in rank order

INSTITUTION	Rank	Score
COLUMBIA (N.Y.)	1	4.93
NORTHWESTERN (Illinois)	2	4.91
MISSOURI (Columbia)	3	4.90
MINNESOTA (Minneapolis)	4	4.86
ILLINOIS (Urbana)	5	4.84
WISCONSIN (Madison)	6	4.82
MICHIGAN (Ann Arbor)	7	4.80
STANFORD	8	4.79
TEXAS (Austin)	9	4.75
INDIANA (Bloomington)	10	4.72
IOWA (Iowa City)	11	4.71
MARYLAND (College Park)	12	4.67
N.Y.U.	13	4.62
BOSTON U.	14	4.59
U.S.C. (Los Angeles)	15	4.55
WAYNE STATE (Michigan)	16	4.51
SYRACUSE	17	4.48
MICHIGAN STATE	18	4.44
NORTH CAROLINA (Chapel Hill)	19	4.42
PENN STATE (University Park)	20	4.40
OHIO STATE (Columbus)	21	4.37
OHIO U. (Athens)	22	4.30

A RATING OF GRADUATE PROGRAMS IN LANDSCAPE ARCHITECTURE
Leading Institutions

Seventeen institutions with scores in the 4.0-5.0 range, in rank order

INSTITUTION	Rank	Score
HARVARD	1	4.88
CALIFORNIA, BERKELEY	2	4.83
MICHIGAN (Ann Arbor)	3	4.80
PENNSYLVANIA	4	4.76
SUNY (College of Environmental Science & Forestry)	5	4.74
ILLINOIS (Urbana)	6	4.69
CORNELL (N.Y.)	7	4.68
KANSAS STATE	8	4.61
MASSACHUSETTS (Amherst)	9	4.55
GEORGIA (Athens)	10	4.52
WASHINGTON (Seattle)	11	4.48
NORTH CAROLINA STATE (Raleigh)	12	4.41
OHIO STATE (Columbus)	13	4.40
COLORADO (Denver)	14	4.36
LSU (Baton Rouge)	15	4.32
MINNESOTA (Minneapolis)	16	4.29
VIRGINIA (Charlottesville)	17	4.27

A RATING OF GRADUATE PROGRAMS IN LIBRARY SCIENCE
Leading Institutions

Eighteen institutions with scores in the 4.0-5.0 range, in rank order

INSTITUTION	Rank	Score
CHICAGO	1	4.92
ILLINOIS (Urbana)	2	4.91
MICHIGAN (Ann Arbor)	3	4.90
COLUMBIA (N.Y.)	4	4.89
CALIFORNIA, BERKELEY	5	4.85
RUTGERS (New Brunswick)	6	4.79
PITTSBURGH (Pittsburgh)	7	4.76
INDIANA (Bloomington)	8	4.73
SYRACUSE	9	4.69
UCLA	10	4.63
NORTH CAROLINA (Chapel Hill)	11	4.59
SIMMONS (Massachusetts)	12	4.56
WISCONSIN (Madison)	13	4.50
DREXEL	14	4.43
MARYLAND (College Park)	15	4.40
FLORIDA STATE	16	4.34
TEXAS (Austin)	17	4.30
WASHINGTON (Seattle)	18	4.24

A RATING OF GRADUATE PROGRAMS IN LINGUISTICS
Leading Institutions

Thirty institutions with scores in the 4.0-5.0 range, in rank order

INSTITUTION	Rank	Score
M.I.T.	1	4.91
UCLA	2	4.88
TEXAS (Austin)	3	4.85
CHICAGO	4	4.83
CALIFORNIA, BERKELEY	5	4.82
MASSACHUSETTS (Amherst)	6	4.80
CALIFORNIA, SAN DIEGO	7	4.79
PENNSYLVANIA	8	4.76
STANFORD	9	4.73
ILLINOIS (Urbana)	10	4.71
OHIO STATE (Columbus)	11	4.69
HARVARD	12	4.68
CONNECTICUT (Storrs)	13	4.61
MICHIGAN (Ann Arbor)	14	4.60
WASHINGTON (Seattle)	15	4.56
U.S.C. (Los Angeles)	16	4.54
CUNY (Graduate School)	17	4.51
CORNELL (N.Y.)	18	4.49
ARIZONA (Tucson)	19	4.48
YALE	20	4.43
GEORGETOWN (D.C.)	21	4.36
INDIANA (Bloomington)	22	4.31
BROWN	23	4.28
HAWAII (Manoa)	24	4.25
WISCONSIN (Madison)	25	4.22
N.Y.U.	26	4.18
SUNY (Buffalo)	27	4.15
KANSAS (Lawrence)	28	4.12
MINNESOTA (Minneapolis)	29	4.10
PITTSBURGH (Pittsburgh)	30	4.08

A RATING OF GRADUATE PROGRAMS IN MASS COMMUNICATION/THEORY
Leading Institutions

Eighteen institutions with scores in the 4.0-5.0 range, in rank order

INSTITUTION	Rank	Score
NORTHWESTERN (Illinois)	1	4.89
STANFORD	2	4.87
PENNSYLVANIA	3	4.82
MICHIGAN (Ann Arbor)	4	4.81
IOWA (Iowa City)	5	4.74
U.S.C. (Los Angeles)	6	4.72
MICHIGAN STATE	7	4.69
TEXAS (Austin)	8	4.65
SYRACUSE	9	4.63
MISSOURI (Columbia)	10	4.58
FLORIDA STATE	11	4.53
WISCONSIN (Madison)	12	4.49
WASHINGTON (Seattle)	13	4.46
OHIO STATE (Columbus)	14	4.41
MINNESOTA (Minneapolis)	15	4.37
PURDUE (Lafayette)	16	4.29
SUNY (Buffalo)	17	4.21
KANSAS (Lawrence)	18	4.14

A RATING OF GRADUATE PROGRAMS IN
MASS/ORGANIZATIONAL COMMUNICATION
Leading Institutions

Ten institutions with scores in the 4.0-5.0 range, in rank order

INSTITUTION	Rank	Score
SYRACUSE	1	4.88
INDIANA (Bloomington)	2	4.84
IOWA (Iowa City)	3	4.80
WISCONSIN (Madison)	4	4.79
U.S.C. (Los Angeles)	5	4.77
FLORIDA STATE	6	4.72
MICHIGAN STATE	7	4.70
MARYLAND (College Park)	8	4.67
MINNESOTA (Minneapolis)	9	4.65
PENNSYLVANIA STATE (University Park)	10	4.61

A RATING OF GRADUATE PROGRAMS IN MATERIALS SCIENCE
Leading Institutions

Thirty-eight institutions with scores in the 4.0-5.0 range, in rank order

INSTITUTION	Rank	Score
M.I.T.	1	4.95
CALIFORNIA, BERKELEY	2	4.94
STANFORD	3	4.93
CORNELL (N.Y.)	4	4.92
NORTHWESTERN (Illinois)	5	4.91
CAL TECH	6	4.89
WISCONSIN (Madison)	7	4.87
CARNEGIE-MELLON	8	4.86
LEHIGH	9	4.84
PENN STATE (University Park)	10	4.83
CASE WESTERN RESERVE	11	4.81
RICE	12	4.78
PENNSYLVANIA	13	4.76
JOHNS HOPKINS	14	4.75
UCLA	15	4.72
COLUMBIA (N.Y.)	16	4.71
MICHIGAN (Ann Arbor)	17	4.70
RUTGERS (New Brunswick)	18	4.68
BROWN	19	4.63
TEXAS (Austin)	20	4.62
PURDUE (Lafayette)	21	4.59
FLORIDA (Gainesville)	22	4.57
MICHIGAN STATE	23	4.53
MINNESOTA (Minneapolis)	24	4.51
CINCINNATI	25	4.48
V.P.I. & STATE U.	26	4.43
NORTH CAROLINA STATE (Raleigh)	27	4.42
ROCHESTER (N.Y.)	28	4.40
DUKE	29	4.36
PITTSBURGH (Pittsburgh)	30	4.33
UTAH	31	4.29
DREXEL	32	4.22
SUNY (Stony Brook)	33	4.20
U.S.C. (Los Angeles)	34	4.19
TENNESSEE (Knoxville)	35	4.17
VANDERBILT	36	4.15
VIRGINIA (Charlottesville)	37	4.11
DELAWARE (Newark)	38	4.09

A RATING OF GRADUATE PROGRAMS IN MATHEMATICS
Leading Institutions

Fifty institutions with scores in the 4.0-5.0 range, in rank order

INSTITUTION	Rank	Score
PRINCETON	1	4.96
CALIFORNIA, BERKELEY	2	4.95
HARVARD	3	4.94
M.I.T.	4	4.93
CHICAGO	5	4.92
STANFORD	6	4.91
N.Y.U.	7	4.90
YALE	8	4.89
WISCONSIN (Madison)	9	4.88
COLUMBIA (N.Y.)	10	4.87
MICHIGAN (Ann Arbor)	11	4.86
BROWN	12	4.85
CORNELL (N.Y.)	13	4.84
UCLA	14	4.83
ILLINOIS (Urbana)	15	4.82
CAL TECH	16	4.81
MINNESOTA (Minneapolis)	17	4.80
CUNY (Graduate School)	18	4.78
PENNSYLVANIA	19	4.73
NOTRE DAME	20	4.72
RICE	21	4.70
PURDUE (Lafayette)	22	4.69
RUTGERS (New Brunswick)	23	4.67
WASHINGTON (Seattle)	24	4.65
SUNY (Stony Brook)	25	4.64
INDIANA (Bloomington)	26	4.61
MARYLAND (College Park)	27	4.60
NORTHWESTERN (Illinois)	28	4.59
CALIFORNIA, SAN DIEGO	29	4.55
TEXAS (Austin)	30	4.53
CARNEGIE-MELLON	31	4.50
JOHNS HOPKINS	32	4.48
WASHINGTON (St. Louis)	33	4.46
OHIO STATE (Columbus)	34	4.44
PENN STATE (University Park)	35	4.41
BRANDEIS	36	4.40
VIRGINIA (Charlottesville)	37	4.35
KENTUCKY	38	4.32
COLORADO (Boulder)	39	4.29
NORTH CAROLINA (Chapel Hill)	40	4.25
UTAH	41	4.24
ILLINOIS (Chicago)	42	4.21
ROCHESTER (N.Y.)	43	4.19
RENSSELAER (N.Y.)	44	4.17
SUNY (Buffalo)	45	4.14
TULANE	46	4.12
CALIFORNIA, SANTA BARBARA	47	4.10
U.S.C. (Los Angeles)	48	4.08
MICHIGAN STATE	49	4.06
DUKE	50	4.04

A RATING OF GRADUATE PROGRAMS IN MECHANICAL ENGINEERING
Leading Institutions

Fifty institutions with scores in the 4.0-5.0 range, in rank order

INSTITUTION	Rank	Score
M.I.T.	1	4.95
STANFORD	2	4.94
CALIFORNIA, BERKELEY	3	4.93
CAL TECH	4	4.92
MINNESOTA (Minneapolis)	5	4.91
PRINCETON	6	4.89
PURDUE (Lafayette)	7	4.87
CORNELL (N.Y.)	8	4.86
BROWN	9	4.85
MICHIGAN (Ann Arbor)	10	4.81
UCLA	11	4.80
ILLINOIS (Urbana)	12	4.79
WISCONSIN (Madison)	13	4.75
NORTHWESTERN (Illinois)	14	4.74
RENSSELAER (N.Y.)	15	4.72
TEXAS (Austin)	16	4.71
LEHIGH	17	4.66
JOHNS HOPKINS	18	4.62
PENNSYLVANIA	19	4.59
CARNEGIE-MELLON	20	4.56
COLUMBIA (N.Y.)	21	4.54
GEORGIA TECH	22	4.53
CASE WESTERN RESERVE	23	4.49
CALIFORNIA, DAVIS	24	4.46
RICE	25	4.44
V.P.I. & STATE U.	26	4.43
PENN STATE (University Park)	27	4.41
OHIO STATE (Columbus)	28	4.40
IOWA STATE (Ames)	29	4.38
WASHINGTON (Seattle)	30	4.37
NORTH CAROLINA STATE (Raleigh)	31	4.36
YALE	32	4.34
SUNY (Stony Brook)	33	4.33
ILLINOIS (Chicago)	34	4.32
HOUSTON (Houston)	35	4.29
MARYLAND (College Park)	36	4.28
NOTRE DAME	37	4.27
MICHIGAN STATE	38	4.25
ROCHESTER (N.Y.)	39	4.22
IOWA (Iowa City)	40	4.21
VIRGINIA (Charlottesville)	41	4.19
ILLINOIS INSTITUTE OF TECHNOLOGY	42	4.18
DELAWARE (Newark)	43	4.16
OKLAHOMA STATE	44	4.14
SUNY (Buffalo)	45	4.12
POLYTECHNIC UNIVERSITY (Brooklyn, N.Y.)	46	4.10
RUTGERS (New Brunswick)	47	4.08
OREGON STATE	48	4.07
FLORIDA (Gainesville)	49	4.05
DREXEL	50	4.02

A RATING OF GRADUATE PROGRAMS IN METALLURGICAL ENGINEERING
Leading Institutions

Fifteen institutions with scores in the 4.0-5.0 range, in rank order

INSTITUTION	Rank	Score
CARNEGIE-MELLON	1	4.92
COLUMBIA (N.Y.)	2	4.90
COLORADO SCHOOL OF MINES	3	4.89
GEORGIA TECH	4	4.88
OHIO STATE (Columbus)	5	4.87
PITTSBURGH (Pittsburgh)	6	4.85
PENNSYLVANIA STATE (University Park)	7	4.80
RENSSELAER (N.Y.)	8	4.78
MISSOURI (Rolla)	9	4.77
WASHINGTON (Seattle)	10	4.73
WISCONSIN (Madison)	11	4.72
UTAH (Salt Lake)	12	4.71
FLORIDA (Gainesville)	13	4.70
OKLAHOMA (Norman)	14	4.68
POLYTECHNIC UNIVERSITY (Brooklyn, N.Y.)	15	4.67

A RATING OF GRADUATE PROGRAMS IN METALLURGY
Leading Institutions

Ten institutions with scores in the 4.0-5.0 range, in rank order

INSTITUTION	Rank	Score
M.I.T.	1	4.91
COLORADO SCHOOL OF MINES	2	4.90
COLUMBIA (N.Y.)	3	4.88
CALIFORNIA, BERKELEY	4	4.86
MINNESOTA (Minneapolis)	5	4.82
RENSSELAER (N.Y.)	6	4.79
MICHIGAN STATE	7	4.74
IOWA STATE (Ames)	8	4.71
POLYTECHNIC UNIVERSITY (Brooklyn, N.Y.)	9	4.68
OKLAHOMA (Norman)	10	4.66

A RATING OF GRADUATE PROGRAMS IN METEOROLOGY/ATMOSPHERIC SCIENCES
Leading Institutions

Fifteen institutions with scores in the 4.0-5.0 range, in rank order

INSTITUTION	Rank	Score
CORNELL (N.Y)	1	4.93
M.I.T.	2	4.90
ARIZONA (Tucson)	3	4.88
COLUMBIA (N.Y.)	4	4.86
MARYLAND (College Park)	5	4.85
COLORADO (Boulder)	6	4.83
PENNSYLVANIA STATE (University Park)	7	4.80
TEXAS A&M (College Station)	8	4.77
OKLAHOMA (Norman)	9	4.76
WISCONSIN (Madison)	10	4.72
YALE	11	4.69
PRINCETON	12	4.66
NORTH CAROLINA STATE (Raleigh)	13	4.63
KANSAS (Lawrence)	14	4.61
MISSOURI (Columbia)	15	4.57

A RATING OF GRADUATE PROGRAMS IN MICROBIOLOGY
Leading Institutions

Fifty-two institutions with scores in the 4.0-5.0 range, in rank order

INSTITUTION	Rank	Score
M.I.T.	1	4.95
ROCKEFELLER (N.Y.)	2	4.94
CALIFORNIA, SAN DIEGO	3	4.93
JOHNS HOPKINS	4	4.92
DUKE	5	4.91
WASHINGTON (Seattle)	6	4.90
UCLA	7	4.89
CHICAGO	8	4.88
ILLINOIS (Urbana)	9	4.87
PENNSYLVANIA	10	4.86
HARVARD	11	4.85
CALIFORNIA, DAVIS	12	4.84
WISCONSIN (Madison)	13	4.83
MICHIGAN (Ann Arbor)	14	4.82
STANFORD	15	4.81
COLUMBIA (N.Y.)	16	4.80
CALIFORNIA, SAN FRANCISCO	17	4.79
YALE	18	4.77
N.Y.U.	19	4.76
CALIFORNIA, BERKELEY	20	4.75
ALABAMA (Birmingham)	21	4.73
MINNESOTA (Minneapolis)	22	4.72
RUTGERS (New Brunswick)	23	4.71
PURDUE (Lafayette)	24	4.69
CORNELL (Medical Center)	25	4.68
CORNELL (Ithaca, N.Y.)	26	4.66
MICHIGAN STATE	27	4.63
NORTH CAROLINA (Chapel Hill)	28	4.62
ALBERT EINSTEIN (College of Medicine)	29	4.61
TEXAS (Austin)	30	4.59
CALIFORNIA, IRVINE	31	4.58
VANDERBILT	32	4.55
ROCHESTER (N.Y.)	33	4.53
FLORIDA (Gainesville)	34	4.51
VIRGINIA (Charlottesville)	35	4.47
OREGON (Eugene)	36	4.45
TUFTS	37	4.43
V.P.I. & STATE U.	38	4.41
INDIANA (Bloomington)	39	4.39
IOWA (Iowa City)	40	4.38
MASSACHUSETTS (Amherst)	41	4.37
PITTSBURGH (Pittsburgh)	42	4.34
BAYLOR (College of Medicine)	43	4.31
ILLINOIS (U. Medical Center)	44	4.27
PENN STATE (University Park)	45	4.23
SUNY (Buffalo)	46	4.22
MARYLAND (College Park)	47	4.19
WAYNE STATE (Michigan)	48	4.17
TEXAS (U. Health Sci. Ctr., Houston)	49	4.16
U.S.C. (Los Angeles)	50	4.15
NORTHWESTERN (Illinois)	51	4.13
OREGON STATE	52	4.10

A RATING OF GRADUATE PROGRAMS IN MUSIC
Leading Institutions

Thirty-eight institutions with scores in the 4.0-5.0 range, in rank order

INSTITUTION	Rank	Score
CALIFORNIA, BERKELEY	1	4.92
CHICAGO	2	4.91
HARVARD	3	4.89
PRINCETON	4	4.87
YALE	5	4.86
CORNELL (N.Y.)	6	4.84
ILLINOIS (Urbana)	7	4.82
COLUMBIA (N.Y.)	8	4.78
MICHIGAN (Ann Arbor)	9	4.76
UCLA	10	4.74
PENNSYLVANIA	11	4.72
N.Y.U.	12	4.70
STANFORD	13	4.68
ROCHESTER (N.Y.)	14	4.65
NORTH CAROLINA (Chapel Hill)	15	4.62
INDIANA (Bloomington)	16	4.57
U.S.C. (Los Angeles)	17	4.56
BRANDEIS	18	4.50
IOWA (Iowa City)	19	4.48
TEXAS (Austin)	20	4.45
CUNY (Graduate School)	21	4.42
RUTGERS (New Brunswick)	22	4.38
NORTHWESTERN (Illinois)	23	4.35
OHIO STATE (Columbus)	24	4.33
NORTH TEXAS (Denton)	25	4.32
SUNY (Buffalo)	26	4.25
WASHINGTON (Seattle)	27	4.22
MARYLAND (College Park)	28	4.19
CALIFORNIA, SANTA BARBARA	29	4.18
FLORIDA STATE	30	4.16
JULLIARD SCHOOL (N.Y.)	31	4.14
MINNESOTA (Minneapolis)	32	4.12
WISCONSIN (Madison)	33	4.10
BOSTON U.	34	4.09
KANSAS (Lawrence)	35	4.08
PITTSBURGH (Pittsburgh)	36	4.07
CINCINNATI	37	4.06
OREGON (Eugene)	38	4.05

A RATING OF GRADUATE PROGRAMS IN
NEAR/MIDDLE EASTERN LANGUAGES
Leading Institutions

Ten institutions with scores in the 4.0-5.0 range, in rank order

INSTITUTION	Rank	Score
HARVARD	1	4.89
CALIFORNIA, BERKELEY	2	4.86
COLUMBIA (N.Y.)	3	4.83
GEORGETOWN (D.C.)	4	4.80
YALE	5	4.77
WISCONSIN (Madison)	6	4.74
WASHINGTON (Seattle)	7	4.72
N.Y.U.	8	4.69
UCLA	9	4.65
INDIANA (Bloomington)	10	4.62

A RATING OF GRADUATE PROGRAMS IN NEAR/MIDDLE EASTERN STUDIES
Leading Institutions

Ten institutions with scores in the 4.0-5.0 range, in rank order

INSTITUTION	Rank	Score
CHICAGO	1	4.86
HARVARD	2	4.84
PENNSYLVANIA	3	4.81
MICHIGAN (Ann Arbor)	4	4.78
COLUMBIA (N.Y.)	5	4.73
CORNELL (N.Y.)	6	4.70
PRINCETON	7	4.66
UCLA	8	4.61
JOHNS HOPKINS (Baltimore)	9	4.58
N.Y.U.	10	4.55

A RATING OF GRADUATE PROGRAMS IN NUCLEAR ENGINEERING
Leading Institutions

Twenty-six institutions with scores in the 4.0-5.0 range, in rank order

INSTITUTION	Rank	Score
M.I.T.	1	4.92
MICHIGAN (Ann Arbor)	2	4.91
CORNELL (N.Y.)	3	4.89
CALIFORNIA, BERKELEY	4	4.88
GEORGIA TECH	5	4.87
ILLINOIS (Urbana)	6	4.84
RENSSELAER (N.Y.)	7	4.83
TEXAS A&M (College Station)	8	4.81
OHIO STATE (Columbus)	9	4.77
WISCONSIN (Madison)	10	4.73
PURDUE (Lafayette)	11	4.72
VIRGINIA (Charlottesville)	12	4.68
UCLA	13	4.66
PENN STATE (University Park)	14	4.64
FLORIDA (Gainesville)	15	4.61
NORTHWESTERN (Illinois)	16	4.58
NORTH CAROLINA STATE (Raleigh)	17	4.56
CINCINNATI	18	4.51
ARIZONA (Tucson)	19	4.48
WASHINGTON (Seattle)	20	4.46
MISSOURI (Columbia)	21	4.42
KANSAS STATE	22	4.38
MARYLAND (College Park)	23	4.34
MISSOURI (Rolla)	24	4.30
COLUMBIA (N.Y.)	25	4.26
OKLAHOMA (Norman)	26	4.21

A RATING OF GRADUATE PROGRAMS IN OCCUPATIONAL THERAPY
Leading Institutions

Fifteen institutions with scores in the 4.0-5.0 range, in rank order

INSTITUTION	Rank	Score
N.Y.U.	1	4.89
BOSTON U.	2	4.83
COLUMBIA (N.Y.)	3	4.79
TUFTS	4	4.75
TEMPLE (Philadelphia)	5	4.70
NORTH CAROLINA (Chapel Hill)	6	4.65
OHIO STATE (Columbus)	7	4.62
WASHINGTON (Seattle)	8	4.58
COLORADO STATE	9	4.52
U.S.C. (Los Angeles)	10	4.51
WISCONSIN (Madison)	11	4.41
FLORIDA (Gainesville)	12	4.33
WAYNE STATE (Michigan)	13	4.28
WASHINGTON (St. Louis)	14	4.23
SUNY (Buffalo)	15	4.19

A RATING OF GRADUATE PROGRAMS IN OPERATIONS RESEARCH
Leading Institutions

Twenty-five institutions with scores in the 4.0-5.0 range, in rank order

INSTITUTION	Rank	Score
CALIFORNIA, BERKELEY	1	4.93
COLUMBIA (N.Y.)	2	4.92
STANFORD	3	4.91
M.I.T.	4	4.90
CORNELL (N.Y.)	5	4.88
MICHIGAN (Ann Arbor)	6	4.85
NORTHWESTERN (Illinois)	7	4.83
RENSSELAER (N.Y.)	8	4.82
CARNEGIE-MELLON	9	4.81
CASE WESTERN RESERVE	10	4.76
N.Y.U.	11	4.72
WISCONSIN (Madison)	12	4.66
NORTH CAROLINA (Chapel Hill)	13	4.63
GEORGIA TECH	14	4.62
PURDUE (Lafayette)	15	4.59
TEXAS (Austin)	16	4.56
YALE	17	4.50
V.P.I. & STATE U.	18	4.43
JOHNS HOPKINS	19	4.41
UCLA	20	4.38
MASSACHUSETTS (Amherst)	21	4.33
NORTH CAROLINA STATE (Raleigh)	22	4.30
SYRACUSE	23	4.25
SOUTHERN METHODIST	24	4.22
HOUSTON (Houston)	25	4.19

A RATING OF GRADUATE PROGRAMS IN ORGANIC CHEMISTRY
Leading Institutions

Sixteen institutions with scores in the 4.0-5.0 range, in rank order

INSTITUTION	Rank	Score
MINNESOTA (Minneapolis)	1	4.91
HARVARD	2	4.89
PURDUE (Lafayette)	3	4.86
OHIO STATE (Columbus)	4	4.83
M.I.T.	5	4.80
MICHIGAN (Ann Arbor)	6	4.78
MARYLAND (College Park)	7	4.77
COLUMBIA (N.Y.)	8	4.75
TEXAS A&M (College Station)	9	4.71
RUTGERS (New Brunswick)	10	4.68
FLORIDA (Gainesville)	11	4.63
PITTSBURGH (Pittsburgh)	12	4.59
MISSOURI (Columbia)	13	4.55
YALE	14	4.52
NOTRE DAME	15	4.49
RENSSELAER (N.Y.)	16	4.44

A RATING OF GRADUATE PROGRAMS IN PETROLEUM ENGINEERING
Leading Institutions

Fourteen institutions with scores in the 4.0-5.0 range, in rank order

INSTITUTION	Rank	Score
TEXAS (Austin)	1	4.91
STANFORD	2	4.90
U.S.C. (Los Angeles)	3	4.85
TULSA	4	4.82
TEXAS A&M (College Station)	5	4.79
OKLAHOMA (Norman)	6	4.76
LSU (Baton Rouge)	7	4.68
CALIFORNIA, BERKELEY	8	4.65
KANSAS (Lawrence)	9	4.62
PENN STATE (University Park)	10	4.58
COLORADO (Mines)	11	4.53
MISSOURI (Rolla)	12	4.46
HOUSTON (Houston)	13	4.43
NEW MEXICO (Mining & Technology)	14	4.39

A RATING OF GRADUATE PROGRAMS IN PHILOSOPHY
Leading Institutions

Forty-five institutions with scores in the 4.0-5.0 range, in rank order

INSTITUTION	Rank	Score
PRINCETON	1	4.94
HARVARD	2	4.93
PITTSBURGH (Pittsburgh)	3	4.92
CALIFORNIA, BERKELEY	4	4.91
UCLA	5	4.90
STANFORD	6	4.89
CHICAGO	7	4.86
MICHIGAN (Ann Arbor)	8	4.84
CORNELL (N.Y.)	9	4.81
M.I.T.	10	4.80
BROWN	11	4.77
MASSACHUSETTS (Amherst)	12	4.75
COLUMBIA (N.Y.)	13	4.74
INDIANA (Bloomington)	14	4.70
NORTH CAROLINA (Chapel Hill)	15	4.66
WISCONSIN (Madison)	16	4.62
YALE	17	4.61
MINNESOTA (Minneapolis)	18	4.57
NOTRE DAME	19	4.54
BOSTON U.	20	4.49
ILLINOIS (Chicago)	21	4.48
CALIFORNIA, IRVINE	22	4.44
TEXAS (Austin)	23	4.42
U.S.C. (Los Angeles)	24	4.38
OHIO STATE (Columbus)	25	4.37
ARIZONA (Tucson)	26	4.36
SYRACUSE	27	4.33
JOHNS HOPKINS	28	4.32
CUNY (Graduate School)	29	4.30
PENNSYLVANIA	30	4.28
ROCHESTER (N.Y.)	31	4.26
ILLINOIS (Urbana)	32	4.23
CALIFORNIA, SAN DIEGO	33	4.22
CATHOLIC U. (D.C.)	34	4.19
NORTHWESTERN (Illinois)	35	4.15
TEMPLE (Philadelphia)	36	4.14
IOWA (Iowa City)	37	4.13
WASHINGTON (St. Louis)	38	4.12
WASHINGTON (Seattle)	39	4.10
FORDHAM (N.Y.)	40	4.07
RUTGERS (New Brunswick)	41	4.05
VANDERBILT	42	4.04
PENN STATE (University Park)	43	4.03
SUNY (Buffalo)	44	4.02
CALIFORNIA, SANTA BARBARA	45	4.01

A RATING OF GRADUATE PROGRAMS IN PHYSICAL CHEMISTRY
Leading Institutions

Sixteen institutions with scores in the 4.0-5.0 range, in rank order

INSTITUTION	Rank	Score
MINNESOTA (Minneapolis)	1	4.90
OHIO STATE (Columbus)	2	4.86
HARVARD	3	4.85
COLUMBIA (N.Y.)	4	4.82
M.I.T.	5	4.79
PURDUE (Lafayette)	6	4.78
MICHIGAN (Ann Arbor)	7	4.76
TEXAS A&M (College Station)	8	4.75
RUTGERS (New Brunswick)	9	4.73
MARYLAND (College Park)	10	4.70
MISSOURI (Columbia)	11	4.66
PITTSBURGH (Pittsburgh)	12	4.62
YALE	13	4.60
FLORIDA (Gainesville)	14	4.55
NOTRE DAME	15	4.53
RENSSELAER (N.Y.)	16	4.51

A RATING OF GRADUATE PROGRAMS IN PHYSICAL THERAPY
Leading Institutions

Sixteen institutions with scores in the 4.0-5.0 range, in rank order

INSTITUTION	Rank	Score
BOSTON U.	1	4.91
COLUMBIA (College of Physicians and Surgeons, N.Y.)	2	4.89
DUKE U. (Medical Center)	3	4.86
LONG ISLAND U. (Brooklyn)	4	4.71
U.S.C. (Los Angeles)	5	4.69
EMORY	6	4.62
HAHNEMANN U. (Pennsylvania)	7	4.55
ALABAMA (Birmingham)	8	4.51
U.S. ARMY-BAYLOR U.	9	4.43
TEXAS WOMAN'S U.	10	4.39
PACIFIC (Oregon)	11	4.32
INDIANAPOLIS, U. OF (Indiana)	12	4.23
MIAMI (Florida)	13	4.15
IOWA (Iowa City)	14	4.13
PHILADELPHIA COLLEGE OF PHARMACY & SCIENCE	15	4.10
BEAVER COLLEGE (Pennsylvania)	16	4.08

A RATING OF GRADUATE PROGRAMS IN PHYSICS
Leading Institutions

Fifty-one institutions with scores in the 4.0-5.0 range, in rank order

INSTITUTION	Rank	Score
HARVARD	1	4.95
CAL TECH	2	4.94
CORNELL (N.Y.)	3	4.93
PRINCETON	4	4.92
M.I.T.	5	4.91
CALIFORNIA, BERKELEY	6	4.90
STANFORD	7	4.89
CHICAGO	8	4.88
ILLINOIS (Urbana)	9	4.87
COLUMBIA (N.Y.)	10	4.85
YALE	11	4.84
CALIFORNIA, SAN DIEGO	12	4.82
PENNSYLVANIA	13	4.81
MICHIGAN (Ann Arbor)	14	4.80
UCLA	15	4.75
WISCONSIN (Madison)	16	4.73
WASHINGTON (Seattle)	17	4.72
SUNY (Stony Brook)	18	4.71
MARYLAND (College Park)	19	4.70
ROCKEFELLER (N.Y.)	20	4.69
CALIFORNIA, SANTA BARBARA	21	4.68
TEXAS (Austin)	22	4.67
CARNEGIE-MELLON	23	4.64
MINNESOTA (Minneapolis)	24	4.61
ROCHESTER (N.Y.)	25	4.59
BROWN	26	4.56
JOHNS HOPKINS	27	4.54
MICHIGAN STATE	28	4.51
N.Y.U.	29	4.49
BRANDEIS	30	4.48
PITTSBURGH (Pittsburgh)	31	4.47
RUTGERS (New Brunswick)	32	4.44
COLORADO (Boulder)	33	4.42
INDIANA (Bloomington)	34	4.40
NORTHWESTERN (Illinois)	35	4.38
CUNY (Graduate School)	36	4.37
NORTH CAROLINA (Chapel Hill)	37	4.32
CALIFORNIA, IRVINE	38	4.31
DUKE	39	4.30
ARIZONA (Tucson)	40	4.29
RICE	41	4.27
SYRACUSE	42	4.23
VIRGINIA (Charlottesville)	43	4.20
OHIO STATE (Columbus)	44	4.18
CASE WESTERN RESERVE	45	4.17
IOWA STATE (Ames)	46	4.15
FLORIDA STATE	47	4.14
WASHINGTON (St. Louis)	48	4.12
RENSSELAER (N.Y.)	49	4.10
DARTMOUTH	50	4.09
IOWA (Iowa City)	51	4.08

A RATING OF GRADUATE PROGRAMS IN PHYSIOLOGY
Leading Institutions

Thirty-five institutions with scores in the 4.0-5.0 range, in rank order

INSTITUTION	Rank	Score
ROCKEFELLER (N.Y.)	1	4.93
CALIFORNIA, SAN FRANCISCO	2	4.92
WASHINGTON (Seattle)	3	4.90
YALE	4	4.88
PENNSYLVANIA	5	4.86
HARVARD	6	4.83
UCLA	7	4.79
DUKE	8	4.75
MICHIGAN (Ann Arbor)	9	4.73
WASHINGTON (St. Louis)	10	4.68
CALIFORNIA, DAVIS	11	4.64
COLUMBIA (N.Y.)	12	4.60
SUNY (Buffalo)	13	4.57
VIRGINIA (Charlottesville)	14	4.56
MISSOURI (Columbia)	15	4.55
NORTH CAROLINA (Chapel Hill)	16	4.51
CORNELL (N.Y.)	17	4.48
MICHIGAN STATE	18	4.43
MINNESOTA (Minneapolis)	19	4.41
CHICAGO	20	4.38
PENN STATE (University Park)	21	4.36
IOWA (Iowa City)	22	4.33
ROCHESTER (N.Y.)	23	4.29
CALIFORNIA, SAN DIEGO	24	4.28
TEXAS HEALTH SCIENCE CENTER (Houston)	25	4.24
ALBERT EINSTEIN (College of Medicine, N.Y.)	26	4.23
CALIFORNIA, BERKELEY	27	4.19
STANFORD	28	4.17
VANDERBILT	29	4.15
JOHNS HOPKINS	30	4.13
NORTHWESTERN (Illinois)	31	4.11
CALIFORNIA, IRVINE	32	4.09
ALABAMA (Birmingham)	33	4.08
COLORADO STATE	34	4.06
ARIZONA (Tucson)	35	4.03

A RATING OF GRADUATE PROGRAMS IN PLANETARY SCIENCES
Leading Institutions

Ten institutions with scores in the 4.0-5.0 range, in rank order

INSTITUTION	Rank	Score
CORNELL (N.Y.)	1	4.94
CAL TECH	2	4.92
CHICAGO	3	4.90
COLUMBIA (N.Y.)	4	4.88
M.I.T.	5	4.85
HARVARD	6	4.82
ARIZONA (Tucson)	7	4.79
UCLA	8	4.74
RENSSELAER (N.Y.)	9	4.70
BROWN	10	4.66

A RATING OF GRADUATE PROGRAMS IN PLASMA PHYSICS
Leading Institutions

Eight institutions with scores in the 4.0-5.0 range, in rank order

INSTITUTION	Rank	Score
CAL TECH	1	4.88
PRINCETON	2	4.86
COLUMBIA (N.Y.)	3	4.84
MINNESOTA (Minneapolis)	4	4.81
MARYLAND (College Park)	5	4.78
RENSSELAER (N.Y.)	6	4.73
YALE	7	4.70
COLORADO (Boulder)	8	4.67

A RATING OF GRADUATE PROGRAMS IN POLITICAL SCIENCE
Leading Institutions

Thirty-six institutions with scores in the 4.0-5.0 range, in rank order

INSTITUTION	Rank	Score
YALE	1	4.94
MICHIGAN (Ann Arbor)	2	4.93
CALIFORNIA, BERKELEY	3	4.92
HARVARD	4	4.91
CHICAGO	5	4.90
M.I.T.	6	4.89
STANFORD	7	4.88
WISCONSIN (Madison)	8	4.83
MINNESOTA (Minneapolis)	9	4.81
CORNELL (N.Y.)	10	4.79
PRINCETON	11	4.75
COLUMBIA (N.Y.)	12	4.73
NORTHWESTERN (Illinois)	13	4.70
UCLA	14	4.68
INDIANA (Bloomington)	15	4.65
NORTH CAROLINA (Chapel Hill)	16	4.64
PENNSYLVANIA	17	4.62
ILLINOIS (Urbana)	18	4.58
OHIO STATE (Columbus)	19	4.55
NOTRE DAME	20	4.53
DUKE	21	4.52
JOHNS HOPKINS	22	4.46
IOWA (Iowa City)	23	4.44
VIRGINIA (Charlottesville)	24	4.41
TEXAS (Austin)	25	4.38
MICHIGAN STATE	26	4.33
PITTSBURGH (Pittsburgh)	27	4.30
WASHINGTON (Seattle)	28	4.27
CALIFORNIA, SAN DIEGO	29	4.23
CUNY (Graduate School)	30	4.20
MASSACHUSETTS (Amherst)	31	4.17
ROCHESTER (N.Y.)	32	4.15
RUTGERS (New Brunswick)	33	4.14
WASHINGTON (St. Louis)	34	4.10
OREGON (Eugene)	35	4.09
VANDERBILT	36	4.08

A RATING OF GRADUATE PROGRAMS IN POLYMER SCIENCES/PLASTICS ENGINEERING
Leading Institutions

Nine institutions with scores in the 4.0-5.0 range, in rank order

INSTITUTION	Rank	Score
M.I.T.	1	4.88
CORNELL (N.Y.)	2	4.84
PRINCETON	3	4.80
RENSSELAER (N.Y.)	4	4.76
GEORGIA TECH	5	4.72
PENNSYLVANIA STATE (University Park)	6	4.68
POLYTECHNIC UNIVERSITY (Brooklyn, N.Y.)	7	4.64
FLORIDA (Gainesville)	8	4.61
LEHIGH	9	4.58

A RATING OF GRADUATE PROGRAMS IN PSYCHOLOGY
Leading Institutions

Forty-eight institutions with scores in the 4.0-5.0 range, in rank order

INSTITUTION	Rank	Score
STANFORD	1	4.74
YALE	2	4.73
PENNSYLVANIA	3	4.72
MICHIGAN (Ann Arbor)	4	4.71
MINNESOTA (Minneapolis)	5	4.70
HARVARD	6	4.69
CALIFORNIA, BERKELEY	7	4.68
ILLINOIS (Urbana)	8	4.67
UCLA	9	4.66
CHICAGO	10	4.65
CALIFORNIA, SAN DIEGO	11	4.64
CARNEGIE-MELLON	12	4.63
INDIANA (Bloomington)	13	4.62
COLUMBIA (N.Y.)	14	4.61
COLORADO (Boulder)	15	4.60
WISCONSIN (Madison)	16	4.59
OREGON (Eugene)	17	4.58
M.I.T.	18	4.57
PRINCETON	19	4.56
WASHINGTON (Seattle)	20	4.54
CORNELL (N.Y.)	21	4.52
TEXAS (Austin)	22	4.50
BROWN	23	4.48
NORTH CAROLINA (Chapel Hill)	24	4.47
NORTHWESTERN (Illinois)	25	4.44
JOHNS HOPKINS	26	4.42
SUNY (Stony Brook)	27	4.37
PENN STATE (University Park)	28	4.34
DUKE	29	4.31
CUNY (Graduate School)	30	4.28
OHIO STATE (Columbus)	31	4.27
RUTGERS (New Brunswick)	32	4.25
IOWA (Iowa City)	33	4.23
KANSAS (Lawrence)	34	4.21
PITTSBURGH (Pittsburgh)	35	4.20
PURDUE (Lafayette)	36	4.18
N.Y.U.	37	4.16
U.S.C. (Los Angeles)	38	4.15
VIRGINIA (Charlottesville)	39	4.14
CONNECTICUT (Storrs)	40	4.12
CALIFORNIA, SANTA BARBARA	41	4.10
ROCHESTER (N.Y.)	42	4.09
VANDERBILT	43	4.08
CALIFORNIA, IRVINE	44	4.07
MICHIGAN STATE	45	4.06
MASSACHUSETTS (Amherst)	46	4.05
SUNY (Buffalo)	47	4.04
UTAH	48	4.02

A RATING OF GRADUATE PROGRAMS IN PSYCHOLOGY/NEUROPSYCHOLOGY
Leading Institutions

Thirteen institutions with scores in the 4.0-5.0 range, in rank order

INSTITUTION	Rank	Score
CHICAGO	1	4.70
JOHNS HOPKINS	2	4.63
DUKE	3	4.60
CORNELL (N.Y.)	4	4.55
NORTHWESTERN U. MEDICAL SCHOOL (Illinois)	5	4.50
TEXAS (Austin)	6	4.46
EMORY	7	4.42
CUNY (Graduate School)	8	4.39
SUNY (Stony Brook)	9	4.33
CALIFORNIA, RIVERSIDE	10	4.31
DELAWARE (Newark)	11	4.26
OKLAHOMA U. OF (Health Sciences Center)	12	4.24
NEW MEXICO U. OF	13	4.20

A RATING OF GRADUATE PROGRAMS IN PSYCHOLOGY/NEUROSCIENCE
Leading Institutions

Twenty-three institutions with scores in the 4.0-5.0 range, in rank order

INSTITUTION	Rank	Score
M.I.T.	1	4.71
WASHINGTON (St. Louis)	2	4.66
ILLINOIS (Urbana)	3	4.62
CORNELL (N.Y.)	4	4.58
NORTHWESTERN (Illinois)	5	4.55
PRINCETON	6	4.50
MICHIGAN STATE	7	4.48
PURDUE (Lafayette)	8	4.44
VIRGINIA (Charlottesville)	9	4.40
CALIFORNIA, RIVERSIDE	10	4.39
DELAWARE (Newark)	11	4.38
COLORADO (Boulder)	12	4.35
NEW MEXICO	13	4.30
SUNY (Binghampton)	14	4.26
TULANE	15	4.22
MASSACHUSETTS (Amherst)	16	4.20
TEXAS (Dallas)	17	4.18
WAYNE STATE (Michigan)	18	4.17
ILLINOIS (Chicago)	19	4.13
ARIZONA STATE	20	4.09
FLORIDA STATE	21	4.05
CONNECTICUT (Storrs)	22	4.03
OREGON HEALTH SCIENCES U. (Portland)	23	4.01

A RATING OF GRADUATE PROGRAMS IN PUBLIC ADMINISTRATION
Leading Institutions

Nineteen institutions with scores in the 4.0-5.0 range, in rank order

INSTITUTION	Rank	Score
SYRACUSE	1	4.92
HARVARD	2	4.90
INDIANA (Bloomington)	3	4.88
U.S.C. (Los Angeles)	4	4.87
CALIFORNIA, BERKELEY	5	4.84
TEXAS (Austin)	6	4.81
PRINCETON	7	4.78
PITTSBURGH (Pittsburgh)	8	4.72
MICHIGAN (Ann Arbor)	9	4.70
GEORGIA (Athens)	10	4.67
CARNEGIE-MELLON	11	4.65
MINNESOTA (Minneapolis)	12	4.61
OHIO STATE (Columbus)	13	4.55
AMERICAN (D.C.)	14	4.51
NORTH CAROLINA (Chapel Hill)	15	4.46
SUNY (Albany)	16	4.42
GEORGE WASHINGTON	17	4.36
FLORIDA STATE	18	4.32
KANSAS (Lawrence)	19	4.24

A RATING OF GRADUATE PROGRAMS IN RADIO/TV/FILM
Leading Institutions

Ten institutions with scores in the 4.0-5.0 range, in rank order

INSTITUTION	Rank	Score
U.S.C. (Los Angeles)	1	4.91
UCLA	2	4.90
N.Y.U.	3	4.88
NORTHWESTERN (Illinois)	4	4.85
INDIANA (Bloomington)	5	4.82
FLORIDA STATE	6	4.80
COLUMBIA (N.Y.)	7	4.76
TEXAS (Austin)	8	4.73
NORTH CAROLINA (Chapel Hill)	9	4.71
TEMPLE (Philadelphia)	10	4.68

A RATING OF GRADUATE PROGRAMS IN RUSSIAN
Leading Institutions

Ten institutions with scores in the 4.0-5.0 range, in rank order

INSTITUTION	Rank	Score
HARVARD	1	4.90
COLUMBIA (N.Y.)	2	4.86
CORNELL (N.Y.)	3	4.82
PENNSYLVANIA	4	4.80
WASHINGTON (Seattle)	5	4.76
ILLINOIS (Urbana)	6	4.71
NORTH CAROLINA (Chapel Hill)	7	4.68
BROWN	8	4.62
MICHIGAN STATE	9	4.57
OHIO STATE (Columbus)	10	4.50

A RATING OF GRADUATE PROGRAMS IN SLAVIC LANGUAGES
Leading Institutions

Sixteen institutions with scores in the 4.0-5.0 range, in rank order

INSTITUTION	Rank	Score
HARVARD	1	4.90
COLUMBIA (N.Y.)	2	4.87
INDIANA (Bloomington)	3	4.84
CORNELL (N.Y.)	4	4.80
WISCONSIN (Madison)	5	4.77
WASHINGTON (Seattle)	6	4.75
ILLINOIS (Urbana)	7	4.72
MICHIGAN (Ann Arbor)	8	4.69
CALIFORNIA, BERKELEY	9	4.66
STANFORD	10	4.63
OHIO STATE (Columbus)	11	4.60
CHICAGO	12	4.57
NORTH CAROLINA (Chapel Hill)	13	4.53
UCLA	14	4.51
BROWN	15	4.49
YALE	16	4.44

A RATING OF GRADUATE PROGRAMS IN SOCIAL PSYCHOLOGY
Leading Institutions

Eleven institutions with scores in the 4.0-5.0 range, in rank order

INSTITUTION	Rank	Score
CHICAGO	1	4.61
MICHIGAN (Ann Arbor)	2	4.56
HARVARD	3	4.52
N.Y.U.	4	4.48
COLUMBIA (N.Y.)	5	4.46
WAYNE STATE (Michigan)	6	4.43
RUTGERS (New Brunswick)	7	4.39
SUNY (Buffalo)	8	4.38
INDIANA (Bloomington)	9	4.36
OREGON (Eugene)	10	4.31
CONNECTICUT (Storrs)	11	4.26

A RATING OF GRADUATE PROGRAMS IN SOCIAL WELFARE/SOCIAL WORK
Leading Institutions

Thirty-one institutions with scores in the 4.0-5.0 range, in rank order

INSTITUTION	Rank	Score
CHICAGO	1	4.68
COLUMBIA (N.Y.)	2	4.66
MICHIGAN (Ann Arbor)	3	4.60
WISCONSIN (Madison)	4	4.54
PENNSYLVANIA	5	4.53
CASE WESTERN RESERVE	6	4.52
BRANDEIS	7	4.47
PITTSBURGH (Pittsburgh)	8	4.46
WASHINGTON (St. Louis)	9	4.42
MINNESOTA (Minneapolis)	10	4.40
OHIO STATE (Columbus)	11	4.38
CALIFORNIA, BERKELEY	12	4.36
YESHIVA (N.Y.)	13	4.33
RUTGERS (New Brunswick)	14	4.31
U.S.C. (Los Angeles)	15	4.30
CATHOLIC U. (D.C.)	16	4.29
MICHIGAN STATE	17	4.27
SAINT LOUIS U.	18	4.25
TEXAS (Austin)	19	4.22
TULANE	20	4.19
UTAH	21	4.17
DENVER	22	4.16
UCLA	23	4.15
FLORIDA STATE	24	4.12
CUNY (Hunter College)	25	4.09
ILLINOIS (Chicago Circle)	26	4.07
MARYLAND (Baltimore)	27	4.06
SMITH COLLEGE (Massachusetts)	28	4.05
WASHINGTON (Seattle)	29	4.04
HOWARD (D.C.)	30	4.02
BRYN MAWR	31	4.01

A RATING OF GRADUATE PROGRAMS IN SOCIOLOGY
Leading Institutions

Forty-three institutions with scores in the 4.0-5.0 range, in rank order

INSTITUTION	Rank	Score
WISCONSIN (Madison)	1	4.90
MICHIGAN (Ann Arbor)	2	4.89
CHICAGO	3	4.88
HARVARD	4	4.87
NORTH CAROLINA (Chapel Hill)	5	4.86
PENNSYLVANIA	6	4.85
STANFORD	7	4.84
WASHINGTON (Seattle)	8	4.81
UCLA	9	4.80
COLUMBIA (N.Y.)	10	4.77
INDIANA (Bloomington)	11	4.73
TEXAS (Austin)	12	4.72
ARIZONA (Tucson)	13	4.70
SUNY (Stony Brook)	14	4.69
ILLINOIS (Urbana)	15	4.68
YALE	16	4.66
CORNELL (N.Y.)	17	4.64
NORTHWESTERN (Illinois)	18	4.61
PRINCETON	19	4.60
MINNESOTA (Minneapolis)	20	4.59
DUKE	21	4.58
MASSACHUSETTS (Amherst)	22	4.55
N.Y.U.	23	4.52
U.S.C. (Los Angeles)	24	4.50
WASHINGTON STATE	25	4.48
CALIFORNIA, BERKELEY	26	4.46
CALIFORNIA, SAN DIEGO	27	4.43
CUNY (Graduate School)	28	4.42
CALIFORNIA, SANTA BARBARA	29	4.39
SUNY (Albany)	30	4.37
RUTGERS (New Brunswick)	31	4.35
MICHIGAN STATE	32	4.34
BROWN	33	4.32
JOHNS HOPKINS	34	4.28
BOSTON U.	35	4.25
MARYLAND (College Park)	36	4.24
VANDERBILT	37	4.20
PITTSBURGH (Pittsburgh)	38	4.19
BRANDEIS	39	4.15
SUNY (Binghampton)	40	4.12
CALIFORNIA, DAVIS	41	4.10
ILLINOIS (Chicago)	42	4.08
VIRGINIA (Charlottesville)	43	4.06

A RATING OF GRADUATE PROGRAMS IN SPANISH
Leading Institutions

Forty institutions with scores in the 4.0-5.0 range, in rank order

INSTITUTION	Rank	Score
PENNSYLVANIA	1	4.91
HARVARD	2	4.90
TEXAS (Austin)	3	4.89
CALIFORNIA, BERKELEY	4	4.86
YALE	5	4.85
MICHIGAN (Ann Arbor)	6	4.83
WISCONSIN (Madison)	7	4.82
UCLA	8	4.80
STANFORD	9	4.78
INDIANA (Bloomington)	10	4.75
CORNELL (N.Y.)	11	4.73
CALIFORNIA, SAN DIEGO	12	4.71
ILLINOIS (Urbana)	13	4.69
BROWN	14	4.67
COLUMBIA (N.Y.)	15	4.66
PRINCETON	16	4.63
MINNESOTA (Minneapolis)	17	4.59
PITTSBURGH (Pittsburgh)	18	4.58
KENTUCKY	19	4.54
NORTH CAROLINA (Chapel Hill)	20	4.51
DUKE	21	4.49
KANSAS (Lawrence)	22	4.43
CALIFORNIA, IRVINE	23	4.41
VIRGINIA (Charlottesville)	24	4.39
SUNY (Buffalo)	25	4.33
WASHINGTON (Seattle)	26	4.28
CALIFORNIA, SANTA BARBARA	27	4.27
PENN STATE (University Park)	28	4.23
N.Y.U.	29	4.19
MARYLAND (College Park)	30	4.18
NEW MEXICO (Albuquerque)	31	4.17
ARIZONA (Tucson)	32	4.15
CUNY (Graduate School)	33	4.13
RUTGERS (New Brunswick)	34	4.12
MASSACHUSETTS (Amherst)	35	4.11
VANDERBILT	36	4.10
JOHNS HOPKINS	37	4.08
SUNY (Albany)	38	4.07
IOWA (Iowa City)	39	4.05
CALIFORNIA, DAVIS	40	4.04

A RATING OF GRADUATE PROGRAMS IN STATISTICS
Leading Institutions

Twenty-seven institutions with scores in the 4.0-5.0 range, in rank order

INSTITUTION	Rank	Score
HARVARD	1	4.90
PRINCETON	2	4.87
CHICAGO	3	4.84
CORNELL (N.Y.)	4	4.82
PENNSYLVANIA	5	4.80
JOHNS HOPKINS	6	4.77
INDIANA (Bloomington)	7	4.74
ILLINOIS (Urbana)	8	4.71
CALIFORNIA, BERKELEY	9	4.70
MICHIGAN (Ann Arbor)	10	4.69
COLUMBIA (N.Y.)	11	4.66
SMU (Dallas)	12	4.64
CARNEGIE-MELLON	13	4.61
IOWA STATE (Ames)	14	4.58
PENNSYLVANIA STATE (University Park)	15	4.55
MINNESOTA (Minneapolis)	16	4.53
TEXAS A&M (College Station)	17	4.52
WISCONSIN (Madison)	18	4.49
YALE	19	4.44
WASHINGTON (St. Louis)	20	4.41
NORTHWESTERN (Illinois)	21	4.38
OHIO STATE (Columbus)	22	4.34
RENSSELAER (N.Y.)	23	4.30
PURDUE (Lafayette)	24	4.27
V.P.I. & STATE U.	25	4.24
N.Y.U.	26	4.20
MISSOURI (Columbia)	27	4.17

A RATING OF GRADUATE PROGRAMS IN URBAN DESIGN
Leading Institutions

Eight institutions with scores in the 4.0-5.0 range, in rank order

INSTITUTION	Rank	Score
CORNELL (N.Y.)	1	4.88
TEXAS A&M (College Station)	2	4.86
COLUMBIA (N.Y.)	3	4.82
PENNSYLVANIA	4	4.78
HARVARD	5	4.73
WASHINGTON (Seattle)	6	4.69
WASHINGTON (St. Louis)	7	4.64
RICE	8	4.58

A RATING OF GRADUATE PROGRAMS IN ZOOLOGY
Leading Institutions

Thirty-eight institutions with scores in the 4.0-5.0 range, in rank order

INSTITUTION	Rank	Score
HARVARD	1	4.93
CALIFORNIA, BERKELEY	2	4.92
WASHINGTON (Seattle)	3	4.91
YALE	4	4.87
UCLA	5	4.86
DUKE	6	4.84
WISCONSIN	7	4.81
STANFORD	8	4.80
TEXAS (Austin)	9	4.77
CHICAGO	10	4.76
CORNELL (N.Y.)	11	4.74
CALIFORNIA, DAVIS	12	4.72
NORTH CAROLINA (Chapel Hill)	13	4.68
GEORGIA (Athens)	14	4.67
INDIANA (Bloomington)	15	4.63
CALIFORNIA, IRVINE	16	4.57
ARIZONA (Tucson)	17	4.52
MARYLAND (College Park)	18	4.49
COLORADO (Boulder)	19	4.46
OHIO STATE (Columbus)	20	4.44
FLORIDA (Gainesville)	21	4.41
MINNESOTA (Minneapolis)	22	4.39
MICHIGAN STATE	23	4.37
IOWA STATE (Ames)	24	4.33
OREGON STATE	25	4.31
ARIZONA STATE	26	4.28
RUTGERS (New Brunswick)	27	4.27
OREGON (Eugene)	28	4.21
TENNESSEE (Knoxville)	29	4.18
MASSACHUSETTS (Amherst)	30	4.17
WASHINGTON STATE	31	4.15
COLORADO STATE	32	4.13
NOTRE DAME	33	4.12
OKLAHOMA (Norman)	34	4.11
SUNY (College of Envir. Sci. & Forestry, Syracuse)	35	4.10
V.P.I. & STATE U.	36	4.09
CONNECTICUT (Storrs)	37	4.08
UTAH STATE	38	4.07

The GOURMAN REPORT
PART II

PROFESSIONAL PROGRAMS

A Rating of International Law Schools

A Rating of Law Schools in Canada

A Rating of U.S.A. Law Schools

A RATING OF LAW SCHOOLS

INTERNATIONAL UNIVERSITIES
Leading Institutions

Fifty-three institutions with scores in the 4.0-5.0 range, in rank order

INSTITUTION	COUNTRY	Rank	Score
PARIS (All Law Campuses)	France	1	4.93
OXFORD	United Kingdom	2	4.92
CAMBRIDGE	United Kingdom	3	4.91
HEIDELBERG	Federal Republic of Germany	4	4.89
LYON III	France	5	4.88
MUNICH	Federal Republic of Germany	6	4.86
MONTPELLIER I	France	7	4.85
BRUSSELS	Belgium	8	4.84
GÖTTINGEN	Federal Republic of Germany	9	4.82
ERLANGEN-NÜRNBERG	Federal Republic of Germany	10	4.81
AIX-MARSEILLE II	France	11	4.80
EDINBURGH	United Kingdom (Scotland)	12	4.79
BORDEAUX I	France	13	4.77
BONN	Federal Republic of Germany	14	4.75
LILLE II	France	15	4.74
DIJON	France	16	4.73
NANCY II	France	17	4.72
BESANCON	France	18	4.71
GRENOBLE II	France	19	4.69
CLERMONT-FERRAND	France	20	4.68
ROUEN	France	21	4.67
REIMS	France	22	4.66
COLOGNE	Federal Republic of Germany	23	4.65
RENNES I	France	24	4.64
VIENNA	Austria	25	4.63
KIEL	Federal Republic of Germany	26	4.62
STOCKHOLM	Sweden	27	4.61
NICE	France	28	4.60
CAEN	France	29	4.53
POITIERS	France	30	4.52
TOULOUSE I	France	31	4.51
LIMOGES	France	32	4.50
NANTES	France	33	4.49
COPENHAGEN	Denmark	34	4.48
MAINZ	Federal Republic of Germany	35	4.43
ORLEANS	France	36	4.41
SAINT-ETIENNE	France	37	4.40
TOKYO	Japan	38	4.39
FREIBURG	Federal Republic of Germany	39	4.37
TÜEBINGEN	Federal Republic of Germany	40	4.36
INNSBRUCK	Austria	41	4.35
MÜNSTER	Federal Republic of Germany	42	4.34
WÜRZBURG	Federal Republic of Germany	43	4.33
DUBLIN	Ireland	44	4.32
HEBREW	Israel	45	4.27

A RATING OF LAW SCHOOLS

INTERNATIONAL UNIVERSITIES (Continued)
Leading Institutions

Fifty-three institutions with scores in the 4.0-5.0 range, in rank order

INSTITUTION	COUNTRY	Rank	Score
MADRID	Spain	46	4.26
MARBURG	Federal Republic of Germany	47	4.24
GENEVA	Switzerland	48	4.23
LONDON	United Kingdom	49	4.22
FRIBOURG	Switzerland	50	4.17
ROME	Italy	51	4.16
AMSTERDAM	Netherlands	52	4.14
ATHENS	Greece	53	4.07

A RATING OF LAW SCHOOLS IN CANADA

Leading Institutions

INSTITUTION	Rank	Score
UNIVERSITY OF TORONTO	1	4.69
UNIVERSITY OF BRITISH COLUMBIA	2	4.65
McGILL UNIVERSITY	3	4.63
YORK UNIVERSITY	4	4.52
UNIVERSITY OF OTTAWA	5	4.01
DALHOUSIE UNIVERSITY	6	3.62
UNIVERSITY OF MANITOBA	7	3.60
UNIVERSITY OF ALBERTA	8	3.52
QUEEN'S UNIVERSITY	9	3.41
UNIVERSITY OF VICTORIA	10	3.38
UNIVERSITY OF WINDSOR	11	3.22
UNIVERSITY OF CALGARY	12	3.21
UNIVERSITY OF WESTERN ONTARIO	13	3.17
UNIVERSITY OF SASKATCHEWAN	14	3.12

A RATING OF LAW SCHOOLS

U.S.A. LAW SCHOOLS
Very Strong

Twenty institutions with scores in the 4.6-5.0 range, in rank order

INSTITUTION	Rank	Score
HARVARD UNIVERSITY	1	4.93
THE UNIVERSITY OF MICHIGAN (Ann Arbor)	2	4.92
YALE UNIVERSITY	3	4.91
THE UNIVERSITY OF CHICAGO	4	4.90
UNIVERSITY OF CALIFORNIA, BERKELEY (Boalt Hall)	5	4.89
STANFORD UNIVERSITY	6	4.88
COLUMBIA UNIVERSITY (N.Y.)	7	4.87
DUKE UNIVERSITY	8	4.85
UNIVERSITY OF PENNSYLVANIA	9	4.83
CORNELL (N.Y.)	10	4.79
NEW YORK UNIVERSITY	11	4.78
UNIVERSITY OF TEXAS (Austin)	12	4.76
UNIVERSITY OF CALIFORNIA, LOS ANGELES	13	4.75
NORTHWESTERN (Chicago)	14	4.73
UNIVERSITY OF VIRGINIA	15	4.72
VANDERBILT	16	4.71
GEORGETOWN (D.C.)	17	4.69
UNIVERSITY OF NOTRE DAME	18	4.68
UNIVERSITY OF MINNESOTA (Minneapolis)	19	4.64
UNIVERSITY OF CALIFORNIA, SAN FRANCISCO (Hastings)	20	4.62

A RATING OF LAW SCHOOLS

U.S.A. LAW SCHOOLS (Continued)
Strong

Twenty-three institutions with scores in the 4.0-4.5 range, in rank order

INSTITUTION	Rank	Score
IOWA (Iowa City)	21	4.50
UNIVERSITY OF WISCONSIN (Madison)	22	4.49
BOSTON UNIVERSITY	23	4.48
FORDHAM UNIVERSITY (N.Y.)	24	4.47
UNIVERSITY OF NORTH CAROLINA (Chapel Hill)	25	4.46
UNIVERSITY OF WASHINGTON (Seattle)	26	4.45
UNIVERSITY OF SOUTHERN CALIFORNIA	27	4.44
UNIVERSITY OF CALIFORNIA, DAVIS	28	4.43
TULANE UNIVERSITY	29	4.42
INDIANA UNIVERSITY (Bloomington)	30	4.41
UNIVERSITY OF UTAH	31	4.40
THE GEORGE WASHINGTON UNIVERSITY	32	4.39
THE OHIO STATE UNIVERSITY (Columbus)	33	4.38
McGEORGE SCHOOL OF LAW	34	4.37
SOUTHERN METHODIST UNIVERSITY	35	4.36
ALBANY LAW SCHOOL (Union University)	36	4.35
LOYOLA UNIVERSITY (Los Angeles)	37	4.34
UNIVERSITY OF ILLINOIS (Urbana)	38	4.33
STATE UNIVERSITY OF NEW YORK AT BUFFALO	39	4.32
MARQUETTE UNIVERSITY	40	4.31
WASHINGTON (St. Louis)	41	4.30
BOSTON COLLEGE	42	4.29
HOFSTRA UNIVERSITY (N.Y.)	43	4.20

A RATING OF LAW SCHOOLS

U.S.A. LAW SCHOOLS (Continued)
Good

Thirty-one institutions with scores in the 3.6-3.9 range, in rank order

INSTITUTION	Rank	Score
EMORY UNIVERSITY	44	3.90
THE CATHOLIC UNIVERSITY OF AMERICA	45	3.89
TEMPLE UNIVERSITY	46	3.88
UNIVERSITY OF GEORGIA (Athens)	47	3.87
UNIVERSITY OF DENVER	48	3.86
UNIVERSITY OF HOUSTON	49	3.85
AMERICAN UNIVERSITY (D.C.)	50	3.84
ITT CHICAGO-KENT COLLEGE OF LAW	51	3.83
SYRACUSE UNIVERSITY	52	3.82
UNIVERSITY OF SAN DIEGO	53	3.81
UNIVERSITY OF SAN FRANCISCO	54	3.80
UNIVERSITY OF MISSOURI (Columbia)	55	3.79
UNIVERSITY OF FLORIDA (Gainesville)	56	3.78
UNIVERSITY OF MARYLAND (Baltimore)	57	3.77
CARDOZA SCHOOL OF LAW (N.Y.)	58	3.76
UNIVERSITY OF PITTSBURGH (Pittsburgh)	59	3.75
CASE WESTERN RESERVE	60	3.74
RUTGERS UNIVERSITY THE STATE U. OF NEW JERSEY (Newark)	61	3.73
UNIVERSITY OF SANTA CLARA	62	3.72
UNIVERSITY OF KANSAS	63	3.71
VILLANOVA UNIVERSITY	64	3.70
RUTGERS UNIVERSITY THE STATE U. OF NEW JERSEY (Camden)	65	3.69
PEPPERDINE UNIVERSITY	66	3.68
UNIVERSITY OF OREGON	67	3.67
WAYNE STATE UNIVERSITY (Michigan)	68	3.66
SAINT LOUIS UNIVERSITY	69	3.65
ST. JOHN'S UNIVERSITY (N.Y.)	70	3.64
BRIGHAM YOUNG UNIVERSITY	71	3.63
BROOKLYN LAW SCHOOL	72	3.62
WILLIAMETTE UNIVERSITY	73	3.61
VALPARAISO UNIVERSITY	74	3.60

A RATING OF LAW SCHOOLS

U.S.A. LAW SCHOOLS (Continued)
Acceptable Plus

Forty-three institutions with scores in the 3.0-3.5 range, in rank order

INSTITUTION	Rank	Score
UNIVERSITY OF COLORADO (Boulder)	75	3.50
LOYOLA UNIVERSITY (Chicago)	76	3.49
GONZAGA UNIVERSITY	77	3.48
SOUTHWESTERN UNIVERSITY (Los Angeles)	78	3.47
UNIVERSITY OF DETROIT MERCY	79	3.46
COLLEGE OF WILLIAM & MARY	80	3.45
SETON HALL UNIVERSITY	81	3.44
GOLDEN GATE UNIVERSITY	82	3.43
FLORIDA STATE UNIVERSITY	83	3.42
UNIVERSITY OF OKLAHOMA (Norman)	84	3.41
DE PAUL UNIVERSITY	85	3.40
LOUISIANA STATE UNIVERSITY (Baton Rouge)	86	3.39
UNIVERSITY OF CONNECTICUT (Hartford)	87	3.38
UNIVERSITY OF MISSOURI (Kansas City)	88	3.37
NEW YORK LAW SCHOOL	89	3.36
UNIVERSITY OF MIAMI (Florida)	90	3.35
DRAKE UNIVERSITY	91	3.34
UNIVERSITY OF ARIZONA (Tucson)	92	3.33
DUQUESNE UNIVERSITY	93	3.32
BAYLOR UNIVERSITY	94	3.31
ARIZONA STATE UNIVERSITY	95	3.30
UNIVERSITY OF LOUISVILLE	96	3.29
UNIVERSITY OF CINCINNATI	97	3.28
DICKINSON SCHOOL OF LAW	98	3.27
UNIVERSITY OF KENTUCKY	99	3.26
UNIVERSITY OF MISSISSIPPI	100	3.25
UNIVERSITY OF ALABAMA	101	3.24
UNIVERSITY OF NEBRASKA (Lincoln)	102	3.23
DETROIT COLLEGE OF LAW	103	3.22
THE UNIVERSITY OF TULSA	104	3.21
WASHBURN UNIVERSITY OF TOPEKA	105	3.20
WEST VIRGINIA UNIVERSITY	106	3.19
TEXAS TECH UNIVERSITY	107	3.18
LEWIS & CLARK COLLEGE	108	3.17
SOUTHERN ILLINOIS UNIVERSITY (Carbondale)	109	3.16
INDIANA UNIVERSITY (Indianapolis)	110	3.15
WAKE FOREST UNIVERSITY	111	3.14
SUFFOLK UNIVERSITY (Massachusetts)	112	3.12
NORTHEASTERN UNIVERSITY (Massachusetts)	113	3.10
CREIGHTON UNIVERSITY	114	3.09
THE JOHN MARSHALL LAW SCHOOL	115	3.08
NEW ENGLAND SCHOOL OF LAW	116	3.07
CALIFORNIA WESTERN SCHOOL OF LAW	117	3.05

A RATING OF LAW SCHOOLS

U.S.A. LAW SCHOOLS (Continued)
Adequate

Fifty-eight institutions with scores in the 2.1-2.9 range, in rank order

INSTITUTION	Rank	Score
UNIVERSITY OF TENNESSEE (Knoxville)	118	2.95
MERCER UNIVERSITY	119	2.94
WASHINGTON & LEE UNIVERSITY	120	2.93
UNIVERSITY OF SOUTH CAROLINA	121	2.92
WILLIAM MITCHELL COLLEGE OF LAW	122	2.91
THOMAS M. COOLEY LAW SCHOOL	123	2.90
THE UNIVERSITY OF AKRON	124	2.89
UNIVERSITY OF PUGET SOUND (Washington)	125	2.88
HOWARD UNIVERSITY (D.C.)	126	2.87
UNIVERSITY OF ARKANSAS (Fayetteville)	127	2.86
UNIVERSITY OF NEW MEXICO (Albuquerque)	128	2.85
UNIVERSITY OF MONTANA (Missoula)	129	2.84
THE CLEVELAND STATE UNIVERSITY	130	2.80
CAPITAL UNIVERSITY	131	2.78
HAMLINE UNIVERSITY (Minnesota)	132	2.76
GEORGE MASON UNIVERSITY	133	2.73
UNIVERSITY OF IDAHO	134	2.71
SAMFORD UNIVERSITY	135	2.70
OKLAHOMA UNIVERSITY	136	2.69
WESTERN NEW ENGLAND COLLEGE (Massachusetts)	137	2.68
OHIO NORTHERN UNIVERSITY	138	2.67
UNIVERSITY OF HAWAII (Manoa)	139	2.66
DELAWARE LAW SCHOOL OF WIDENER COLLEGE	140	2.65
UNIVERSITY OF RICHMOND	141	2.64
MEMPHIS STATE UNIVERSITY	142	2.63
UNIVERSITY OF DAYTON	143	2.62
FRANKLIN PIERCE COLLEGE	144	2.60
UNIVERSITY OF WYOMING	145	2.59
UNIVERSITY OF BALTIMORE	146	2.58
STETSON UNIVERSITY	147	2.56
NOVA UNIVERSITY (Florida)	148	2.55
UNIVERSITY OF MAINE (Portland)	149	2.54
WHITTIER COLLEGE OF LAW (Los Angeles)	150	2.53
ST. MARY'S UNIVERSITY (Texas)	151	2.52
VERMONT LAW SCHOOL	152	2.51
LOYOLA UNIVERSITY (New Orleans)	153	2.50
UNIVERSITY OF TOLEDO	154	2.49
UNIVERSITY OF SOUTH DAKOTA	155	2.48
UNIVERSITY OF ARKANSAS (Little Rock)	156	2.47
NORTHERN ILLINOIS UNIVERSITY	157	2.43

U.S.A. LAW SCHOOLS (Continued)
Adequate

Fifty-eight institutions with scores in the 2.1-2.9 range, in rank order

INSTITUTION	Rank	Score
PACE UNIVERSITY (N.Y.)	158	2.40
UNIVERSITY OF NORTH DAKOTA	159	2.35
TEXAS SOUTHERN UNIVERSITY	160	2.33
UNIVERSITY OF PUERTO RICO	161	2.29
SOUTH TEXAS COLLEGE OF LAW	162	2.27
NORTHERN KENTUCKY UNIVERSITY	163	2.24
BRIDGEPORT SCHOOL OF LAW	164	2.22
CATHOLIC UNIVERSITY OF PUERTO RICO	165	2.20
NORTH CAROLINA CENTRAL UNIVERSITY	166	2.17
CAMPBELL UNIVERSITY (North Carolina)	167	2.16
INTER-AMERICAN UNIVERSITY OF PUERTO RICO	168	2.15
MISSISSIPPI COLLEGE SCHOOL OF LAW	169	2.14
TOURO COLLEGE OF LAW (N.Y.)	170	2.13
GEORGIA STATE UNIVERSITY (Atlanta)	171	2.12
CUNY LAW SCHOOL AT QUEENS COLLEGE	172	2.10
SOUTHERN UNIVERSITY (Baton Rouge)	173	2.08
WIDENER UNIVERSITY AT HARRISBURG (Pennsylvania)	174	2.07
DISTRICT OF COLUMBIA SCHOOL OF LAW (D.C.)	175	2.06

The GOURMAN REPORT
PART III

A RATING OF DENTAL SCHOOLS IN CANADA
Leading Institutions

Ten institutions with scores in the 4.0-5.0 range, in rank order

INSTITUTION	Rank	Score
McGILL UNIVERSITY	1	4.92
UNIVERSITY OF TORONTO	2	4.89
UNIVERSITY OF BRITISH COLUMBIA	3	4.87
UNIVERSITÉ DE MONTREAL	4	4.79
UNIVERSITÉ LAVAL	5	4.72
UNIVERSITY OF MANITOBA	6	4.69
UNIVERSITY OF WESTERN ONTARIO	7	4.60
UNIVERSITY OF ALBERTA	8	4.53
DALHOUSIE UNIVERSITY	9	4.48
UNIVERSITY OF SASKATCHEWAN	10	4.38

A RATING OF U.S.A. DENTAL SCHOOLS
Leading Institutions

Fifty-four institutions with scores in the 4.0-5.0 range, in rank order

INSTITUTION	Rank	Score
HARVARD (Boston)	1	4.94
CALIFORNIA (San Francisco)	2	4.93
MICHIGAN (Ann Arbor)	3	4.92
COLUMBIA (New York)	4	4.91
PENNSYLVANIA (Philadelphia)	5	4.89
UCLA (Los Angeles)	6	4.88
OHIO STATE (Columbus)	7	4.87
TUFTS (Boston)	8	4.84
NORTHWESTERN (Chicago)	9	4.80
N.Y.U. (New York)	10	4.78
MINNESOTA (Minneapolis)	11	4.77
ILLINOIS (Chicago)	12	4.73
WASHINGTON (Seattle)	13	4.65
SUNY (Buffalo)	14	4.59
TEMPLE (Philadelphia)	15	4.56
CREIGHTON (Omaha)	16	4.54
SOUTHERN CALIFORNIA (Los Angeles)	17	4.52
MARQUETTE (Milwaukee)	18	4.49
CASE WESTERN RESERVE (Cleveland)	19	4.46
PITTSBURGH (Pittsburgh)	20	4.44
NORTH CAROLINA (Chapel Hill)	21	4.43
INDIANA (Indianapolis)	22	4.42
IOWA (Iowa City)	23	4.39
SUNY (Stony Brook)	24	4.37
BAYLOR (Dallas)	25	4.36
TEXAS (Houston)	26	4.35
OREGON HEALTH SCIENCES UNIVERSITY (Portland)	27	4.34
LOUISVILLE (Louisville)	28	4.33
BOSTON U. (Boston)	29	4.32
PACIFIC (San Francisco)	30	4.31
LOMA LINDA (Loma Linda)	31	4.30
TEXAS (San Antonio)	32	4.29
MISSOURI (Kansas City)	33	4.28
LOUISIANA STATE (New Orleans)	34	4.27
ALABAMA (Birmingham)	35	4.26
TENNESSEE (Memphis)	36	4.25
DETROIT-MERCY (Detroit)	37	4.24
CONNECTICUT (Farmington)	38	4.23
MEDICAL UNIVERSITY OF SOUTH CAROLINA (Charleston)	39	4.22
WEST VIRGINIA (Morgantown)	40	4.19
MARYLAND (Baltimore)	41	4.18
NEBRASKA (Lincoln)	42	4.17
VIRGINIA COMMONWEALTH (Richmond)	43	4.16
MEDICAL COLLEGE OF GEORGIA (Augusta)	44	4.15
MEHARRY MEDICAL COLLEGE (Nashville)	45	4.14

A RATING OF U.S.A. DENTAL SCHOOLS (Continued)
Leading Institutions

Fifty-four institutions with scores in the 4.0-5.0 range, in rank order

INSTITUTION	Rank	Score
NEW JERSEY DENTAL SCHOOL (Newark)	46	4.12
COLORADO (Denver)	47	4.11
OKLAHOMA (Oklahoma City)	48	4.10
FLORIDA (Gainesville)	49	4.09
KENTUCKY (Lexington)	50	4.08
SOUTHERN ILLINOIS (Alton)	51	4.07
MISSISSIPPI (Jackson)	52	4.06
HOWARD (D.C.)	53	4.05
PUERTO RICO (San Juan)	54	4.04

A RATING OF MEDICAL SCHOOLS IN CANADA
Leading Institutions

Sixteen institutions with scores in the 4.0-5.0 range, in rank order

INSTITUTION	Rank	Score
McGILL UNIVERSITY		
Faculty of Medicine	1	4.90
UNIVERSITY OF TORONTO		
Faculty of Medicine	2	4.89
UNIVERSITY OF BRITISH COLUMBIA		
Faculty of Medicine	3	4.86
UNIVERSITY OF MONTREAL		
Faculty of Medicine	4	4.79
McMASTER UNIVERSITY		
School of Medicine	5	4.75
QUEEN'S UNIVERSITY		
Faculty of Medicine	6	4.69
LAVAL UNIVERSITY		
Faculty of Medicine	7	4.63
UNIVERSITY OF MANITOBA		
Faculty of Medicine	8	4.57
UNIVERSITY OF OTTAWA		
School of Medicine	9	4.52
UNIVERSITY OF WESTERN ONTARIO		
Faculty of Medicine	10	4.49
UNIVERSITY OF ALBERTA		
Faculty of Medicine	11	4.47
UNIVERSITY OF CALGARY		
Faculty of Medicine	12	4.44
MEMORIAL UNIVERSITY OF NEWFOUNDLAND		
School of Medicine	13	4.38
DALHOUSIE UNIVERSITY		
Faculty of Medicine	14	4.34
UNIVERSITY OF SHERBROOKE		
Faculty of Medicine	15	4.26
UNIVERSITY OF SASKATCHEWAN		
College of Medicine	16	4.17

A RATING OF MEDICAL SCHOOLS

INTERNATIONAL UNIVERSITIES
Leading Institutions

Fifty-five institutions with scores in the 4.0-5.0 range, in rank order

INSTITUTION	COUNTRY	Rank	Score
PARIS (University Medical and Academic Departments) U. of Paris V, VI, VII, XI, XII, XIII	France	1	4.93
OXFORD	United Kingdom	2	4.92
CAMBRIDGE	United Kingdom	3	4.91
HEIDELBERG	Federal Republic of Germany	4	4.90
MUNICH	Federal Republic of Germany	5	4.89
LYON I	France	6	4.88
VIENNA	Austria	7	4.87
MONTPELLIER I	France	8	4.85
ZURICH	Switzerland	9	4.83
GÖTTINGEN	Federal Republic of Germany	10	4.82
EDINBURGH	United Kingdom (Scotland)	11	4.81
LILLE (U.E.R.) II	France	12	4.79
BRUSSELS	Belgium	13	4.77
DIJON	France	14	4.74
LILLE (Faculte Libre de Medicine)	France	15	4.73
GENEVA	Switzerland	16	4.72
KEIO	Japan	17	4.68
ERLANGEN-NURNBERG	Federal Republic of Germany	18	4.67
TOKYO (Medical & Dental)	Japan	19	4.64
AIX-MARSEILLE II	France	20	4.60
NANCY I	France	21	4.58
NICE I	France	22	4.57
REIMS	France	23	4.56
CLERMONT-FERRAND	France	24	4.55
RENNES I	France	25	4.54
ROUEN	France	26	4.53
BORDEAUX II	France	27	4.47
BONN	Federal Republic of Germany	28	4.38
WÜRZBURG	Federal Republic of Germany	29	4.37
HEBREW	Israel	30	4.34
LONDON (12 Campuses)	United Kingdom	31	4.33
FREIBURG	Federal Republic of Germany	32	4.32
HAMBURG	Federal Republic of Germany	33	4.31
AMIENS	France	34	4.30
BESANCON	France	35	4.29
GRENOBLE I	France	36	4.28
MARBURG	Federal Republic of Germany	37	4.27
TUBINGEN	Federal Republic of Germany	38	4.26
POITIERS	France	39	4.25
LIMOGES	France	40	4.24

INTERNATIONAL UNIVERSITIES (Continued)
Leading Institutions

Fifty-five institutions with scores in the 4.0-5.0 range, in rank order

INSTITUTION	COUNTRY	Rank	Score
SAINT-ETIENNE	France	41	4.23
MAINZ	Federal Republic of Germany	42	4.22
STRASBOURG I	France	43	4.21
CAEN	France	44	4.20
STOCKHOLM	Sweden	45	4.19
LOUVAIN	Belgium	46	4.18
AMSTERDAM	Netherlands	47	4.17
ROYAL COLLEGE OF SURGEONS	Ireland	48	4.16
LEIDEN	Netherlands	49	4.14
TOURS	France	50	4.13
TOULOUSE III	France	51	4.12
FRANFURT	Federal Republic of Germany	52	4.11
ANGERS	France	53	4.10
MUNSTER	Federal Republic of Germany	54	4.09
NANTES	France	55	4.07

A RATING OF MEDICAL SCHOOLS

U.S.A. MEDICAL SCHOOLS
Very Strong

Nineteen institutions with scores in the 4.6-5.0 range, in rank order

INSTITUTION	Rank	Score
HARVARD MEDICAL SCHOOL (Boston)	1	4.94
JOHNS HOPKINS UNIVERSITY		
School of Medicine (Baltimore)	2	4.93
UNIVERSITY OF PENNSYLVANIA		
School of Medicine (Philadelphia)	3	4.92
UNIVERSITY OF CALIFORNIA		
School of Medicine (San Francisco)	4	4.91
YALE UNIVERSITY		
School of Medicine (New Haven)	5	4.90
UNIVERSITY OF CHICAGO		
Pritzker School of Medicine (Chicago)	6	4.88
COLUMBIA UNIVERSITY		
College of Physicians & Surgeons (New York)	7	4.87
STANFORD UNIVERSITY		
School of Medicine (Palo Alto)	8	4.86
CORNELL UNIVERSITY		
School of Medicine (New York)	9	4.83
UNIVERSITY OF MICHIGAN		
Medical School (Ann Arbor)	10	4.81
UNIVERSITY OF CALIFORNIA		
School of Medicine (Los Angeles)	11	4.79
DUKE UNIVERSITY		
School of Medicine (Durham)	12	4.73
NEW YORK UNIVERSITY		
School of Medicine (New York)	13	4.70
NORTHWESTERN UNIVERSITY		
Medical School (Chicago)	14	4.68
UNIVERSITY OF MINNESOTA		
Medical School (Minneapolis)	15	4.67
TULANE UNIVERSITY		
Medical School (New Orleans)	16	4.65
UNIVERSITY OF ROCHESTER		
School of Medicine & Dentistry (Rochester)	17	4.63
WASHINGTON UNIVERSITY		
School of Medicine (St. Louis)	18	4.61
VANDERBILT UNIVERSITY		
School of Medicine (Nashville)	19	4.57

A RATING OF MEDICAL SCHOOLS

U.S.A. MEDICAL SCHOOLS (Continued)
Strong

Thirty-two institutions with scores in the 4.0-4.5 range, in rank order

INSTITUTION	Rank	Score
UNIVERSITY OF CALIFORNIA		
School of Medicine (San Diego)	20	4.50
UNIVERSITY OF VIRGINIA		
School of Medicine (Charlottesville)	21	4.49
UNIVERSITY OF NORTH CAROLINA		
School of Medicine (Chapel Hill)	22	4.48
TUFTS UNIVERSITY		
School of Medicine (Boston)	23	4.47
UNIVERSITY OF CALIFORNIA		
School of Medicine (Davis)	24	4.46
BOSTON UNIVERSITY		
School of Medicine (Boston)	25	4.45
INDIANA UNIVERSITY		
School of Medicine (Indianapolis)	26	4.44
UNIVERSITY OF WISCONSIN		
Medical School (Madison)	27	4.43
UNIVERSITY OF ILLINOIS		
College of Medicine (Chicago)	28	4.42
UNIVERSITY OF IOWA		
College of Medicine (Iowa City)	29	4.41
UNIVERSITY OF WASHINGTON		
School of Medicine (Seattle)	30	4.40
GEORGETOWN UNIVERSITY		
School of Medicine (Washington D.C.)	31	4.39
OHIO STATE UNIVERSITY		
College of Medicine (Columbus)	32	4.38
STATE UNIVERSITY OF NEW YORK AT BUFFALO		
School of Medicine	33	4.37
GEORGE WASHINGTON UNIVERSITY		
School of Medicine (Washington D.C.)	34	4.36
UNIVERSITY OF CALIFORNIA		
College of Medicine (Irvine)	35	4.35

A RATING OF MEDICAL SCHOOLS

U.S.A. MEDICAL SCHOOLS (Continued)
Strong

Thirty-two institutions with scores in the 4.0-4.5 range, in rank order

INSTITUTION	Rank	Score
BAYLOR COLLEGE OF MEDICINE (Houston)	36	4.34
BOWMAN GRAY SCHOOL OF MEDICINE (Winston-Salem)	37	4.33
EMORY UNIVERSITY		
School of Medicine (Atlanta)	38	4.32
UNIVERSITY OF PITTSBURGH		
School of Medicine (Pittsburgh)	39	4.31
LOMA LINDA UNIVERSITY		
School of Medicine (Loma Linda)	40	4.30
LOYOLA UNIVERSITY OF CHICAGO		
Stritch School of Medicine	41	4.28
UNIVERSITY OF LOUISVILLE		
School of Medicine (Louisville)	42	4.27
TEMPLE UNIVERSITY		
School of Medicine (Philadelphia)	43	4.26
SAINT LOUIS UNIVERSITY		
School of Medicine (St. Louis)	44	4.25
DARTMOUTH MEDICAL SCHOOL (Hanover)	45	4.23
UNIVERSITY OF SOUTHERN CALIFORNIA		
School of Medicine (Los Angeles)	46	4.21
UNIVERSITY OF MISSOURI		
School of Medicine (Columbia)	47	4.18
WAYNE STATE UNIVERSITY		
School of Medicine (Detroit)	48	4.17
ALBERT EINSTEIN		
College of Medicine of Yeshiva University (New York)	49	4.16
STATE UNIVERSITY OF NEW YORK AT STONY BROOK		
School of Medicine	50	4.15
BROWN UNIVERSITY PROGRAM IN MEDICINE (Providence)	51	4.13

A RATING OF MEDICAL SCHOOLS

U.S.A. MEDICAL SCHOOLS (Continued)
Good

Twenty-nine institutions with scores in the 3.6-3.9 range, in rank order

INSTITUTION	Rank	Score
CASE WESTERN RESERVE UNIVERSITY		
School of Medicine (Cleveland)	52	3.89
UNIVERSITY OF COLORADO		
School of Medicine (Denver)	53	3.88
UNIVERSITY OF CONNECTICUT		
School of Medicine (Farmington)	54	3.87
UNIVERSITY OF KANSAS		
School of Medicine (Kansas City)	55	3.85
CREIGHTON UNIVERSITY		
School of Medicine (Omaha)	56	3.84
MOUNT SINAI		
School of Medicine of the City University of New York	57	3.83
UNIVERSITY OF MARYLAND		
School of Medicine (Baltimore)	58	3.82
HEALTH SCIENCES UNIVERSITY		
School of Medicine (Portland)	59	3.81
ALBANY MEDICAL COLLEGE		
of Union University (Albany)	60	3.80
UNIVERSITY OF UTAH		
College of Medicine (Salt Lake City)	61	3.79
UNIVERSITY OF FLORIDA		
College of Medicine (Gainesville)	62	3.78
LOUISIANA STATE UNIVERSITY		
School of Medicine (New Orleans)	63	3.77
UNIVERSITY OF MIAMI		
School of Medicine (Miami, Florida)	64	3.76
MICHIGAN STATE UNIVERSITY		
College of Human Medicine (East Lansing)	65	3.75
UNIVERSITY OF TEXAS		
Southwestern Medical School (Dallas)	66	3.74
UNIVERSITY OF MISSOURI		
School of Medicine (Kansas City)	67	3.73
UNIVERSITY OF TEXAS MEDICAL BRANCH (Galveston)	68	3.72
UNIVERSITY OF TEXAS MEDICAL SCHOOL (San Antonio)	69	3.71
PENNSYLVANIA STATE UNIVERSITY		
College of Medicine, The Milton S. Hershey Medical Ctr. (Hershey)	70	3.70
STATE UNIVERSITY OF NEW YORK		
College of Medicine (Brooklyn)	71	3.69
UNIVERSITY OF CINCINNATI		
College of Medicine (Cincinnati)	72	3.68
STATE UNIVERSITY OF NEW YORK		
College of Medicine (Syracuse)	73	3.67
MAYO MEDICAL SCHOOL (Rochester)	74	3.66
UNIVERSITY OF ALABAMA		
School of Medicine (Birmingham)	75	3.65
UNIVERSITY OF NEBRASKA		
College of Medicine (Omaha)	76	3.64
UNIVERSITY OF KENTUCKY		
College of Medicine (Lexington)	77	3.63
UNIVERSITY OF VERMONT		
College of Medicine (Burlington)	78	3.62
LOUISIANA STATE UNIVERSITY		
School of Medicine (Shreveport)	79	3.61
UNIVERSITY OF TENNESSEE		
College of Medicine (Memphis)	80	3.60

A RATING OF MEDICAL SCHOOLS

U.S.A. MEDICAL SCHOOLS (Continued)
Acceptable Plus

Forty-five institutions with scores in the 3.0-3.5 range, in rank order

INSTITUTION	Rank	Score
NEW YORK MEDICAL COLLEGE (New York)	81	3.51
JEFFERSON MEDICAL COLLEGE		
of Thomas Jefferson University (Philadelphia)	82	3.50
UNIVERSITY OF OKLAHOMA		
School of Medicine (Oklahoma City)	83	3.49
WEST VIRGINIA UNIVERSITY		
School of Medicine (Morgantown)	84	3.48
UNIVERSITY OF TEXAS MEDICAL SCHOOL (Houston)	85	3.47
UNIVERSITY OF ARKANSAS		
School of Medicine (Little Rock)	86	3.46
HAHNEMANN UNIVERSITY SCHOOL OF MEDICINE (Philadelphia)	87	3.45
UMDNJ-NEW JERSEY MEDICAL SCHOOL (Newark)	88	3.44
UNIVERSITY OF ARIZONA		
College of Medicine (Tucson)	89	3.43
UNIVERSITY OF SOUTH FLORIDA		
College of Medicine (Tampa)	90	3.42
MEDICAL UNIVERSITY OF SOUTH CAROLINA		
College of Medicine (Charleston)	91	3.41
UNIVERSITY OF MISSISSIPPI		
School of Medicine (Jackson)	92	3.40
MEDICAL COLLEGE OF PENNSYLVANIA (Philadelphia)	93	3.39
MeHARRY MEDICAL COLLEGE		
School of Medicine (Nashville)	94	3.38
RUSH MEDICAL COLLEGE (Chicago)	95	3.37
MEDICAL COLLEGE OF VIRGINIA (Richmond)	96	3.35
MEDICAL COLLEGE OF GEORGIA (Augusta)	97	3.34
MEDICAL COLLEGE OF OHIO (Toledo)	98	3.33
CHICAGO MEDICAL SCHOOL		
University of Health Sciences (Chicago)	99	3.32
HOWARD UNIVERSITY		
College of Medicine (Washington D.C.)	100	3.31
UNIVERSITY OF NEW MEXICO		
School of Medicine (Albuquerque)	101	3.30
SOUTHERN ILLINOIS UNIVERSITY		
School of Medicine (Springfield)	102	3.29
TEXAS TECH UNIVERSITY		
School of Medicine (Lubbock)	103	3.28
UMDNJ-RUTGERS MEDICAL SCHOOL (Piscataway)	104	3.27
UNIVERSITY OF HAWAII		
School of Medicine (Honolulu)	105	3.26

A RATING OF MEDICAL SCHOOLS

U.S.A. MEDICAL SCHOOLS (Continued)
Acceptable Plus

Forty-five institutions with scores in the 3.0-3.5 range, in rank order

INSTITUTION	Rank	Score
UNIVERSITY OF MASSACHUSETTS		
Medical School (Worcester)	106	3.25
MEDICAL COLLEGE OF WISCONSIN (Milwaukee)	107	3.24
UNIVERSITY OF PUERTO RICO		
School of Medicine (San Juan)	108	3.23
UNIVERSITY OF SOUTH CAROLINA		
School of Medicine (Columbia)	109	3.22
UNIVERSITY OF NEVADA		
School of Medical Science (Reno)	110	3.21
UNIFORMED SERVICES UNIVERSITY OF THE HEALTH SCIENCES		
School of Medicine (Bethesda)	111	3.19
UNIVERSITY OF NORTH DAKOTA		
School of Medicine (Grand Forks)	112	3.18
UNIVERSITY OF SOUTH DAKOTA		
School of Medicine (Vermillion)	113	3.17
NORTHEASTERN OHIO UNIVERSITIES		
College of Medicine (Rootstown)	114	3.16
EAST CAROLINA UNIVERSITY		
School of Medicine (Greenville)	115	3.15
MARSHALL UNIVERSITY		
School of Medicine (Huntington)	116	3.14
EASTERN VIRGINIA MEDICAL SCHOOL (Norfolk)	117	3.13
EAST TENNESSEE STATE UNIVERSITY		
College of Medicine (Johnson City)	118	3.12
UNIVERSITY OF SOUTH CAROLINA		
College of Medicine (Mobile)	119	3.11
TEXAS A&M UNIVERSITY		
College of Medicine (College Station)	120	3.10
WRIGHT STATE UNIVERSITY		
School of Medicine (Dayton)	121	3.09
MOREHOUSE SCHOOL OF MEDICINE (Atlanta)	122	3.07
MERCER UNIVERSITY		
School of Medicine (Macon)	123	3.04
PONCE SCHOOL OF MEDICINE (Ponce)	124	3.03
UNIVERSIDAD CENTRAL DEL CARIBE		
School of Medicine (Cayey)	125	3.02

A RATING OF GRADUATE PROGRAMS IN VETERINARY MEDICINE/SCIENCES
Leading Institutions

Twenty-six institutions with scores in the 4.0-5.0 range, in rank order

INSTITUTION	Rank	Score
CALIFORNIA, DAVIS	1	4.93
CORNELL (N.Y.)	2	4.91
PENNSYLVANIA	3	4.86
OHIO STATE (Columbus)	4	4.83
COLORADO STATE	5	4.82
MICHIGAN STATE	6	4.79
IOWA STATE (Ames)	7	4.75
MINNESOTA (Minneapolis)	8	4.73
PURDUE (Lafayette)	9	4.69
KANSAS STATE	10	4.67
TEXAS A&M (College Station)	11	4.65
WISCONSIN (Madison)	12	4.63
ILLINOIS (Urbana)	13	4.58
TUFTS	14	4.55
FLORIDA (Gainesville)	15	4.54
GEORGIA (Athens)	16	4.47
LSU (Baton Rouge)	17	4.43
NORTH CAROLINA STATE (Raleigh)	18	4.38
V.P.I. & STATE U.	19	4.32
AUBURN U. (Auburn)	20	4.28
MISSOURI (Columbia)	21	4.22
TENNESSEE (Knoxville)	22	4.18
WASHINGTON STATE (Pullman)	23	4.12
MISSISSIPPI STATE U.	24	4.09
OKLAHOMA STATE	25	4.06
TUSKEGEE U. (Tuskegee)	26	4.02

The GOURMAN REPORT
PART IV

PROFESSIONAL PROGRAMS

A Rating of U.S.A. Nursing Schools

A Rating of U.S.A. Optometry Schools

A Rating of Pharmacy Schools in Canada

A Rating of U.S.A. Pharmacy Schools

A Rating of U.S.A. Public Health Schools

A RATING OF GRADUATE PROGRAMS IN NURSING
Leading Institutions

Thirty institutions with scores in the 4.6-5.0 range, in rank order

INSTITUTION	Rank	Score
CALIFORNIA, SAN FRANCISCO	1	4.95
CASE WESTERN RESERVE	2	4.94
MICHIGAN (Ann Arbor)	3	4.93
N.Y.U.	4	4.92
WASHINGTON (Seattle)	5	4.91
PENNSYLVANIA	6	4.90
ILLINOIS (Chicago)	7	4.89
PITTSBURGH (Pittsburgh)	8	4.88
WAYNE STATE (Michigan)	9	4.87
CATHOLIC U.	10	4.86
YALE	11	4.84
COLUMBIA (N.Y.)	12	4.83
UCLA	13	4.82
INDIANA (Indianapolis)	14	4.81
TEXAS (Austin)	15	4.80
OHIO STATE (Columbus)	16	4.79
MINNESOTA (Minneapolis)	17	4.78
COLORADO (Denver)	18	4.77
WISCONSIN (Madison)	19	4.76
MARYLAND (Baltimore)	20	4.75
UTAH	21	4.73
SUNY (Buffalo)	22	4.72
CUNY (Hunter)	23	4.71
COLUMBIA (Teachers College)	24	4.70
NORTH CAROLINA (Chapel Hill)	25	4.69
NORTH CAROLINA (Chapel Hill) School of Public Health	26	4.68
THE HEALTH SCIENCES UNIVERSITY (Portland)	27	4.67
VANDERBILT	28	4.66
ROCHESTER (N.Y.)	29	4.63
RUSH U. (Chicago)	30	4.61

A RATING OF GRADUATE PROGRAMS IN NURSING (Continued)
Leading Institutions

Twenty-three institutions with scores in the 4.0-4.5 range, in rank order

INSTITUTION	Rank	Score
TEXAS HEALTH SCIENCE CENTER (San Antonio)	31	4.50
IOWA (Iowa City)	32	4.48
ARIZONA (Tucson)	33	4.47
ST. LOUIS U.	34	4.46
ALABAMA (Birmingham)	35	4.45
EMORY	36	4.42
LOYOLA (Chicago)	37	4.38
KANSAS (Kansas City)	38	4.35
MEDICAL COLLEGE OF GEORGIA	39	4.33
TENNESSEE (Memphis)	40	4.31
FLORIDA (Gainesville)	41	4.30
SYRACUSE	42	4.27
LSU (New Orleans)	43	4.25
LOMA LINDA (California)	44	4.23
CINCINNATI	45	4.22
MARQUETTE	46	4.20
VIRGINIA (Charlottesville)	47	4.18
PENN STATE (University Park)	48	4.16
BOSTON COLLEGE	49	4.14
KENTUCKY	50	4.11
CONNECTICUT (Storrs)	51	4.09
VIRGINIA COMMONWEALTH	52	4.04
ADELPHI (N.Y.)	53	4.01

A RATING OF GRADUATE PROGRAMS IN NURSING (Continued)
Leading Institutions

Twenty institutions with scores in the 3.6-3.9 range, in rank order

INSTITUTION	Rank	Score
TEXAS WOMAN'S U.	54	3.89
ARIZONA STATE	55	3.87
MISSOURI (Columbia)	56	3.86
ARKANSAS (Little Rock)	57	3.83
NEBRASKA (Omaha)	58	3.82
OKLAHOMA (Oklahoma City)	59	3.80
NORTHERN ILLINOIS	60	3.78
RUTGERS (Newark)	61	3.77
SOUTH CAROLINA (Columbia)	62	3.76
SUNY (Binghampton)	63	3.74
TEXAS HEALTH SCIENCE CENTER (Houston)	64	3.73
DE PAUL	65	3.72
DELAWARE (Newark)	66	3.71
WISCONSIN (Milwaukee)	67	3.69
B.Y.U.	68	3.68
CALIFORNIA STATE (Los Angeles)	69	3.66
THE SAGE COLLEGES	70	3.65
SOUTHERN MISSISSIPPI	71	3.64
CALIFORNIA STATE (Fresno)	72	3.62
PUERTO RICO (San Juan)	73	3.61

A RATING OF GRADUATE PROGRAMS IN OPTOMETRY
Leading Institutions

Sixteen institutions with scores in the 4.0-5.0 range, in rank order

INSTITUTION	Rank	Score
UNIVERSITY OF CALIFORNIA, BERKELEY		
School of Optometry	1	4.94
THE OHIO STATE UNIVERSITY		
College of Optometry	2	4.92
INDIANA UNIVERSITY		
School of Optometry	3	4.91
UNIVERSITY OF ALABAMA AT BIRMINGHAM		
School of Optometry	4	4.89
UNIVERSITY OF HOUSTON		
College of Optometry	5	4.83
SOUTHERN CALIFORNIA COLLEGE		
College of Optometry	6	4.82
SUNY STATE		
College of Optometry	7	4.74
ILLINOIS COLLEGE		
College of Optometry	8	4.73
PENNSYLVANIA		
College of Optometry	9	4.70
NEW ENGLAND		
College of Optometry	10	4.65
FERRIS STATE		
College of Optometry	11	4.61
PACIFIC UNIVERSITY		
College of Optometry	12	4.55
UNIVERSITY OF MISSOURI–ST. LOUIS		
School of Optometry	13	4.52
SOUTHERN COLLEGE		
College of Optometry	14	4.38
NORTHEASTERN STATE UNIVERSITY		
College of Optometry	15	4.17
INTER AMERICAN UNIVERSITY OF PUERTO RICO		
School of Optometry	16	4.08

A RATING OF PHARMACY SCHOOLS IN CANADA

CANADIAN PHARMACY SCHOOLS
Leading Institutions

Eight institutions with scores in the 4.0-5.0 range, in rank order

INSTITUTION	Rank	Score
UNIVERSITY OF TORONTO	1	4.85
UNIVERSITY OF BRITISH COLUMBIA	2	4.82
UNIVERSITY OF MONTREAL	3	4.74
UNIVERSITY OF LAVAL	4	4.69
UNIVERSITY OF MANITOBA	5	4.61
UNIVERSITY OF ALBERTA	6	4.51
DALHOUSIE UNIVERSITY	7	4.46
UNIVERSITY OF SASKATCHEWAN	8	4.38

A RATING OF PHARMACY SCHOOLS

U.S.A. PHARMACY SCHOOLS
Leading Institutions

Thirty institutions with scores in the 4.6-5.0 range, in rank order

INSTITUTION	Rank	Score
UNIVERSITY OF CALIFORNIA, SAN FRANCISCO		
School of Pharmacy	1	4.93
UNIVERSITY OF MICHIGAN College of Pharmacy	2	4.92
UNIVERSITY OF MINNESOTA College of Pharmacy	3	4.91
STATE UNIVERSITY OF NEW YORK AT BUFFALO		
School of Pharmacy	4	4.89
UNIVERSITY OF SOUTHERN CALIFORNIA School of Pharmacy	5	4.88
UNIVERSITY OF WISCONSIN, MADISON School of Pharmacy	6	4.87
OHIO STATE UNIVERSITY College of Pharmacy	7	4.86
PURDUE UNIVERSITY		
School of Pharmacy & Pharmacal Sciences	8	4.85
UNIVERSITY OF ILLINOIS AT CHICAGO		
College of Pharmacy	9	4.84
WAYNE STATE UNIVERSITY		
College of Pharmacy & Allied Health Professions	10	4.83
CREIGHTON UNIVERSITY School of Pharmacy	11	4.81
UNIVERSITY OF MARYLAND School of Pharmacy	12	4.80
UNIVERSITY OF KENTUCKY College of Pharmacy	13	4.79
UNIVERSITY OF UTAH College of Pharmacy	14	4.78
UNIVERSITY OF THE PACIFIC School of Pharmacy	15	4.77
THE UNIVERSITY OF TEXAS AT AUSTIN College of Pharmacy	16	4.76
UNIVERSITY OF NEBRASKA College of Pharmacy	17	4.75
DUQUESNE UNIVERSITY School of Pharmacy	18	4.74
UNIVERSITY OF CINCINNATI College of Pharmacy	19	4.73
ST. JOHN'S UNIVERSITY		
College of Pharmacy & Allied Health Professions	20	4.71
UNIVERSITY OF TENNESSEE		
Center for the Health Sciences College of Pharmacy	21	4.70
UNIVERSITY OF FLORIDA		
College of Pharmacy J. Hillis Miller Health Center	22	4.69
MASSACHUSETTS College of Pharmacy	23	4.68
PHILADELPHIA College of Pharmacy and Science	24	4.67
MEDICAL UNIVERSITY OF SOUTH CAROLINA		
College of Pharmacy	25	4.66
VIRGINIA COMMONWEALTH UNIVERSITY		
School of Pharmacy Medical College of Virginia	26	4.65
THE UNIVERSITY OF IOWA College of Pharmacy	27	4.64
THE UNIVERSITY OF NORTH CAROLINA AT CHAPEL HILL		
School of Pharmacy	28	4.63
UNIVERSITY OF ARIZONA College of Pharmacy	29	4.62
UNIVERSITY OF GEORGIA College of Pharmacy	30	4.61

A RATING OF PHARMACY SCHOOLS

U.S.A. PHARMACY SCHOOLS (Continued)
Leading Institutions

Twenty institutions with scores in the 4.0-4.5 range, in rank order

INSTITUTION	Rank	Score
UNIVERSITY OF MISSOURI, KANSAS CITY		
School of Pharmacy	31	4.51
UNIVERSITY OF PITTSBURGH		
School of Pharmacy	32	4.50
TEMPLE UNIVERSITY		
School of Pharmacy	33	4.48
UNION UNIVERSITY ALBANY		
College of Pharmacy	34	4.46
UNIVERSITY OF WASHINGTON		
School of Pharmacy	35	4.44
BUTLER UNIVERSITY		
College of Pharmacy	36	4.41
RUTGERS, THE STATE UNIVERSITY OF NEW JERSEY		
College of Pharmacy	37	4.39
LONG ISLAND UNIVERSITY		
Arnold & Marie Schwartz College of Pharmacy & Health Sciences	38	4.38
UNIVERSITY OF HOUSTON		
College of Pharmacy	39	4.36
UNIVERSITY OF KANSAS		
School of Pharmacy	40	4.32
WASHINGTON STATE UNIVERSITY		
College of Pharmacy	41	4.31
UNIVERSITY OF CONNECTICUT		
School of Pharmacy	42	4.26
UNIVERSITY OF COLORADO		
School of Pharmacy	43	4.24
MERCER UNIVERSITY SOUTHERN		
School of Pharmacy	44	4.23
OHIO NORTHERN UNIVERSITY		
College of Pharmacy	45	4.19
UNIVERSITY OF TOLEDO		
College of Pharmacy	46	4.17
OREGON STATE UNIVERSITY		
School of Pharmacy	47	4.14
DRAKE UNIVERSITY		
College of Pharmacy	48	4.13
UNIVERSITY OF OKLAHOMA		
College of Pharmacy	49	4.07
UNIVERSITY OF RHODE ISLAND		
College of Pharmacy	50	4.04

A RATING OF PHARMACY SCHOOLS

U.S.A. PHARMACY SCHOOLS (Continued)
Leading Institutions

Twenty-three institutions with scores in the 3.6-3.9 range, in rank order

INSTITUTION	Rank	Score
AUBURN UNIVERSITY		
School of Pharmacy	51	3.91
SAMFORD UNIVERSITY		
School of Pharmacy	52	3.90
UNIVERSITY OF ARKANSAS FOR MEDICAL SCIENCES		
College of Pharmacy	53	3.89
HOWARD UNIVERSITY		
College of Pharmacy & Pharmacal Sciences	54	3.88
IDAHO STATE UNIVERSITY		
College of Pharmacy	55	3.87
ST. LOUIS		
College of Pharmacy	56	3.86
NORTHEASTERN UNIVERSITY		
College of Pharmacy & Allied Health Professions	57	3.85
FERRIS STATE COLLEGE		
School of Pharmacy	58	3.84
UNIVERSITY OF SOUTH CAROLINA		
College of Pharmacy	59	3.83
UNIVERSITY OF MISSISSIPPI		
School of Pharmacy	60	3.82
FLORIDA AGRICULTURAL & MECHANICAL UNIVERSITY		
School of Pharmacy	61	3.81
UNIVERSITY OF MONTANA		
School of Pharmacy	62	3.79
UNIVERSITY OF NEW MEXICO		
College of Pharmacy	63	3.77
NORTH DAKOTA STATE UNIVERSITY		
College of Pharmacy	64	3.76
SOUTHWESTERN OKLAHOMA STATE UNIVERSITY		
School of Pharmacy	65	3.75
NORTHEAST LOUISIANA UNIVERSITY		
School of Pharmacy	66	3.73
SOUTH DAKOTA STATE UNIVERSITY		
College of Pharmacy	67	3.72
UNIVERSITY OF WYOMING		
School of Pharmacy	68	3.70
WEST VIRGINIA UNIVERSITY		
School of Pharmacy Medical Center	69	3.69
TEXAS SOUTHERN UNIVERSITY		
School of Pharmacy	70	3.66
UNIVERSITY OF PUERTO RICO		
College of Pharmacy	71	3.64
XAVIER UNIVERSITY OF LOUISIANA		
College of Pharmacy	72	3.63
CAMPBELL UNIVERSITY		
School of Pharmacy	73	3.61

A RATING OF GRADUATE PROGRAMS IN PUBLIC HEALTH
Leading Institutions

Twenty-two institutions with scores in the 4.0-5.0 range, in rank order

INSTITUTION	Rank	Score
THE JOHNS HOPKINS UNIVERSITY		
School of Hygiene & Public Health	1	4.94
UNIVERSITY OF CALIFORNIA (Berkeley)		
School of Public Health	2	4.93
HARVARD UNIVERSITY		
School of Public Health	3	4.91
UNIVERSITY OF MICHIGAN (Ann Arbor)		
School of Public Health	4	4.90
UNIVERSITY OF CALIFORNIA AT LOS ANGELES (UCLA)		
School of Public Health	5	4.88
YALE UNIVERSITY		
Department of Epidemiology & Public Health	6	4.86
UNIVERSITY OF MINNESOTA		
School of Public Health	7	4.81
UNIVERSITY OF NORTH CAROLINA (Chapel Hill)		
School of Public Health	8	4.79
COLUMBIA UNIVERSITY		
School of Public Health	9	4.76
TULANE UNIVERSITY		
School of Public Health & Tropical Medicine	10	4.72
UNIVERSITY OF WASHINGTON (Seattle)		
School of Public Health & Community Medicine	11	4.69
UNIVERSITY OF ILLINOIS AT CHICAGO		
School of Public Health	12	4.66
UNIVERSITY OF PITTSBURGH		
Graduate School of Public Health	13	4.62
UNIVERSITY OF TEXAS–HOUSTON		
School of Public Health	14	4.60
UNIVERSITY OF ALABAMA IN BIRMINGHAM		
Department of Public Health	15	4.59
UNIVERSITY OF OKLAHOMA		
College of Public Health	16	4.51
LOMA LINDA UNIVERSITY		
School of Public Health	17	4.48
UNIVERSITY OF MASSACHUSETTS (Amherst)		
Division of Public Health, School of Health Sciences	18	4.46
BOSTON UNIVERSITY		
School of Public Health	19	4.41
UNIVERSITY OF PUERTO RICO		
School of Public Health	20	4.38
UNIVERSITY OF HAWAII		
School of Public Health	21	4.33
UNIVERSITY OF SOUTH CAROLINA		
School of Public Health	22	4.27

The GOURMAN REPORT
PART V

**A RATING OF RESEARCH LIBRARIES
IN THE UNITED STATES**

A RATING OF RESEARCH LIBRARIES
Leading Institutions

Forty-one institutions with scores in the 4.0-5.0 range, in rank order

INSTITUTION	Rank	Score
HARVARD	1	4.95
YALE	2	4.93
ILLINOIS (Urbana)	3	4.92
CALIFORNIA, BERKELEY	4	4.90
MICHIGAN (Ann Arbor)	5	4.89
COLUMBIA (N.Y.)	6	4.87
STANFORD	7	4.86
TEXAS (Austin)	8	4.83
CHICAGO	9	4.81
UCLA	10	4.80
CORNELL (N.Y.)	11	4.78
WISCONSIN (Madison)	12	4.74
WASHINGTON (Seattle)	13	4.71
MINNESOTA (Minneapolis)	14	4.69
INDIANA (Bloomington)	15	4.68
OHIO STATE (Columbus)	16	4.65
PRINCETON	17	4.63
PENNSYLVANIA	18	4.62
DUKE	19	4.61
NORTHWESTERN (Illinois)	20	4.58
NORTH CAROLINA (Chapel Hill)	21	4.54
MICHIGAN STATE	22	4.52
N.Y.U.	23	4.48
ARIZONA (Tucson)	24	4.47
VIRGINIA (Charlottesville)	25	4.45
IOWA (Iowa City)	26	4.41
PITTSBURGH (Pittsburgh)	27	4.39
PENN STATE (University Park)	28	4.36
RUTGERS (New Brunswick)	29	4.32
FLORIDA (Gainesville)	30	4.29
SUNY (Buffalo)	31	4.28
KANSAS (Lawrence)	32	4.25
M.I.T.	33	4.24
NOTRE DAME	34	4.23
SYRACUSE	35	4.20
U.S.C. (Los Angeles)	36	4.19
GEORGIA (Athens)	37	4.18
CALIFORNIA, DAVIS	38	4.14
CALIFORNIA, SAN DIEGO	39	4.11
MARYLAND (College Park)	40	4.08
CALIFORNIA, SANTA BARBARA	41	4.06

The GOURMAN REPORT
PART VI

**A RATING OF GRADUATE SCHOOLS
IN ENGINEERING
ON THE APPROVED LIST OF
THE GOURMAN REPORT**

A RATING OF GRADUATE SCHOOLS IN ENGINEERING

RATING CATEGORIES	Numerical Range
Very Strong	4.51-4.99
Strong	4.01-4.49
Good	3.61-3.99
Acceptable	3.01-3.59

INSTITUTIONS IN ALPHABETICAL ORDER

INSTITUTION	Gourman Ranking	Gourman Score
UNIVERSITY OF AKRON Akron, Ohio	104	3.51
UNIVERSITY OF ALABAMA University, Alabama	90	3.72
UNIVERSITY OF ALABAMA IN BIRMINGHAM Birmingham, Alabama	133	3.12
UNIVERSITY OF ALABAMA IN HUNTSVILLE Huntsville, Alabama	116	3.32
ARIZONA STATE UNIVERSITY Tempe, Arizona	37	4.33
UNIVERSITY OF ARIZONA Tucson, Arizona	33	4.37
UNIVERSITY OF ARKANSAS Fayetteville, Arkansas	73	3.89
AUBURN UNIVERSITY Auburn, Alabama	70	3.94
BOSTON UNIVERSITY Boston, Massachusetts	92	3.68
BRIGHAM YOUNG UNIVERSITY Provo, Utah	131	3.15
BROWN UNIVERSITY Providence, Rhode Island	58	4.09
CALIFORNIA INSTITUTE OF TECHNOLOGY Pasadena, California	6	4.87
UNIVERSITY OF CALIFORNIA, BERKELEY Berkeley, California	2	4.92
UNIVERSITY OF CALIFORNIA, DAVIS Davis, California	32	4.38

A RATING OF GRADUATE SCHOOLS IN ENGINEERING (Continued)

INSTITUTIONS IN ALPHABETICAL ORDER

INSTITUTION	Gourman Ranking	Gourman Score
UNIVERSITY OF CALIFORNIA, IRVINE Irvine, California	93	3.67
UNIVERSITY OF CALIFORNIA, LOS ANGELES (UCLA) Los Angeles, California	28	4.44
UNIVERSITY OF CALIFORNIA, SAN DIEGO La Jolla, California	49	4.18
UNIVERSITY OF CALIFORNIA, SANTA BARBARA Santa Barbara, California	78	3.84
CARNEGIE-MELLON UNIVERSITY Pittsburgh, Pennsylvania	11	4.78
CASE WESTERN RESERVE UNIVERSITY Cleveland, Ohio	23	4.52
CATHOLIC UNIVERSITY OF AMERICA Washington, D.C.	99	3.61
UNIVERSITY OF CENTRAL FLORIDA Orlando, Florida	128	3.19
UNIVERSITY OF CINCINNATI Cincinnati, Ohio	39	4.30
CLARKSON UNIVERSITY Potsdam, New York	86	3.76
CLEMSON UNIVERSITY Clemson, South Carolina	71	3.92
CLEVELAND STATE UNIVERSITY Cleveland, Ohio	127	3.20
COLORADO SCHOOL OF MINES Golden, Colorado	47	4.21
COLORADO STATE UNIVERSITY Fort Collins, Colorado	67	3.99
UNIVERSITY OF COLORADO AT BOULDER Boulder, Colorado	60	4.07
UNIVERSITY OF COLORADO AT DENVER Denver, Colorado	137	3.05

A RATING OF GRADUATE SCHOOLS IN ENGINEERING (Continued)

RATING CATEGORIES	Numerical Range
Very Strong	4.51-4.99
Strong	4.01-4.49
Good	3.61-3.99
Acceptable	3.01-3.59

INSTITUTIONS IN ALPHABETICAL ORDER

INSTITUTION	Gourman Ranking	Gourman Score
COLUMBIA UNIVERSITY New York, New York	17	4.68
UNIVERSITY OF CONNECTICUT Storrs, Connecticut	103	3.54
CORNELL UNIVERSITY Ithaca, New York	5	4.88
DARTMOUTH COLLEGE Hanover, New Hampshire	66	4.01
UNIVERSITY OF DAYTON Dayton, Ohio	101	3.57
UNIVERSITY OF DELAWARE Newark, Delaware	36	4.34
UNIVERSITY OF DETROIT MERCY Detroit, Michigan	134	3.11
DREXEL UNIVERSITY Philadelphia, Pennsylvania	38	4.32
DUKE UNIVERSITY Durham, North Carolina	65	4.02
FLORIDA ATLANTIC UNIVERSITY Boca Raton, Florida	136	3.07
FLORIDA INSTITUTE OF TECHNOLOGY Melbourne, Florida	138	3.03
UNIVERSITY OF FLORIDA Gainesville, Florida	26	4.47
GEORGE WASHINGTON UNIVERSITY Washington, D.C.	87	3.75
GEORGIA INSTITUTE OF TECHNOLOGY Atlanta, Georgia	7	4.85

INSTITUTIONS IN ALPHABETICAL ORDER

INSTITUTION	Gourman Ranking	Gourman Score
HARVARD UNIVERSITY Cambridge, Massachusetts	19	4.64
UNIVERSITY OF HAWAII AT MANOA Honolulu, Hawaii	125	3.22
UNIVERSITY OF HOUSTON Houston, Texas	42	4.26
HOWARD UNIVERSITY Washington, D.C.	135	3.10
UNIVERSITY OF IDAHO Moscow, Idaho	118	3.29
ILLINOIS INSTITUTE OF TECHNOLOGY Chicago, Illinois	81	3.81
UNIVERSITY OF ILLINOIS AT CHICAGO Chicago, Illinois	107	3.45
UNIVERSITY OF ILLINOIS AT URBANA-CHAMPAIGN Urbana, Illinois	3	4.91
IOWA STATE UNIVERSITY Ames, Iowa	34	4.36
UNIVERSITY OF IOWA Iowa City, Iowa	59	4.08
JOHNS HOPKINS UNIVERSITY Baltimore, Maryland	44	4.24
KANSAS STATE UNIVERSITY Manhattan, Kansas	77	3.85
UNIVERSITY OF KANSAS Lawrence, Kansas	51	4.16
UNIVERSITY OF KENTUCKY Lexington, Kentucky	79	3.83
LEHIGH UNIVERSITY Bethlehem, Pennsylvania	27	4.45
LOUISIANA STATE UNIVERSITY Baton Rouge, Louisiana	48	4.20
LOUISIANA TECH UNIVERSITY Ruston, Louisiana	110	3.40
UNIVERSITY OF LOWELL Lowell, Massachusetts	108	3.43

A RATING OF GRADUATE SCHOOLS IN ENGINEERING (Continued)

RATING CATEGORIES	Numerical Range
Very Strong	4.51-4.99
Strong	4.01-4.49
Good	3.61-3.99
Acceptable	3.01-3.59

INSTITUTIONS IN ALPHABETICAL ORDER

INSTITUTION	Gourman Ranking	Gourman Score
UNIVERSITY OF MAINE AT ORONO Orono, Maine	119	3.28
MARQUETTE UNIVERSITY Milwaukee, Wisconsin	132	3.13
UNIVERSITY OF MARYLAND College Park, Maryland	30	4.41
MASSACHUSETTS INSTITUTE OF TECHNOLOGY Cambridge, Massachusetts	1	4.94
UNIVERSITY OF MASSACHUSETTS AT AMHERST Amherst, Massachusetts	46	4.22
UNIVERSITY OF MIAMI Coral Gables, Florida	112	3.38
MICHIGAN STATE UNIVERSITY East Lansing, Michigan	40	4.28
MICHIGAN TECHNOLOGICAL UNIVERSITY Houghton, Michigan	84	3.78
UNIVERSITY OF MICHIGAN Ann Arbor, Michigan	10	4.80
UNIVERSITY OF MINNESOTA Minneapolis, Minnesota	15	4.71
MISSISSIPPI STATE UNIVERSITY Mississippi State, Mississippi	88	3.74
UNIVERSITY OF MISSISSIPPI University, Mississippi	121	3.26
UNIVERSITY OF MISSOURI–COLUMBIA Columbia, Missouri	61	4.06
UNIVERSITY OF MISSOURI–ROLLA Rolla, Missouri	57	4.10

INSTITUTIONS IN ALPHABETICAL ORDER

INSTITUTION	Gourman Ranking	Gourman Score
MONTANA STATE UNIVERSITY Bozeman, Montana	120	3.27
UNIVERSITY OF NEBRASKA–LINCOLN Lincoln, Nebraska	91	3.70
UNIVERSITY OF NEW HAMPSHIRE Durham, New Hampshire	113	3.37
NEW MEXICO STATE UNIVERSITY Las Cruces, New Mexico	129	3.18
UNIVERSITY OF NEW MEXICO Albuquerque, New Mexico	80	3.82
STATE UNIVERSITY OF NEW YORK AT BUFFALO Buffalo, New York	53	4.14
STATE UNIVERSITY OF NEW YORK AT STONY BROOK Stony Brook, New York	72	3.90
CITY COLLEGE OF THE CITY UNIVERSITY OF NEW YORK New York, New York	85	3.77
NORTH CAROLINA STATE UNIVERSITY AT RALEIGH Raleigh, North Carolina	55	4.12
NORTH DAKOTA STATE UNIVERSITY Fargo, North Dakota	124	3.23
NORTHWESTERN UNIVERSITY Evanston, Illinois	21	4.58
UNIVERSITY OF NOTRE DAME Notre Dame, Indiana	50	4.17
OHIO STATE UNIVERSITY Columbus, Ohio	12	4.76
OHIO UNIVERSITY Athens, Ohio	111	3.39
OKLAHOMA STATE UNIVERSITY Stillwater, Oklahoma	69	3.96
UNIVERSITY OF OKLAHOMA Norman, Oklahoma	75	3.87
OLD DOMINION UNIVERSITY Norfolk, Virginia	122	3.25
OREGON STATE UNIVERSITY Corvallis, Oregon	83	3.79

A RATING OF GRADUATE SCHOOLS IN ENGINEERING (Continued)

RATING CATEGORIES	Numerical Range
Very Strong	4.51-4.99
Strong	4.01-4.49
Good	3.61-3.99
Acceptable	3.01-3.59

INSTITUTIONS IN ALPHABETICAL ORDER

INSTITUTION	Gourman Ranking	Gourman Score
PENNSYLVANIA STATE UNIVERSITY University Park, Pennsylvania	18	4.66
UNIVERSITY OF PENNSYLVANIA Philadelphia, Pennsylvania	14	4.73
UNIVERSITY OF PITTSBURGH Pittsburgh, Pennsylvania	52	4.15
POLYTECHNIC UNIVERSITY Brooklyn, New York	62	4.05
PRINCETON UNIVERSITY Princeton, New Jersey	16	4.70
PURDUE UNIVERSITY West Lafayette, Indiana	8	4.83
RENSSELAER POLYTECHNIC INSTITUTE Troy, New York	20	4.61
UNIVERSITY OF RHODE ISLAND Kingston, Rhode Island	115	3.33
RICE UNIVERSITY Houston, Texas	22	4.55
UNIVERSITY OF ROCHESTER Rochester, New York	63	4.04
THE STATE UNIVERSITY OF NEW JERSEY, RUTGERS New Brunswick, New Jersey	56	4.11
UNIVERSITY OF SOUTH CAROLINA Columbia, South Carolina	109	3.41
SOUTH DAKOTA SCHOOL OF MINES AND TECHNOLOGY Rapid City, South Dakota	130	3.16
UNIVERSITY OF SOUTHERN CALIFORNIA Los Angeles, California	29	4.43

A RATING OF GRADUATE SCHOOLS IN ENGINEERING (Continued)

INSTITUTIONS IN ALPHABETICAL ORDER

INSTITUTION	Gourman Ranking	Gourman Score
SOUTHERN ILLINOIS UNIVERSITY–CARBONDALE Carbondale, Illinois	117	3.30
SOUTHERN METHODIST UNIVERSITY Dallas, Texas	96	3.64
STANFORD UNIVERSITY Stanford, California	4	4.90
STEVENS INSTITUTE OF TECHNOLOGY Hoboken, New Jersey	68	3.97
SYRACUSE UNIVERSITY Syracuse, New York	54	4.13
UNIVERSITY OF TENNESSEE AT KNOXVILLE Knoxville, Tennessee	45	4.23
TEXAS A&M UNIVERSITY College Station, Texas	25	4.49
TEXAS TECH UNIVERSITY Lubbock, Texas	74	3.88
UNIVERSITY OF TEXAS AT ARLINGTON Arlington, Texas	102	3.55
UNIVERSITY OF TEXAS AT AUSTIN Austin, Texas	9	4.81
UNIVERSITY OF TOLEDO Toledo, Ohio	126	3.21
TUFTS UNIVERSITY Medford, Massachusetts	97	3.63
TULANE UNIVERSITY New Orleans, Louisiana	98	3.61
UNIVERSITY OF TULSA Tulsa, Oklahoma	106	3.46
UTAH STATE UNIVERSITY Logan, Utah	76	3.86
UNIVERSITY OF UTAH Salt Lake City, Utah	35	4.35
VANDERBILT UNIVERSITY Nashville, Tennessee	82	3.80
UNIVERSITY OF VERMONT Burlington, Vermont	139	3.01

A RATING OF GRADUATE SCHOOLS IN ENGINEERING (Continued)

RATING CATEGORIES	Numerical Range
Very Strong	4.51-4.99
Strong	4.01-4.49
Good	3.61-3.99
Acceptable	3.01-3.59

INSTITUTIONS IN ALPHABETICAL ORDER

INSTITUTION	Gourman Ranking	Gourman Score
VIRGINIA POLYTECHNIC INSTITUTE AND STATE UNIVERSITY Blacksburg, Virginia	64	4.03
UNIVERSITY OF VIRGINIA Charlottesville, Virginia	31	4.40
WASHINGTON STATE UNIVERSITY Pullman, Washington	89	3.73
WASHINGTON UNIVERSITY St. Louis, Missouri	41	4.27
UNIVERSITY OF WASHINGTON Seattle, Washington	24	4.51
WAYNE STATE UNIVERSITY Detroit, Michigan	94	3.66
WEST VIRGINIA UNIVERSITY Morgantown, West Virginia	105	3.49
WICHITA STATE UNIVERSITY Wichita, Kansas	123	3.24
UNIVERSITY OF WISCONSIN–MADISON Madison, Wisconsin	13	4.75
UNIVERSITY OF WISCONSIN–MILWAUKEE Milwaukee, Wisconsin	95	3.65
WORCESTER POLYTECHNIC INSTITUTE Worcester, Massachusetts	100	3.59
UNIVERSITY OF WYOMING Laramie, Wyoming	114	3.35
YALE UNIVERSITY New Haven, Connecticut	43	**4.25**

The GOURMAN REPORT
PART VII

A RATING OF EMBA/MANAGEMENT SCHOOLS
ON THE APPROVED LIST OF
THE GOURMAN REPORT

A RATING OF GRADUATE PROGRAMS IN EMBA/MANAGEMENT
Leading Institutions

Thirteen institutions with scores in the 4.0-5.0 range, in rank order

INSTITUTION	Rank	Score
PENNSYLVANIA (Wharton)	1	4.91
CHICAGO	2	4.90
COLUMBIA (N.Y.)	3	4.88
UCLA (Anderson)	4	4.86
INDIANA (Bloomington)	5	4.84
NORTHWESTERN (Kellog)	6	4.81
ILLINOIS (Urbana)	7	4.75
N.Y.U. (Stern)	8	4.72
PITTSBURGH (Katz)	9	4.71
TEXAS (Austin)	10	4.68
DUKE (Fuqua)	11	4.64
PURDUE (Krannert)	12	4.59
U.S.C. (Los Angeles)	13	4.50

The GOURMAN REPORT
PART VIII

A RATING OF MBA/MANAGEMENT SCHOOLS
ON THE APPROVED LIST OF
THE GOURMAN REPORT

A RATING OF MBA/MANAGEMENT SCHOOLS

RATING CATEGORIES	Numerical Range
Very Strong	4.59-4.99
Strong	4.01-4.58
Good	3.59-3.99
Acceptable	3.01-3.58

STATE AND SCHOOL	Gourman State Ranking	Gourman National Ranking	Gourman National Score
ALABAMA			
University of Alabama (Tuscaloosa)	1	62	3.85
University of Alabama at Birmingham	2	98	3.05
ALASKA			
No MBA Programs Approved By The Gourman Report			
ARIZONA			
University of Arizona (Tucson) (Eller)	1	49	4.13
Arizona State University (Tempe)	2	53	4.07
ARKANSAS			
University of Arkansas (Fayetteville)	1	87	3.19
CALIFORNIA			
Stanford University	1	3	4.93
University of California, Los Angeles (UCLA) (Anderson)	2	7	4.88
University of California, Berkeley (Haas)	3	9	4.85
University of Southern California	4	30	4.51
University of California, Irvine	5	58	3.98
Golden Gate University	6	77	3.41
COLORADO			
University of Colorado (Boulder)	1	63	3.84
University of Denver	2	76	3.44

STATE AND SCHOOL	Gourman State Ranking	Gourman National Ranking	Gourman National Score
CONNECTICUT			
Yale University	1	46	4.16
DELAWARE			
No MBA Programs Approved By The Gourman Report			
DISTRICT OF COLUMBIA			
George Washington University	1	36	4.39
FLORIDA			
University of Florida	1	40	4.29
Rollins College (Crummer)	2	54	4.06
Florida State University	3	70	3.67
University of Miami	4	78	3.39
GEORGIA			
Emory University	1	35	4.42
Georgia Institute of Technology (Allen)	2	39	4.30
Georgia State University	3	51	4.10
University of Georgia (Terry)	4	56	4.02
HAWAII			
No MBA Programs Approved By The Gourman Report			
IDAHO			
No MBA Programs Approved By The Gourman Report			

A RATING OF MBA/MANAGEMENT SCHOOLS (Continued)

RATING CATEGORIES	Numerical Range
Very Strong	4.59-4.99
Strong	4.01-4.58
Good	3.59-3.99
Acceptable	3.01-3.58

STATE AND SCHOOL	Gourman State Ranking	Gourman National Ranking	Gourman National Score
ILLINOIS			
University of Chicago	1	5	4.91
Northwestern University (Kellog)	2	11	4.82
University of Illinois (Urbana-Champaign)	3	13	4.79
University of Illinois at Chicago	4	80	3.36
DePaul University	5	99	3.04
Southern Illinois University at Carbondale	6	100	3.02
INDIANA			
Indiana University (Bloomington)	1	8	4.86
Purdue University (West Lafayette) (Krannert) ..	2	22	4.64
University of Notre Dame	3	47	4.15
IOWA			
University of Iowa (Iowa City)	1	31	4.49
KANSAS			
University of Kansas	1	60	3.92
KENTUCKY			
University of Kentucky	1	66	3.78
LOUISIANA			
Tulane University (Freeman)	1	45	4.17
Louisiana State University (Baton Rouge)	2	55	4.03
Louisiana Tech University	3	96	3.07

STATE AND SCHOOL	Gourman State Ranking	Gourman National Ranking	Gourman National Score
MAINE			
No MBA Programs Approved By The Gourman Report			
MARYLAND			
University of Maryland (College Park)	1	74	3.52
MASSACHUSETTS			
Harvard University	1	1	4.95
M.I.T. (Sloan)	2	4	4.92
Boston University	3	59	3.95
University of Massachusetts (Amherst)	4	64	3.82
MICHIGAN			
University of Michigan (Ann Arbor)	1	10	4.84
Michigan State University (Broad)	2	25	4.59
MINNESOTA			
University of Minnesota (Minneapolis)	1	28	4.53
MISSISSIPPI			
Mississippi State University	1	86	3.22
University of Mississippi	2	91	3.15
MISSOURI			
Washington University (St. Louis) (Olin)	1	33	4.47
University of Missouri (Columbia)	2	65	3.81
Saint Louis University	3	72	3.59
MONTANA			
No MBA Programs Approved By The Gourman Report			

RATING CATEGORIES	Numerical Range
Very Strong	4.59-4.99
Strong	4.01-4.58
Good	3.59-3.99
Acceptable	3.01-3.58

STATE AND SCHOOL	Gourman State Ranking	Gourman National Ranking	Gourman National Score
NEBRASKA			
University of Nebraska (Lincoln)	1	81	3.33
NEVADA			
No MBA Programs Approved By The Gourman Report			
NEW HAMPSHIRE			
Dartmouth College (Tuck)	1	16	4.74
NEW JERSEY			
Rutgers University (Newark)	1	80	3.34
NEW MEXICO			
University of New Mexico	1	83	3.28
NEW YORK			
Columbia University	1	6	4.89
Cornell University (Johnson)	2	14	4.78
New York University (New York City) (Stern) ...	3	15	4.75
Baruch College (CUNY)	4	32	4.48
University of Rochester (Simon)	5	37	4.37
State University of New York at Buffalo	6	42	4.25
Syracuse University	7	48	4.14
Rensselaer Polytechnic Institute (Troy)	8	60	3.92
Pace University (Lubin)	9	75	3.47
Clarkson University	10	97	3.06

STATE AND SCHOOL	Gourman State Ranking	Gourman National Ranking	Gourman National Score
NORTH CAROLINA			
Duke University (Fuqua)	1	19	4.70
University of North Carolina (Chapel Hill) (Kenan/Flagler)	2	23	4.61
NORTH DAKOTA			
No MBA Programs Approved By The Gourman Report			
OHIO			
Ohio State University (Columbus)	1	26	4.57
Case Western Reserve (Weatherhead)	2	29	4.52
University of Cincinnati	3	71	3.63
Kent State University	4	94	3.09
OKLAHOMA			
University of Oklahoma (Norman)	1	93	3.10
OREGON			
University of Oregon (Eugene)	1	43	4.23
PENNSYLVANIA			
University of Pennsylvania (Wharton)	1	2	4.94
Carnegie-Mellon University	2	12	4.81
University of Pittsburgh (Pittsburgh) (Katz)	3	17	4.73
Penn State University (University Park) (Smeal)	4	34	4.44
Lehigh	5	44	4.20
Drexel University	6	61	3.88
Temple University (Philadelphia)	7	68	3.72
RHODE ISLAND			
No MBA Programs Approved By The Gourman Report			

A RATING OF MBA/MANAGEMENT SCHOOLS (Continued)

RATING CATEGORIES	Numerical Range
Very Strong	4.59-4.99
Strong	4.01-4.58
Good	3.59-3.99
Acceptable	3.01-3.58

STATE AND SCHOOL	Gourman State Ranking	Gourman National Ranking	Gourman National Score
SOUTH CAROLINA			
University of South Carolina	1	52	4.08
SOUTH DAKOTA			
No MBA Programs Approved By The Gourman Report			
TENNESSEE			
Vanderbilt University (Owen)	1	57	4.01
Tennessee University (Knoxville)	2	69	3.71
Memphis State University	3	82	3.31
TEXAS			
University of Texas (Austin)	1	18	4.71
Texas A&M University (College Station)	2	27	4.55
University of Houston (University Park)	3	41	4.26
Southern Methodist University (Cox)	4	50	4.11
Baylor University	5	85	3.25
Texas Tech University	6	88	3.18
University of Texas (Arlington)	7	92	3.12
University of North Texas State	8	95	3.08
UTAH			
University of Utah	1	38	4.33

STATE AND SCHOOL	Gourman State Ranking	Gourman National Ranking	Gourman National Score
VERMONT			
No MBA Programs Approved By The Gourman Report			
VIRGINIA			
University of Virginia (Darden)	1	21	4.66
V.P.I. & State University	2	84	3.27
Virginia Commonwealth University	3	89	3.17
WASHINGTON			
University of Washington (Seattle)	1	24	4.60
Washington State University	2	90	3.16
WEST VIRGINIA			
No MBA Programs Approved By The Gourman Report			
WISCONSIN			
University of Wisconsin (Madison)	1	20	4.68
University of Wisconsin (Milwaukee)	2	73	3.55
WYOMING			
No MBA Programs Approved By The Gourman Report			

The GOURMAN REPORT
PART IX

A RATING OF DOCTORAL SCHOOLS
IN BUSINESS AND MANAGEMENT
ON THE APPROVED LIST OF
THE GOURMAN REPORT

A RATING OF DOCTORAL SCHOOLS
IN BUSINESS AND MANAGEMENT

RATING CATEGORIES	Numerical Range
Very Strong	4.59-4.99
Strong	4.01-4.58
Good	3.59-3.99
Acceptable	3.01-3.58

SCHOOL (In Alphabetical Order)	Gourman National Ranking	Gourman National Score
UNIVERSITY OF ALABAMA .... Graduate School of Business University, Alabama	61	3.72
UNIVERSITY OF ALABAMA AT BIRMINGHAM .... Graduate School of Management Birmingham, Alabama	88	3.01
UNIVERSITY OF ARIZONA .... College of Business and Public Administration Tucson, Arizona	42	4.16
ARIZONA STATE UNIVERSITY .... College of Business Tempe, Arizona	44	4.10
UNIVERSITY OF ARKANSAS .... College of Business Administration Fayetteville, Arkansas	79	3.24
BARUCH COLLEGE – The City University of New York .... School of Business and Public Administration New York, New York	32	4.44
BOSTON UNIVERSITY .... School of Management Boston, Massachusetts	62	3.68
UNIVERSITY OF CALIFORNIA, BERKELEY .... School of Business Administration Berkeley, California	9	4.84
UNIVERSITY OF CALIFORNIA, IRVINE .... Graduate School of Management Irvine, California	56	3.84

A RATING OF DOCTORAL SCHOOLS
IN BUSINESS AND MANAGEMENT (Continued)

SCHOOL (In Alphabetical Order)	Gourman National Ranking	Gourman National Score
UNIVERSITY OF CALIFORNIA, LOS ANGELES (UCLA) ...... Graduate School of Management Los Angeles, California	7	4.87
CARNEGIE-MELLON UNIVERSITY .... Graduate School of Industrial Administration Pittsburgh, Pennsylvania	12	4.80
CASE WESTERN RESERVE UNIVERSITY .... Weatherhead School of Management Cleveland, Ohio	26	4.55
UNIVERSITY OF CHICAGO .... Graduate School of Business Chicago, Illinois	6	4.90
UNIVERSITY OF CINCINNATI .... College of Business Administration Cincinnati, Ohio	58	3.78
UNIVERSITY OF COLORADO .... Graduate School of Business Administration Boulder, Colorado	50	4.01
COLUMBIA UNIVERSITY .... Graduate School of Business New York, New York	5	4.91
CORNELL UNIVERSITY .... Johnson Graduate School of Management Ithaca, New York	15	4.72
DREXEL UNIVERSITY .... College of Business and Administration Philadelphia, Pennsylvania	66	3.60
DUKE UNIVERSITY .... Fuqua School of Business Durham, North Carolina	21	4.63
UNIVERSITY OF FLORIDA .... Graduate School of Business Administration Gainesville, Florida	38	4.28

A RATING OF DOCTORAL SCHOOLS
IN BUSINESS AND MANAGEMENT (Continued)

RATING CATEGORIES	Numerical Range
Very Strong	4.59-4.99
Strong	4.01-4.58
Good	3.59-3.99
Acceptable	3.01-3.58

SCHOOL (In Alphabetical Order)	Gourman National Ranking	Gourman National Score
FLORIDA STATE UNIVERSITY .... College of Business Tallahassee, Florida	68	3.55
GEORGE WASHINGTON UNIVERSITY .... School of Government and Business Administration Washington, D.C.	36	4.33
UNIVERSITY OF GEORGIA .... College of Business Administration Athens, Georgia	49	4.02
GEORGIA INSTITUTE OF TECHNOLOGY .... College of Management Atlanta, Georgia	46	4.05
GEORGIA STATE UNIVERSITY .... College of Business Administration Atlanta, Georgia	51	3.99
GOLDEN GATE UNIVERSITY .... Graduate College San Francisco, California	69	3.53
HARVARD UNIVERSITY .... Graduate School of Business Administration Boston, Massachusetts	1	4.95
UNIVERSITY OF HOUSTON .... College of Business Administration Houston, Texas	39	4.25
UNIVERSITY OF ILLINOIS AT CHICAGO .... College of Business Administration Chicago, Illinois	73	3.41

SCHOOL (In Alphabetical Order)	Gourman National Ranking	Gourman National Score
UNIVERSITY OF ILLINOIS AT URBANA-CHAMPAIGN .... College of Commerce and Business Administration Champaign, Illinois	16	4.70
INDIANA UNIVERSITY .... The Graduate School of Business Bloomington, Indiana	8	4.85
UNIVERSITY OF IOWA .... College of Business Administration Iowa City, Iowa	27	4.53
UNIVERSITY OF KANSAS .... School of Business Lawrence, Kansas	47	4.04
KENT STATE UNIVERSITY .... Graduate School of Management Kent, Ohio	81	3.17
UNIVERSITY OF KENTUCKY .... College of Business and Economics Lexington, Kentucky	64	3.63
LEHIGH UNIVERSITY .... College of Business and Economics Bethlehem, Pennsylvania	53	3.93
LOUISIANA STATE UNIVERSITY .... College of Business Administration Baton Rouge, Louisiana	57	3.81
LOUISIANA TECH UNIVERSITY .... College of Administration and Business Ruston, Louisiana	86	3.03
UNIVERSITY OF MARYLAND .... College of Business and Management College Park, Maryland	54	3.91
UNIVERSITY OF MASSACHUSETTS – AMHERST .... School of Management Amherst, Massachusetts	67	3.58

A RATING OF DOCTORAL SCHOOLS
IN BUSINESS AND MANAGEMENT (Continued)

RATING CATEGORIES	Numerical Range
Very Strong	4.59-4.99
Strong	4.01-4.58
Good	3.59-3.99
Acceptable	3.01-3.58

SCHOOL (In Alphabetical Order)	Gourman National Ranking	Gourman National Score
MASSACHUSETTS INSTITUTE OF TECHNOLOGY Alfred P. Sloan School of Management Cambridge, Massachusetts	4	4.92
MEMPHIS STATE UNIVERSITY The Fogelman College of Business and Economics Memphis, Tennessee	74	3.38
UNIVERSITY OF MICHIGAN Graduate School of Business Administration Ann Arbor, Michigan	10	4.83
MICHIGAN STATE UNIVERSITY The Graduate School of Business Administration East Lansing, Michigan	24	4.60
UNIVERSITY OF MINNESOTA School of Management Minneapolis, Minnesota	31	4.45
UNIVERSITY OF MISSISSIPPI School of Administration University, Mississippi	85	3.06
MISSISSIPPI STATE UNIVERSITY College of Business and Industry Mississippi State, Mississippi	77	3.31
UNIVERSITY OF MISSOURI – COLUMBIA College of Business and Public Administration Columbia, Missouri	43	4.14
UNIVERSITY OF NEBRASKA – LINCOLN College of Business Administration Lincoln, Nebraska	71	3.47

SCHOOL (In Alphabetical Order)	Gourman National Ranking	Gourman National Score
UNIVERSITY OF NEW MEXICO . . . . The Robert O. Anderson Graduate School of Management Albuquerque, New Mexico	84	3.09
NEW YORK UNIVERSITY . . . . Graduate School of Business Administration New York, New York	13	4.78
UNIVERSITY OF NORTH CAROLINA AT CHAPEL HILL . . . . . . School of Business Administration Chapel Hill, North Carolina	22	4.62
UNIVERSITY OF NORTH TEXAS . . . . College of Business Administration Denton, Texas	87	3.02
NORTHWESTERN UNIVERSITY . . . . J.L. Kellogg Graduate School of Management Evanston, Illinois	11	4.81
OHIO STATE UNIVERSITY . . . . College of Administrative Science Columbus, Ohio	25	4.59
UNIVERSITY OF OKLAHOMA . . . . College of Business Administration Norman, Oklahoma	80	3.21
UNIVERSITY OF OREGON . . . . Graduate School of Management Eugene, Oregon	45	4.08
PACE UNIVERSITY . . . . Lubin Schools of Business New York, New York	70	3.52
UNIVERSITY OF PENNSYLVANIA . . . . The Wharton School Philadelphia, Pennsylvania	2	4.94
PENNSYLVANIA STATE UNIVERSITY . . . . College of Business Administration University Park, Pennsylvania	40	4.22

RATING CATEGORIES	Numerical Range
Very Strong	4.59-4.99
Strong	4.01-4.58
Good	3.59-3.99
Acceptable	3.01-3.58

SCHOOL (In Alphabetical Order)	Gourman National Ranking	Gourman National Score
UNIVERSITY OF PITTSBURGH .... Graduate School of Business Pittsburgh, Pennsylvania	16	4.70
PURDUE UNIVERSITY .... Krannert Graduate School of Management West Lafayette, Indiana	17	4.68
RENSSELAER POLYTECHNIC INSTITUTE .... School of Management Troy, New York	41	4.19
UNIVERSITY OF ROCHESTER .... Graduate School of Management Rochester, New York	37	4.31
RUTGERS – The State University of New Jersey, Newark Campus Graduate School of Management Newark, New Jersey	59	3.77
ST. LOUIS UNIVERSITY .... School of Business and Administration St. Louis, Missouri	63	3.64
UNIVERSITY OF SOUTH CAROLINA .... Graduate School of Business Columbia, South Carolina	52	3.96
UNIVERSITY OF SOUTHERN CALIFORNIA .... Graduate School of Business Administration Los Angeles, California	30	4.47
SOUTHERN ILLINOIS UNIVERSITY AT CARBONDALE ...... College of Business and Administration Carbondale, Illinois	82	3.15

A RATING OF DOCTORAL SCHOOLS
IN BUSINESS AND MANAGEMENT (Continued)

SCHOOL (In Alphabetical Order)	Gourman National Ranking	Gourman National Score
STANFORD UNIVERSITY . . . . Graduate School of Business Stanford, California	3	4.93
STATE UNIVERSITY OF NEW YORK AT BUFFALO . . . . School of Management Buffalo, New York	33	4.41
SYRACUSE UNIVERSITY . . . . School of Management Syracuse, New York	48	4.03
TEMPLE UNIVERSITY . . . . School of Business Administration Philadelphia, Pennsylvania	65	3.62
UNIVERSITY OF TENNESSEE AT KNOXVILLE . . . . College of Business Administration Knoxville, Tennessee	60	3.74
UNIVERSITY OF TEXAS AT ARLINGTON . . . . College of Business Administration Arlington, Texas	78	3.27
UNIVERSITY OF TEXAS AT AUSTIN . . . . Graduate School of Business Austin, Texas	14	4.76
TEXAS A&M UNIVERSITY . . . . College of Business Administration College Station, Texas	28	4.51
TEXAS TECH UNIVERSITY . . . . College of Business Administration Lubbock, Texas	76	3.32
UNIVERSITY OF UTAH . . . . Graduate School of Business Salt Lake City, Utah	35	4.36
VANDERBILT UNIVERSITY . . . . Owen Graduate School of Management Nashville, Tennessee	55	3.88

A RATING OF DOCTORAL SCHOOLS
IN BUSINESS AND MANAGEMENT (Continued)

RATING CATEGORIES	Numerical Range
Very Strong	4.59-4.99
Strong	4.01-4.58
Good	3.59-3.99
Acceptable	3.01-3.58

SCHOOL (In Alphabetical Order)	Gourman National Ranking	Gourman National Score
UNIVERSITY OF VIRGINIA .... Colgate Darden Graduate School of Business Administration Charlottesville, Virginia	23	4.61
VIRGINIA COMMONWEALTH UNIVERSITY .... School of Business Richmond, Virginia	83	3.12
VIRGINIA POLYTECHNIC INSTITUTE AND STATE UNIVERSITY College of Business Blacksburg, Virginia	72	3.44
UNIVERSITY OF WASHINGTON .... Graduate School of Business Administration Seattle, Washington	18	4.67
WASHINGTON UNIVERSITY .... The Graduate School of Business Administration St. Louis, Missouri	34	4.40
UNIVERSITY OF WISCONSIN – MADISON .... School of Business Madison, Wisconsin	20	4.64
UNIVERSITY OF WISCONSIN – MILWAUKEE .... School of Business Administration Milwaukee, Wisconsin	75	3.36
YALE UNIVERSITY .... Yale School of Organization and Management New Haven, Connecticut	29	4.49

The GOURMAN REPORT
PART X

**A RATING OF SELECTIVE DOCTORAL PROGRAMS
IN BUSINESS AND MANAGEMENT
ON THE APPROVED LIST
OF THE GOURMAN REPORT**

- **Accounting**
- **Finance**
- **Management/Organizational Behavior**
- **Marketing**

A RATING OF SELECTIVE DOCTORAL PROGRAMS
IN BUSINESS AND MANAGEMENT

RATING CATEGORIES	Numerical Range
Very Strong	4.59-4.99
Strong	4.01-4.58
Good	3.59-3.99
Acceptable	3.01-3.58

SCHOOL (In Alphabetical Order)	ACCOUNTING		FINANCE		MANAGEMENT/ ORGANIZATIONAL BEHAVIOR		MARKETING	
	Gourman Rank	Score	Gourman Rank	Score	Gourman Rank	Score	Gourman Rank	Score
University of Alabama .... Graduate School of Business University, Alabama	61	3.73	61	3.70	61	3.68	61	3.76
University of Alabama at Birmingham Graduate School of Management Birmingham, Alabama	88	3.01	88	3.01	88	3.02	88	3.01
University of Arizona .... College of Business and Public Administration Tucson, Arizona	42	4.21	42	4.32	40	4.26	40	4.34
Arizona State University .... College of Business Tempe, Arizona	44	4.15	44	4.26	43	4.18	43	4.28
University of Arkansas .... College of Business Administration Fayetteville, Arkansas	79	3.27	79	3.23	78	3.24	79	3.28
Baruch College – The City University of New York .... School of Business and Public Administration New York, New York	26	4.59	32	4.52	33	4.46	32	4.48
Boston University .... School of Management Boston, Massachusetts	62	3.71	62	3.68	62	3.66	63	3.70
University of California, Berkeley .... School of Business Administration Berkeley, California	9	4.85	9	4.86	9	4.87	8	4.88

SCHOOL (In Alphabetical Order)	ACCOUNTING		FINANCE		MANAGEMENT/ ORGANIZATIONAL BEHAVIOR		MARKETING	
	Gourman Rank	Score	Gourman Rank	Score	Gourman Rank	Score	Gourman Rank	Score
University of California, irvine ...... Graduate School of Management Irvine, California	66	3.61	66	3.60	66	3.60	66	3.61
University of California, Los Angeles (UCLA) .... Graduate School of Management Los Angeles, California	8	4.87	7	4.89	7	4.89	7	4.89
Carnegie-Mellon University .... Graduate School of Industrial Administration Pittsburgh, Pennsylvania	11	4.82	12	4.82	12	4.84	12	4.83
Case Western Reserve University ... Weatherhead School of Management Cleveland, Ohio	17	4.75	27	4.58	28	4.54	29	4.52
University of Chicago .... Graduate School of Business Chicago, Illinois	5	4.90	5	4.91	6	4.90	5	4.91
University of Cincinnati .... College of Business Administration Cincinnati, Ohio	58	3.81	57	3.83	57	3.80	58	3.82
University of Colorado .... Graduate School of Business Administration Boulder, Colorado	50	4.01	50	4.05	50	4.02	50	4.06
Columbia University .... Graduate School of Business New York, New York	4	4.91	6	4.90	5	4.91	6	4.90
Cornell University .... Johnson Graduate School of Management Ithaca, New York	15	4.77	16	4.76	16	4.78	16	4.78
Drexel University .... College of Business and Administration Philadelphia, Pennsylvania	56	3.85	58	3.80	56	3.82	57	3.84

RATING CATEGORIES	Numerical Range
Very Strong	4.59-4.99
Strong	4.01-4.58
Good	3.59-3.99
Acceptable	3.01-3.58

SCHOOL (In Alphabetical Order)	ACCOUNTING		FINANCE		MANAGEMENT/ ORGANIZATIONAL BEHAVIOR		MARKETING	
	Gourman Rank	Score	Gourman Rank	Score	Gourman Rank	Score	Gourman Rank	Score
Duke University .... Fuqua School of Business Durham, North Carolina	22	4.64	21	4.66	21	4.69	21	4.66
University of Florida .... Graduate School of Business Administration Gainesville, Florida	38	4.32	38	4.42	38	4.30	37	4.38
Florida State University .... College of Business Tallahassee, Florida	68	3.56	68	3.55	68	3.54	67	3.59
George Washington University ..... School of Government and Business Administration Washington, D.C.	36	4.38	36	4.47	37	4.34	35	4.42
University of Georgia .... College of Business Administration Athens, Georgia	49	4.03	48	4.14	49	4.04	49	4.09
Georgia Institute of Technology ..... College of Management Atlanta, Georgia	46	4.09	46	4.20	45	4.14	45	4.22
Georgia State University .... College of Business Administration Atlanta, Georgia	51	3.98	52	3.97	51	3.96	52	3.97
Golden Gate University .... Graduate College San Francisco, California	69	3.53	69	3.52	69	3.51	69	3.55

SCHOOL (In Alphabetical Order)	ACCOUNTING Gourman Rank	Score	FINANCE Gourman Rank	Score	MANAGEMENT/ ORGANIZATIONAL BEHAVIOR Gourman Rank	Score	MARKETING Gourman Rank	Score
Harvard University . . . . Graduate School of Business Administration Boston, Massachusetts	1	4.94	2	4.94	1	4.95	1	4.95
University of Houston . . . . College of Business Administration Houston, Texas	39	4.30	39	4.39	39	4.28	39	4.35
University of Illinois at Chicago . . . . . College of Business Administration Chicago, Illinois	73	3.42	73	3.40	74	3.36	74	3.42
University of Illinois at Urbana-Champaign . . . . College of Commerce and Business Administration Champaign, Illinois	27	4.58	20	4.69	19	4.72	18	4.73
Indiana University . . . . The Graduate School of Business Bloomington, Indiana	7	4.88	8	4.87	8	4.88	9	4.87
University of Iowa . . . . College of Business Administration Iowa City, Iowa	31	4.52	26	4.59	26	4.58	27	4.55
University of Kansas . . . . School of Business Lawrence, Kansas	47	4.06	47	4.16	48	4.06	47	4.16
Kent State University . . . . Graduate School of Management Kent, Ohio	81	3.19	81	3.16	81	3.12	82	3.18
University of Kentucky . . . . College of Business and Economics Lexington, Kentucky	64	3.65	64	3.63	64	3.63	64	3.66
Lehigh University . . . . College of Business and Economics Bethlehem, Pennsylvania	53	3.91	53	3.94	53	3.92	56	3.87

A RATING OF SELECTIVE DOCTORAL PROGRAMS
IN BUSINESS AND MANAGEMENT (Continued)

RATING CATEGORIES	Numerical Range
Very Strong	4.59-4.99
Strong	4.01-4.58
Good	3.59-3.99
Acceptable	3.01-3.58

SCHOOL (In Alphabetical Order)	ACCOUNTING		FINANCE		MANAGEMENT/ ORGANIZATIONAL BEHAVIOR		MARKETING	
	Gourman Rank	Score	Gourman Rank	Score	Gourman Rank	Score	Gourman Rank	Score
Louisiana State University .... College of Business Administration Baton Rouge, Louisiana	54	3.90	54	3.92	54	3.88	53	3.96
Louisiana Tech University .... College of Administration and Business Ruston, Louisiana	86	3.05	86	3.04	86	3.04	86	3.05
University of Maryland .... College of Business and Management College Park, Maryland	57	3.82	56	3.86	58	3.78	55	3.90
University of Massachusetts, Amherst School of Management Amherst, Massachusetts	67	3.59	67	3.57	67	3.56	68	3.57
Massachusetts Institute of Technology Alfred P. Sloan School of Management Cambridge, Massachusetts	3	4.92	4	4.92	4	4.92	4	4.92
Memphis State University .... The Fogelman College of Business and Economics Memphis, Tennessee	74	3.39	74	3.38	73	3.39	73	3.46
University of Michigan .... Graduate School of Business Administration Ann Arbor, Michigan	10	4.84	10	4.85	10	4.86	11	4.85
Michigan State University .... The Graduate School of Business Administration East Lansing, Michigan	24	4.61	24	4.62	24	4.64	24	4.61

SCHOOL (In Alphabetical Order)	ACCOUNTING Gourman Rank	ACCOUNTING Gourman Score	FINANCE Gourman Rank	FINANCE Gourman Score	MANAGEMENT/ ORGANIZATIONAL BEHAVIOR Gourman Rank	MANAGEMENT/ ORGANIZATIONAL BEHAVIOR Gourman Score	MARKETING Gourman Rank	MARKETING Gourman Score
University of Minnesota School of Management Minneapolis, Minnesota	29	4.56	31	4.53	31	4.50	31	4.49
University of Mississippi School of Business Administration University, Mississippi	85	3.07	85	3.05	85	3.05	85	3.06
Mississippi State University College of Business and Industry Mississippi State, Mississippi	77	3.31	77	3.29	77	3.27	76	3.37
University of Missouri, Columbia College of Business and Public Administration Columbia, Missouri	43	4.18	43	4.29	44	4.15	44	4.25
University of Nebraska, Lincoln College of Business Administration Lincoln, Nebraska	71	3.48	71	3.47	70	3.48	71	3.50
University of New Mexico The Robert O. Anderson Graduate School of Management Albuquerque, New Mexico	84	3.11	84	3.08	83	3.08	83	3.13
New York University Graduate School of Business Administration New York, New York	13	4.80	13	4.80	13	4.82	13	4.82
University of North Carolina at Chapel Hill School of Business Administration Chapel Hill, North Carolina	21	4.68	22	4.65	23	4.66	23	4.63
University of North Texas State College of Business Administration Denton, Texas	87	3.03	87	3.02	87	3.03	87	3.03
Northwestern University J.L. Kellogg Graduate School of Management Evanston, Illinois	12	4.81	11	4.84	11	4.85	10	4.86

A RATING OF SELECTIVE DOCTORAL PROGRAMS
IN BUSINESS AND MANAGEMENT (Continued)

RATING CATEGORIES	Numerical Range
Very Strong	4.59-4.99
Strong	4.01-4.58
Good	3.59-3.99
Acceptable	3.01-3.58

SCHOOL (In Alphabetical Order)	ACCOUNTING		FINANCE		MANAGEMENT/ ORGANIZATIONAL BEHAVIOR		MARKETING	
	Gourman Rank	Score	Gourman Rank	Score	Gourman Rank	Score	Gourman Rank	Score
Ohio State University .... College of Administrative Science Columbus, Ohio	25	4.60	25	4.60	25	4.61	25	4.59
University of Oklahoma .... College of Business Administration Norman, Oklahoma	80	3.24	80	3.20	80	3.18	80	3.25
University of Oregon .... Graduate School of Management Eugene, Oregon	40	4.27	40	4.36	41	4.24	41	4.32
Pace University .... Lubin Schools of Business New York, New York	70	3.51	70	3.50	71	3.46	70	3.53
University of Pennsylvania .... The Wharton School Philadelphia, Pennsylvania	2	4.93	1	4.95	2	4.94	2	4.94
Pennsylvania State University ...... College of Business Administration University Park, Pennsylvania	32	4.49	33	4.51	34	4.44	33	4.46
University of Pittsburgh .... Graduate School of Business Pittsburgh, Pennsylvania	16	4.76	15	4.78	15	4.80	15	4.79
Purdue University .... Krannert Graduate School of Management West Lafayette, Indiana	18	4.73	17	4.74	17	4.76	17	4.75

SCHOOL (In Alphabetical Order)	ACCOUNTING		FINANCE		MANAGEMENT/ ORGANIZATIONAL BEHAVIOR		MARKETING	
	Gourman Rank	Score	Gourman Rank	Score	Gourman Rank	Score	Gourman Rank	Score
Rensselaer Polytechnic Institute .... School of Management Troy, New York	48	4.05	49	4.10	47	4.09	48	4.13
University of Rochester .... Graduate School of Management Rochester, New York	37	4.35	37	4.44	36	4.37	36	4.40
Rutgers–The State University of New Jersey, Newark Campus ...... Graduate School of Management Newark, New Jersey	59	3.79	59	3.78	60	3.74	59	3.80
St. Louis University .... School of Business and Administration St. Louis, Missouri	63	3.68	63	3.66	63	3.65	62	3.74
University of South Carolina .... Graduate School of Business Columbia, South Carolina	52	3.96	51	4.01	52	3.93	51	4.03
University of Southern California .... Graduate School of Business Administration Los Angeles, California	30	4.55	29	4.56	30	4.52	28	4.53
Southern Illinois University at Carbondale .... College of Business and Administration Carbondale, Illinois	82	3.15	82	3.14	82	3.11	81	3.22
Stanford University .... Graduate School of Business Stanford, California	6	4.89	3	4.93	3	4.93	3	4.93
State University of New York at Buffalo . School of Management Buffalo, New York	41	4.25	41	4.34	42	4.21	42	4.31
Syracuse University .... School of Management Syracuse, New York	34	4.42	49	4.11	32	4.48	38	4.37

RATING CATEGORIES	Numerical Range
Very Strong	4.59-4.99
Strong	4.01-4.58
Good	3.59-3.99
Acceptable	3.01-3.58

SCHOOL (In Alphabetical Order)	ACCOUNTING		FINANCE		MANAGEMENT/ ORGANIZATIONAL BEHAVIOR		MARKETING	
	Gourman Rank	Score	Gourman Rank	Score	Gourman Rank	Score	Gourman Rank	Score
Temple University .... School of Business Administration Philadelphia, Pennsylvania	65	3.63	65	3.61	65	3.62	65	3.64
University of Tennessee at Knoxville . College of Business Administration Knoxville, Tennessee	60	3.75	60	3.74	59	3.76	60	3.77
University of Texas at Arlington ..... College of Business Administration Arlington, Texas	78	3.29	78	3.25	79	3.21	78	3.31
University of Texas at Austin .... Graduate School of Business Austin, Texas	14	4.78	14	4.79	14	4.81	14	4.80
Texas A&M University .... College of Business Administration College Station, Texas	28	4.57	28	4.57	27	4.57	26	4.57
Texas Tech University .... College of Business Administration Lubbock, Texas	76	3.33	76	3.31	76	3.29	77	3.34
University of Utah .... Graduate School of Business Salt Lake City, Utah	33	4.45	34	4.50	35	4.42	34	4.44
Vanderbilt University .... Owen Graduate School of Management Nashville, Tennessee	55	3.87	55	3.89	55	3.85	54	3.93

SCHOOL (In Alphabetical Order)	ACCOUNTING		FINANCE		MANAGEMENT/ ORGANIZATIONAL BEHAVIOR		MARKETING	
	Gourman Rank	Score	Gourman Rank	Score	Gourman Rank	Score	Gourman Rank	Score
University of Virginia Colgate Darden Graduate School of Business Administration Charlottesville, Virginia	23	4.62	23	4.64	22	4.68	22	4.65
Virginia Commonwealth University School of Business Richmond, Virginia	83	3.13	83	3.12	84	3.07	84	3.10
Virginia Polytechnic Institute and State University College of Business Blacksburg, Virginia	72	3.46	72	3.45	72	3.41	72	3.48
University of Washington Graduate School of Business Administration Seattle, Washington	20	4.70	19	4.71	20	4.70	20	4.69
Washington University The Graduate School of Business Administration St. Louis, Missouri	34	4.42	35	4.49	32	4.48	38	4.37
University of Wisconsin, Madison School of Business Madison, Wisconsin	19	4.71	18	4.72	18	4.74	19	4.71
University of Wisconsin, Milwaukee School of Business Administration Milwaukee, Wisconsin	75	3.37	75	3.35	75	3.32	75	3.39
Yale University Yale School of Organization and Management New Haven, Connecticut	35	4.41	30	4.55	29	4.53	30	4.51

The GOURMAN REPORT
PART XI

**A RATING OF
LEADING INTERNATIONAL UNIVERSITIES**

A RATING OF GRADUATE QUALITY INSTITUTIONS

INTERNATIONAL UNIVERSITIES
Leading Institutions

Forty-nine institutions with scores in the 4.0-5.0 range, in rank order

INSTITUTION	COUNTRY	Rank	Score
PARIS (All Law Campuses)	France	1	4.93
OXFORD	United Kingdom	2	4.92
CAMBRIDGE	United Kingdom	3	4.91
HEIDELBERG	Federal Republic of Germany	4	4.90
MONTPELLIER I, II, III	France	5	4.86
MUNICH	Federal Republic of Germany	6	4.84
LYON I, II, III	France	7	4.82
LILLE I, II, III	France	8	4.81
EDINBURGH	United Kingdom (Scotland)	9	4.80
VIENNA	Austria	10	4.78
AIX-MARSEILLE I, II, III	France	11	4.76
BRUSSELS	Belgium	12	4.74
ZÜRICH	Switzerland	13	4.72
GÖTTINGEN	Federal Republic of Germany	14	4.71
BORDEAUX I, II, III	France	15	4.69
NANCY I, II	France	16	4.66
TORONTO	Canada	17	4.64
McGILL	Canada	18	4.62
GENEVA	Switzerland	19	4.61
TÜEBINGEN	Federal Republic of Germany	20	4.58
ERLANGEN-NÜRNBERG	Federal Republic of Germany	21	4.57
GRENOBLE I, II, III	France	22	4.55
DIJON	France	23	4.53
MARBURG	Federal Republic of Germany	24	4.50
RENNES I, II	France	25	4.46
TOULOUSE I, II, III	France	26	4.45
ROUEN	France	27	4.43
CLERMONT-FERRAND	France	28	4.42
BONN	Federal Republic of Germany	29	4.37
COLOGNE	Federal Republic of Germany	30	4.36
NICE	France	31	4.34
HEBREW	Israel	32	4.33
FRANKFURT	Federal Republic of Germany	33	4.31
LOUVAIN	Belgium	34	4.25
STOCKHOLM	Sweden	35	4.21
MÜNSTER	Federal Republic of Germany	36	4.18
COPENHAGEN	Denmark	37	4.17
MAINZ	Federal Republic of Germany	38	4.16
WÜRZBURG	Federal Republic of Germany	39	4.15
BESANCON	France	40	4.14
AMSTERDAM	Netherlands	41	4.13
LONDON	United Kingdom	42	4.12
TOKYO	Japan	43	4.11
NANTES	France	44	4.10
POITIERS	France	45	4.09
ORLEANS	France	46	4.08
CAEN	France	47	4.06
BOLOGNA	Italy	48	4.05
MADRID	Spain	49	4.04

The GOURMAN REPORT
PART XII

CRIMINAL JUSTICE/CRIMINOLOGY
GRADUATE PROGRAMS
NOT ON THE APPROVED LIST OF
THE GOURMAN REPORT

CRIMINAL JUSTICE/CRIMINOLOGY GRADUATE PROGRAMS
Not On The Approved List of The Gourman Report

IN ALPHABETICAL ORDER

INSTITUTION	STATE
ALBANY STATE COLLEGE	Georgia
AMERICAN INTERNATIONAL COLLEGE	Massachusetts
AMERICAN UNIVERSITY	Washington D.C.
ANNA MARIA COLLEGE	Massachusetts
ARIZONA STATE UNIVERSITY (Tempe)	Arizona
ARMSTRONG STATE COLLEGE	Georgia
AUBURN (Montgomery)	Alabama
BOISE STATE UNIVERSITY	Idaho
BOSTON UNIVERSITY	Massachusetts
BROOKLYN COLLEGE (CUNY)	New York
CALIFORNIA STATE UNIVERSITY (Fresno)	California
CALIFORNIA STATE UNIVERSITY (Long Beach)	California
CALIFORNIA STATE UNIVERSITY (Los Angeles)	California
CALIFORNIA STATE UNIVERSITY (Sacramento)	California
CALIFORNIA STATE UNIVERSITY (San Bernardino)	California
CENTRAL MISSOURI STATE UNIVERSITY	Missouri
CENTRAL STATE UNIVERSITY	Oklahoma
CHAMINADE UNIVERSITY OF HONOLULU	Hawaii
CHICAGO STATE UNIVERSITY	Illinois
CLARK ATLANTIC UNIVERSITY	Georgia
COPPIN STATE COLLEGE	Maryland
EASTERN KENTUCKY UNIVERSITY	Kentucky
EASTERN MICHIGAN UNIVERSITY	Michigan
EAST TENNESSEE STATE UNIVERSITY	Tennessee
FLORIDA INTERNATIONAL UNIVERSITY	Florida
FLORIDA STATE UNIVERSITY (Tallahassee)	Florida
FORDHAM UNIVERSITY	New York
GEORGE WASHINGTON UNIVERSITY	Washington D.C.
GEORGIA STATE UNIVERSITY (Atlanta)	Georgia
GRADUATE SCHOOL AND UNIVERSITY CENTER (CUNY)	New York
GRAMBLING STATE UNIVERSITY	Louisiana
ILLINOIS STATE UNIVERSITY (Normal)	Illinois
INDIANA STATE UNIVERSITY (Terre Haute)	Indiana

IN ALPHABETICAL ORDER

INSTITUTION	STATE
INDIANA UNIVERSITY (Bloomington)	Indiana
INDIANA UNIVERSITY NORTHWEST (Gary)	Indiana
INDIANA UNIVERSITY OF PENNSYLVANIA	Pennsylvania
INDIANA UNIVERSITY–PURDUE UNIVERSITY AT FORT WAYNE	Indiana
JACKSONVILLE STATE UNIVERSITY	Alabama
JERSEY CITY STATE COLLEGE	New Jersey
JOHN JAY COLLEGE OF CRIMINAL JUSTICE OF THE (CUNY)	New York
KENT STATE UNIVERSITY	Ohio
LEWIS UNIVERSITY (Romeoville)	Illinois
LONG ISLAND UNIVERSITY (C.W. Post Campus)	New York
L.S.U. (Baton Rouge)	Louisiana
MARQUETTE UNIVERSITY	Wisconsin
MARSHALL UNIVERSITY	West Virginia
MARYWOOD COLLEGE	Pennsylvania
MEMPHIS STATE UNIVERSITY	Tennessee
MICHIGAN STATE UNIVERSITY	Michigan
MIDDLE TENNESSEE STATE UNIVERSITY	Tennessee
MINOT STATE UNIVERSITY	North Dakota
MOREHEAD STATE UNIVERSITY	Kentucky
NEW MEXICO STATE UNIVERSITY	New Mexico
NORTH CAROLINA CENTRAL UNIVERSITY	North Carolina
NORTHEASTERN STATE UNIVERSITY	Oklahoma
NORTHEASTERN UNIVERSITY	Massachusetts
NORTHEAST LOUISIANA UNIVERSITY	Louisiana
NORTHERN ARIZONA UNIVERSITY	Arizona
OKLAHOMA CITY UNIVERSITY	Oklahoma
PORTLAND STATE UNIVERSITY	Oregon
RADFORD UNIVERSITY	Virginia
RUTGERS, THE STATE UNIVERSITY OF NEW JERSEY (Newark)	New Jersey
SAGINAW VALLEY STATE UNIVERSITY	Michigan
ST. CLOUD STATE UNIVERSITY	Minnesota
SAINT JOSEPH'S UNIVERSITY	Pennsylvania
SALVE REGINA COLLEGE	Rhode Island

CRIMINAL JUSTICE/CRIMINOLOGY GRADUATE PROGRAMS
Not On The Approved List of The Gourman Report (Continued)

IN ALPHABETICAL ORDER

INSTITUTION	STATE
SAM HOUSTON STATE UNIVERSITY	Texas
SAN DIEGO STATE UNIVERSITY	California
SAN JOSE STATE UNIVERSITY	California
SHIPPENSBURGH UNIVERSITY OF PENNSYLVANIA	Pennsylvania
SOUTHEAST MISSOURI STATE UNIVERSITY	Missouri
SOUTHERN ILLINOIS UNIVERSITY (Carbondale)	Illinois
SOUTHWEST TEXAS STATE UNIVERSITY	Texas
SUNY (Albany)	New York
SUNY COLLEGE (Buffalo)	New York
TEMPLE UNIVERSITY (Philadelphia)	Pennsylvania
TENNESSEE STATE UNIVERSITY	Tennessee
TROY STATE UNIVERSITY (Troy)	Alabama
TROY STATE UNIVERSITY IN MONTGOMERY	Alabama
UNIVERSITY OF ALABAMA (Birmingham)	Alabama
UNIVERSITY OF ALABAMA (Tuscaloosa)	Alabama
UNIVERSITY OF ARKANSAS (Little Rock)	Arkansas
UNIVERSITY OF BALTIMORE	Maryland
UNIVERSITY OF CALIFORNIA (Berkeley)	California
UNIVERSITY OF CENTRAL TEXAS	Texas
UNIVERSITY OF CINCINNATI	Ohio
UNIVERSITY OF COLORADO (Denver)	Colorado
UNIVERSITY OF DELAWARE (Newark)	Delaware
UNIVERSITY OF DENVER	Colorado
UNIVERSITY OF DETROIT	Michigan
UNIVERSITY OF ILLINOIS (Chicago)	Illinois
UNIVERSITY OF IOWA (Iowa City)	Iowa
UNIVERSITY OF LOUISVILLE	Kentucky
UNIVERSITY OF LOWELL	Massachusetts
UNIVERSITY OF MARYLAND (College Park)	Maryland
UNIVERSITY OF MISSOURI (Kansas City)	Missouri
UNIVERSITY OF NEBRASKA (Omaha)	Nebraska
UNIVERSITY OF NEW HAVEN	Connecticut
UNIVERSITY OF NORTH CAROLINA (Charlotte)	North Carolina

CRIMINAL JUSTICE/CRIMINOLOGY GRADUATE PROGRAMS
Not On The Approved List of The Gourman Report (Continued)

IN ALPHABETICAL ORDER

INSTITUTION	STATE
UNIVERSITY OF NORTH FLORIDA	Florida
UNIVERSITY OF OREGON (Eugene)	Oregon
UNIVERSITY OF PITTSBURGH (Pittsburgh)	Pennsylvania
UNIVERSITY OF SOUTH CAROLINA (Columbia)	South Carolina
UNIVERSITY OF SOUTHERN CALIFORNIA (Los Angeles)	California
UNIVERSITY OF SOUTHERN MISSISSIPPI	Mississippi
UNIVERSITY OF SOUTH FLORIDA	Florida
UNIVERSITY OF TENNESSEE (Chattanooga)	Tennessee
UNIVERSITY OF TENNESSEE (Knoxville)	Tennessee
UNIVERSITY OF TEXAS (Arlington)	Texas
UNIVERSITY OF WEST VIRGINIA COLLEGE OF GRADUATE STUDIES (Institute)	West Virginia
UNIVERSITY OF WISCONSIN (Milwaukee)	Wisconsin
VALDOSTA STATE COLLEGE	Georgia
VILLANOVA UNIVERSITY	Pennsylvania
VIRGINIA COMMONWEALTH UNIVERSITY	Virginia
WASHINGTON STATE UNIVERSITY	Washington
WAYNE STATE UNIVERSITY	Michigan
WEBSTER UNIVERSITY	Missouri
WESTCHESTER UNIVERSITY OF PENNSYLVANIA	Pennsylvania
WESTERN ILLINOIS UNIVERSITY	Illinois
WESTFIELD STATE COLLEGE	Massachusetts
WICHITA STATE UNIVERSITY	Kansas
XAVIER UNIVERSITY	Ohio
YOUNGSTOWN STATE UNIVERSITY	Ohio

The GOURMAN REPORT
PART XIII

TEACHER EDUCATION
NOT ON THE APPROVED LIST OF
THE GOURMAN REPORT

TEACHER EDUCATION
Not On The Approved List of The Gourman Report

IN ALPHABETICAL ORDER

INSTITUTION	LOCATION
Abilene Christian University	Abilene, Texas
Adams State College	Alamosa, Colorado
Adelphi University	Garden City, New York
Alabama Agricultural and Mechanical University	Normal, Alabama
Alabama State University	Montgomery, Alabama
Alaska Pacific University	Anchorage, Alaska
Albany State College	Albany, Georgia
Alcorn State University	Lorman, Mississippi
Alfred University	Alfred, New York
American International College	Springfield, Massachusetts
American University	Washington, D.C.
Andrews University	Berrien Springs, Michigan
Angelo State University	San Angelo, Texas
Appalachian State University	Boone, North Carolina
Arizona State University	Tempe, Arizona
Arkansas State University	State University, Arkansas
Arkansas Tech University	Russellville, Arkansas
Auburn University	Auburn, Alabama
Auburn University at Montgomery	Montgomery, Alabama
Austin Peay State University	Clarksville, Tennessee
Azusa Pacific University	Azusa, California
Ball State University	Muncie, Indiana
Bank Street College of Education	New York, New York
Barry University	Miami Shores, Florida
Baylor University	Waco, Texas
Bemidji State University	Bemidji, Minnesota
Biola University	La Mirada, California
Bloomsburgh University of Pennsylvania	Bloomsburgh, Pennsylvania
Boise State University	Boise, Idaho

IN ALPHABETICAL ORDER

INSTITUTION	LOCATION
Boston College	Chestnut Hill, Massachusetts
Boston University	Boston, Massachusetts
Bowie State University	Bowie, Maryland
Bowling Green State University	Bowling Green, Ohio
Bradley University	Peoria, Illinois
Bridgewater State College	Bridgewater, Massachusetts
Brigham Young University	Provo, Utah
Bryn Mawr College	Bryn Mawr, Pennsylvania
Bucknell University	Lewisburg, Pennsylvania
Butler University	Indianapolis, Indiana
California Lutheran College	Thousand Oaks, California
California State Polytechnic University, San Luis Obispo	San Luis Obispo, California
California State Polytechnic University, Pomona	Pomona, California
California State University, Bakersfield	Bakersfield, California
California State University, Chico	Chico, California
California State University, Dominguez Hills	Carson, California
California State University, Fresno	Fresno, California
California State University, Fullerton	Fullerton, California
California State University, Hayward	Hayward, California
California State University, Long Beach	Long Beach, California
California State University, Los Angeles	Los Angeles, California
California State University, Northridge	Northridge, California
California State University, Sacramento	Sacramento, California
California State University, San Bernardino	San Bernardino, California
California State University, Stanislaus	Turlock, California
California State University of Pennsylvania	California, Pennsylvania
Canisius College	Buffalo, New York
Catholic University of America	Washington D.C.
Central Connecticut State University	New Britain, Connecticut
Central Michigan University	Mount Pleasant, Michigan

IN ALPHABETICAL ORDER

INSTITUTION	LOCATION
Central Missouri State University	Warrensburg, Missouri
Central State University	Edmond, Oklahoma
Central Washington University	Ellensburg, Washington
Chapman College	Orange, California
Cheyney University of Pennsylvania	Cheyney, Pennsylvania
Chicago State University	Chicago, Illinois
City University of New York, Bernard M. Baruch College	New York, New York
City University of New York, Brooklyn College	Brooklyn, New York
City University of New York, City College	New York, New York
City University of New York, College of Staten Island	Staten Island, New York
City University of New York, Herbert H. Lehman College	Bronx, New York
City University of New York, Hunter College	New York, New York
City University of New York, Queens College	Flushing, New York
Claremont Graduate School	Claremont, California
Clarion University of Pennsylvania	Clarion, Pennsylvania
Clark University	Worcester, Massachusetts
Clemson University	Clemson, South Carolina
Cleveland State University	Cleveland, Ohio
College of William and Mary	Williamsburg, Virginia
Colorado State University	Fort Collins, Colorado
Connecticut College	New London, Connecticut
Cornell University	Ithaca, New York
Corpus Christi State University	Corpus Christi, Texas
Creighton University	Omaha, Nebraska
Delta State University	Cleveland, Mississippi
De Paul University	Chicago, Illinois
Drake University	Des Moines, Iowa
Drury College	Springfield, Missouri
Duquesne University	Pittsburgh, Pennsylvania
East Carolina University	Greenville, North Carolina

IN ALPHABETICAL ORDER

INSTITUTION	LOCATION
East Central University	Ada, Oklahoma
Eastern Connecticut State University	Willimantic, Connecticut
Eastern Illinois University	Charleston, Illinois
Eastern Kentucky University	Richmond, Kentucky
Eastern Michigan University	Ypsilanti, Michigan
Eastern New Mexico University	Portales, New Mexico
Eastern Washington University	Cheney, Washington
East Stroudsburg University of Pennsylvania	East Stroudsburg, Pennsylvania
East Tennessee State University	Johnson City, Tennessee
East Texas State University	Commerce, Texas
Edinboro University of Pennsylvania	Edinboro, Pennsylvania
Emporia State University	Emporia, Kansas
Fairfield University	Fairfield, Connecticut
Fairleigh Dickinson University, Teaneck-Hackensack Campus	Teaneck, New Jersey
Fayetteville State University	Fayetteville, North Carolina
Florida Agricultural and Mechanical University	Tallahassee, Florida
Florida Atlantic University	Boca Raton, Florida
Florida International University	Miami, Florida
Florida State University	Tallahassee, Florida
Fordham University	Bronx, New York
Fort Hays State University	Hays, Kansas
Framingham State College	Framingham, Massachusetts
Frostburg State University	Frostburg, Maryland
Gannon University	Erie, Pennsylvania
George Mason University	Fairfax, Virginia
George Washington University	Washington, D.C.
Georgia College	Milledgeville, Georgia
Georgia Southern University	Statesboro, Georgia
Georgia State University	Atlanta, Georgia

IN ALPHABETICAL ORDER

INSTITUTION	LOCATION
Gonzaga University	Spokane, Washington
Governors State University	Park Forest South, Illinois
Grand Valley State University	Allendale, Michigan
Hamptom University	Hampton, Virginia
Hardin-Simmons University	Abilene, Texas
Harvard University	Cambridge, Massachusetts
Henderson State University	Arkadelphia, Arkansas
Hofstra University	Hempstead, New York
Howard University	Washington, D.C.
Humboldt State University	Arcata, California
Idaho State University	Pocatello, Idaho
Illinois State University	Normal, Illinois
Indiana State University at Terre Haute	Terre Haute, Indiana
Indiana University at South Bend	South Bend, Indiana
Indiana University, Bloomington	Bloomington, Indiana
Indiana University of Pennsylvania	Indiana, Pennsylvania
Indiana University–Purdue University at For Wayne	Fort Wayne, Indiana
Indiana University–Purdue University at Indianapolis	Indianapolis, Indiana
Iowa State University	Ames, Iowa
Jackson State University	Jackson, Mississippi
Jacksonville State University	Jacksonville, Alabama
Jacksonville University	Jacksonville, Florida
James Madison University	Harrisonburg, Virginia
Jersey City State College	Jersey City, New Jersey
John Carroll University	University Heights, Ohio
Johns Hopkins University	Baltimore, Maryland
Kansas State University	Manhattan, Kansas
Kean College of New Jersey	Union, New Jersey

IN ALPHABETICAL ORDER

INSTITUTION	LOCATION
Keene State College	Keene, New Hampshire
Kent State University	Kent, Ohio
Kutztown University of Pennsylvania	Kutztown, Pennsylvania
Lamar University	Beaumont, Texas
Laredo State University	Laredo, Texas
Lehigh University	Bethlehem, Pennsylvania
Loma Linda University	Loma Linda, California
Long Island University, Brooklyn Center	Brooklyn, New York
Long Island University, C.W. Post Campus	Greenvale, New York
Louisiana State University and Agricultural and Mechanical College	Baton Rouge, Louisiana
Louisiana State University in Shreveport	Shreveport, Louisiana
Louisiana Tech University	Ruston, Louisiana
Loyola College	Baltimore, Maryland
Loyola Marymount University	Los Angeles, California
Loyola University, New Orleans	New Orleans, Louisiana
Loyola University of Chicago	Chicago, Illinois
Lynchburg College	Lynchburg, Virginia
Mankato State University	Mankato, Minnesota
Mansfield University of Pennsylvania	Mansfield, Pennsylvania
Marquette University	Milwaukee, Wisconsin
Marshall University	Huntington, West Virginia
Memphis State University	Memphis, Tennessee
Mercer University	Macon, Georgia
Mercer University in Atlanta	Atlanta, Georgia
Miami University	Oxford, Ohio
Michigan State University	East Lansing, Michigan
Middle Tennessee State University	Murfreesboro, Tennessee
Midwestern State University	Wichita Falls, Texas
Millersville University of Pennsylvania	Millersville, Pennsylvania

IN ALPHABETICAL ORDER

INSTITUTION	LOCATION
Mississippi State University	Mississippi State, Mississippi
Montana State University	Bozeman, Montana
Monclair State College	Upper Monclair, New Jersey
Moorhead State University	Moorhead, Minnesota
Morehead State University	Morehead, Kentucky
Morgan State University	Baltimore, Maryland
Murray State University	Murray, Kentucky
National Louis University	Evanston, Illinois
New Mexico Highlands University	Las Vegas, New Mexico
New Mexico State University	Las Cruces, New Mexico
New York University	New York, New York
Niagara University	Niagara, New York
Nicholls State University	Thibodaux, Louisiana
Norfolk State University	Norfolk, Virginia
North Adams State College	North Adams, Massachusetts
North Carolina Agricultural and Technical State University	Greensboro, North Carolina
North Carolina Central University	Durham, North Carolina
North Carolina State University at Raleigh	Raleigh, North Carolina
North Dakota State University	Fargo, North Dakota
Northeastern Illinois University	Chicago, Illinois
Northeastern State University	Tahlequah, Oklahoma
Northeastern University	Boston, Massachusetts
Northeast Louisiana University	Monroe, Louisiana
Northeast Missouri State University	Kirksville, Missouri
Northern Arizona University	Flagstaff, Arizona
Northern Illinois University	DeKalb, Illinois
Northern Kentucky University	Highland Heights, Kentucky
Northern Michigan University	Marquette, Michigan
Northern State University	Aberdeen, South Dakota

IN ALPHABETICAL ORDER

INSTITUTION	LOCATION
Northwestern Oklahoma State University	Alva, Oklahoma
Northwestern State University of Louisiana	Natchitoches, Louisiana
Northwestern University	Evanston, Illinois
Northwest Missouri State University	Maryville, Missouri
Norwich University	Northfield, Vermont
Nova University	Fort Lauderdale, Florida
Oakland University	Rochester, Michigan
Ohio State University	Columbus, Ohio
Ohio University	Athens, Ohio
Oklahoma State University	Stillwater, Oklahoma
Old Dominion University	Norfolk, Virginia
Oral Roberts University	Tulsa, Oklahoma
Oregon State University	Corvallis, Oregon
Pace University	New York, New York
Pacific Lutheran University	Tacoma, Washington
Pacific University	Forest Grove, Oregon
Pennsylvania State University–Capitol Campus	Middletown, Pennsylvania
Pennsylvania State University–University Park Campus	University Park, Pennsylvania
Pepperdine University	Malibu, California
Pittsburg State University	Pittsburg, Kansas
Portland State University	Portland, Oregon
Prairie View A&M University	Prairie View, Texas
Purdue University	West Lafayette, Indiana
Purdue University–Calumet	Hammond, Indiana
Radford University	Radford, Virginia
Roosevelt University	Chicago, Illinois
Rutgers University, New Brunswick	New Brunswick, New Jersey
St. Bonaventure University	St. Bonaventure, New York
St. Cloud State University	St. Cloud, Minnesota

IN ALPHABETICAL ORDER

INSTITUTION	LOCATION
St. John's University	Jamaica, New York
Saint Louis University	St. Louis, Missouri
Samford University	Birmingham, Alabama
Sam Houston State University	Huntsville, Texas
San Diego State University	San Diego, California
San Francisco State University	San Francisco, California
Sangamon State University	Springfield, Illinois
San Jose State University	San Jose, California
Seattle University	Seattle, Washington
Seton Hall University	South Orange, New Jersey
Shippensburg University of Pennsylvania	Shippensburg, Pennsylvania
Simmons College	Boston, Massachusetts
Slippery Rock University of Pennsylvania	Slippery Rock, Pennsylvania
Smith College	Northhampton, Massachusetts
Sonoma State University	Rohnert Park, California
South Dakota State University	Brookings, South Dakota
Southeastern Louisiana University	Hammond, Louisiana
Southeastern Massachusetts University	North Dartmouth, Massachusetts
Southeast Missouri State University	Cape Giradeau, Missouri
Southern Connecticut State University	New Haven, Connecticut
Southern Illinois University at Carbondale	Carbondale, Illinois
Southern Illinois University at Edwardsville	Edwardsville, Illinois
Southern University and Agricultural and Mechanical College	Baton Rouge, Louisiana
Southwestern Oklahoma State University	Weatherford, Oklahoma
Southwest Missouri State University	Springfield, Missouri
Southwest Texas State University	San Marcos, Texas
Stanford University	Stanford, California
State University of New York at Albany	Albany, New York
State University of New York at Binghamton	Binghamton, New York

IN ALPHABETICAL ORDER

INSTITUTION	LOCATION
State University of New York at Buffalo	Buffalo, New York
State University of New York College at Brockport	Brockport, New York
State University of New York College at Buffalo	Buffalo, New York
State University of New York College at Cortland	Cortland, New York
State University of New York College at Fredonia	Fredonia, New York
State University of New York College at Geneseo	Geneseo, New York
State University of New York College at New Paltz	New Paltz, New York
State University of New York College at Oneonta	Oneonta, New York
State University of New York College at Oswego	Oswego, New York
State University of New York College at Plattsburgh	Plattsburgh, New York
State University of New York College at Potsdam	Potsdam, New York
Stephen F. Austin State University	Nacogdoches, Texas
Stetson University	Deland, Florida
Suffolk University	Boston, Massachusetts
Sul Ross State University	Alpine, Texas
Syracuse University	Syracuse, New York
Tarleton State University	Stephenville, Texas
Teachers College, Columbia University	New York, New York
Temple University	Philadelphia, Pennsylvania
Tennessee State University	Nashville, Tennessee
Tennessee Technological University	Cookeville, Tennessee
Texas A&I University at Kingsville	Kingsville, Texas
Texas A&M University	College Station, Texas
Texas Christian University	Fort Worth, Texas
Texas Southern University	Houston, Texas
Texas Tech University	Lubbock, Texas
Texas Woman's University	Denton, Texas
Towson State University	Baltimore, Maryland
Trenton State College	Trenton, New Jersey
Trinity University	San Antonio, Texas

IN ALPHABETICAL ORDER

INSTITUTION	LOCATION
Troy State University	Troy, Alabama
Tufts University	Medford, Massachusetts
Tulane University	New Orleans, Louisiana
Tuskegee University	Tuskegee, Alabama
United States International University	San Diego, California
University of Akron	Akron, Ohio
University of Alabama	University, Alabama
University of Alabama in Birmingham	Birmingham, Alabama
University of Alaska, Anchorage	Anchorage, Alaska
University of Alaska, Fairbanks	Fairbanks, Alaska
University of Arizona	Tucson, Arizona
University of Arkansas	Fayetteville, Arkansas
University of Arkansas at Little Rock	Little Rock, Arkansas
University of Bridgeport	Bridgeport, Connecticut
University of California, Berkeley	Berkeley, California
University of California, Davis	Davis, California
University of California, Los Angeles	Los Angeles, California
University of California, Riverside	Riverside, California
University of California, Santa Barbara	Santa Barbara, California
University of California, Santa Cruz	Santa Cruz, California
University of Central Arkansas	Conway, Arkansas
University of Central Florida	Orlando, Florida
University of Chicago	Chicago, Illinois
University of Cincinnati	Cincinnati, Ohio
University of Colorado at Boulder	Boulder, Colorado
University of Colorado at Colorado Springs	Colorado Springs, Colorado
University of Colorado at Denver	Denver, Colorado
University of Connecticut	Storrs, Connecticut
University of Dallas	Irving, Texas
University of Dayton	Dayton, Ohio

IN ALPHABETICAL ORDER

INSTITUTION	LOCATION
University of Delaware	Newark, Delaware
University of Denver	Denver, Colorado
University of Detroit	Detroit, Michigan
University of Evansville	Evansville, Indiana
University of Florida	Gainesville, Florida
University of Georgia	Athens, Georgia
University of Guam	Mangilao, Guam
University of Hartford	West Hartford, Connecticut
University of Hawaii at Manoa	Honolulu, Hawaii
University of Houston–Clear Lake	Houston, Texas
University of Houston–University Park	Houston, Texas
University of Idaho	Moscow, Idaho
University of Illinois at Chicago	Chicago, Illinois
University of Illinois at Urbana–Champaign	Urbana, Illinois
University of Iowa	Iowa City, Iowa
University of Kansas	Lawrence, Kansas
University of Kentucky	Lexington, Kentucky
University of Louisville	Louisville, Kentucky
University of Lowell	Lowell, Massachusetts
University of Maine at Orono	Orono, Maine
University of Maryland at College Park	College Park, Maryland
University of Maryland, Baltimore County	Catonsville, Maryland
University of Massachusetts at Amherst	Amherst, Massachusetts
University of Massachusetts at Boston	Boston, Massachusetts
University of Miami	Coral Gables, Florida
University of Michigan	Ann Arbor, Michigan
University of Minnesota, Duluth	Duluth, Minnesota
University of Minnesota, Twin Cities	Minneapolis, Minnesota
University of Mississippi	University, Mississippi
University of Missouri–Columbia	Columbia, Missouri

IN ALPHABETICAL ORDER

INSTITUTION	LOCATION
University of Missouri–Kansas City	Kansas City, Missouri
University of Missouri–St. Louis	St. Louis, Missouri
University of Montana	Missoula, Montana
University of Montevallo	Montevallo, Alabama
University of Nebraska at Omaha	Omaha, Nebraska
University of Nebraska–Lincoln	Lincoln, Nebraska
University of Nevada–Las Vegas	Las Vegas, Nevada
University of Nevada–Reno	Reno, Nevada
University of New Hampshire	Durham, New Hampshire
University of New Mexico	Albuquerque, New Mexico
University of New Orleans	New Orleans, Louisiana
University of North Alabama	Florence, Alabama
University of North Carolina at Chapel Hill	Chapel Hill, North Carolina
University of North Carolina at Charlotte	Charlotte, North Carolina
University of North Carolina at Greensboro	Greensboro, North Carolina
University of North Carolina at Wilmington	Wilmington, North Carolina
University of North Dakota	Grand Forks, North Dakota
University of Northern Colorado	Greeley, Colorado
University of Northern Iowa	Cedar Falls, Iowa
University of North Florida	Jacksonville, Florida
University of North Texas	Denton, Texas
University of Oklahoma	Norman, Oklahoma
University of Oregon	Eugene, Oregon
University of Pennsylvania	Philadelphia, Pennsylvania
University of Pittsburgh	Pittsburgh, Pennsylvania
University of Portland	Portland, Oregon
University of Puget Sound	Tacoma, Washington
University of Redlands	Redlands, California
University of Rhode Island	Kingston, Rhode Island
University of Richmond	Richmond, Virginia

IN ALPHABETICAL ORDER

INSTITUTION	LOCATION
University of Rochester	Rochester, New York
University of San Diego	San Diego, California
University of San Francisco	San Francisco, California
University of Santa Clara	Santa Clara, California
University of Scranton	Scranton, Pennsylvania
University of South Alabama	Mobile, Alabama
University of South Carolina	Columbia, South Carolina
University of South Dakota	Vermillion, South Dakota
University of Southern California	Los Angeles, California
University of Southern Mississippi	Hattiesburg, Mississippi
University of South Florida	Tampa, Florida
University of Southwestern Louisiana	Lafayette, Louisiana
University of Tennessee at Chattanooga	Chattanooga, Tennessee
University of Tennessee at Martin	Martin, Tennessee
University of Tennessee	Knoxville, Tennessee
University of Texas at Austin	Austin, Texas
University of Texas at Dallas	Richardson, Texas
University of Texas at El Paso	El Paso, Texas
University of Texas at San Antonio	San Antonio, Texas
University of the District of Columbia	Washington, D.C.
University of the Pacific	Stockton, California
University of Toledo	Toledo, Ohio
University of Tulsa	Tulsa, Oklahoma
University of Utah	Salt Lake City, Utah
University of Vermont	Burlington, Vermont
University of Virginia	Charlottesville, Virginia
University of Washington	Seattle, Washington
University of West Florida	Pensacola, Florida
University of Wisconsin–Eau Claire	Eau Claire, Wisconsin
University of Wisconsin–La Crosse	La Crosse, Wisconsin

IN ALPHABETICAL ORDER

INSTITUTION	LOCATION
University of Wisconsin–Madison	Madison, Wisconsin
University of Wisconsin–Milwaukee	Milwaukee, Wisconsin
University of Wisconsin–Oshkosh	Oshkosh, Wisconsin
University of Wisconsin–Platteville	Platteville, Wisconsin
University of Wisconsin–River Falls	River Falls, Wisconsin
University of Wisconsin–Stevens Point	Stevens Point, Wisconsin
University of Wisconsin–Stout	Menomonie, Wisconsin
University of Wisconsin–Superior	Superior, Wisconsin
University of Wisconsin–Whitewater	Whitewater, Wisconsin
University of Wyoming	Laramie, Wyoming
Utah State University	Logan, Utah
Valdosta State College	Valdosta, Georgia
Vanderbilt University	Nashville, Tennessee
Villanova University	Villanova, Pennsylvania
Virginia Commonwealth University	Richmond, Virginia
Virginia Polytechnic Institute and State University	Blacksburg, Virginia
Virginia State University	Petersburg, Virginia
Wake Forest University	Winston-Salem, North Carolina
Washburn University of Topeka	Topeka, Kansas
Washington State University	Pullman, Washington
Washington University	St. Louis, Missouri
Wayne State University	Detroit, Michigan
Westchester University of Pennsylvania	Westchester, Pennsylvania
Western Carolina University	Cullowhee, North Carolina
Western Illinois University	Macomb, Illinois
Western Kentucky University	Bowling Green, Kentucky
Western Michigan University	Kalamazoo, Michigan
Western Washington University	Bellingham, Washington
West Texas State University	Canyon, Texas
West Virginia University	Morgantown, West Virginia

IN ALPHABETICAL ORDER

INSTITUTION	LOCATION
Wichita State University	Wichita, Kansas
Widener University	Chester, Pennsylvania
William Patterson College of New Jersey	Wayne, New Jersey
Winona State University	Winona, Minnesota
Wright State University	Dayton, Ohio
Xavier University	Cincinnati, Ohio
Yeshiva University	New York, New York
Youngstown State University	Youngstown, Ohio

The GOURMAN REPORT
PART XIV

DEPARTMENTS OF GRADUATE EDUCATION
NOT ON THE APPROVED LIST OF
THE GOURMAN REPORT

DEPARTMENTS OF GRADUATE EDUCATION
Not On The Approved List of The Gourman Report

RATING CATEGORIES	Numerical Range
Very Strong	4.51-4.99
Strong	4.01-4.49
Good	3.61-3.99
Acceptable Plus	3.01-3.59
Adequate	2.51-2.99
Marginal	2.01-2.49

Not Sufficient for Graduate Programs   0.

Department of Graduate Education INSTITUTION	Gourman Overall Academic Score (Combined Areas/Fields)	Administration (Attitude and Policy) (Quality of Leadership at All Levels of Administration)	Curriculum (Attractiveness of Program)	Faculty Effectiveness	Faculty (Quality of Research/ Scholarship)	Library Resources
Abilene Christian University ..... Abilene, TX	0.38	0.35	0.29	0.36	0.	0.31
Adams State College .... Alamosa, CO	0.39	0.36	0.30	0.38	0.	0.32
Adelphi University .... Garden City, NY	0.45	0.37	0.32	0.39	0.	0.34
Alabama Agricultural and Mechanical University .... Normal, AL	0.31	0.32	0.29	0.30	0.	0.28
Alabama State University ...... Montgomery, AL	0.30	0.31	0.28	0.26	0.	0.27
Alaska Pacific University .... Anchorage, AK	0.31	0.29	0.27	0.26	0.	0.25
Albany State College .... Albany, GA	0.29	0.28	0.24	0.25	0.	0.22
Alcorn State University .... Lorman, MS	0.28	0.27	0.23	0.22	0.	0.19
Alfred University .... Alfred, NY	0.32	0.30	0.30	0.31	0.	0.31
American International College .. Springfield, MA	0.31	0.30	0.29	0.29	0.	0.30
American University .... Washington, D.C.	0.62	0.55	0.58	0.55	0.	0.49
Andrews University .... Berrien Springs, MI	0.37	0.36	0.32	0.33	0.	0.30
Angelo State University .... San Angelo, TX	0.41	0.40	0.41	0.38	0.	0.34
Appalachian State University .... Boone, NC	0.41	0.39	0.38	0.39	0.	0.32
Arizona State University .... Tempe, AZ	0.73	0.68	0.72	0.71	0.	0.78
Arkansas State University ...... State University, AR	0.32	0.31	0.30	0.29	0.	0.31
Arkansas Tech University ...... Russellville, AR	0.33	0.32	0.30	0.30	0.	0.28

Department of Graduate Education INSTITUTION	Gourman Overall Academic Score (Combined Areas/Fields)	Administration (Attitude and Policy) (Quality of Leadership at All Levels of Administration)	Curriculum (Attractiveness of Program)	Faculty Effectiveness	Faculty (Quality of Research/ Scholarship)	Library Resources
Auburn University Auburn, AL	0.52	0.51	0.49	0.45	0.	0.46
Auburn University at Montgomery Montgomery, AL	0.28	0.29	0.30	0.31	0.	0.28
Austin Peay State University Clarksville, TN	0.34	0.33	0.31	0.32	0.	0.29
Azusa Pacific University Azusa, CA	0.35	0.34	0.32	0.31	0.	0.30
Ball State University Muncie, IN	0.51	0.46	0.45	0.44	0.	0.41
Bank Street College of Education New York, NY	0.42	0.40	0.39	0.41	0.	0.42
Barry University Miami Shores, FL	0.33	0.31	0.30	0.31	0.	0.31
Baylor University Waco, TX	0.51	0.50	0.49	0.47	0.	0.45
Bemidji State University Bemidji, MN	0.36	0.37	0.35	0.34	0.	0.37
Biola University La Mirada, CA	0.35	0.34	0.31	0.32	0.	0.33
Bloomsburgh University of Pennsylvania Bloomsburgh, PA	0.39	0.37	0.36	0.33	0.	0.35
Boise State University Boise, ID	0.38	0.39	0.37	0.34	0.	0.36
Boston College Chestnut Hill, MA	0.49	0.50	0.51	0.45	0.	0.47
Boston University Boston, MA	0.70	0.66	0.64	0.61	0.	0.56
Bowie State University Bowie, MD	0.26	0.25	0.23	0.22	0.	0.19
Bowling Green State University Bowling Green, OH	0.52	0.48	0.49	0.50	0.	0.49
Bradley University Peoria, IL	0.50	0.47	0.46	0.48	0.	0.49
Bridgewater State College Bridgewater, MA	0.39	0.36	0.35	0.36	0.	0.38
Brigham Young University Provo, UT	0.54	0.52	0.50	0.49	0.	0.51
Bryn Mawr College Bryn Mawr, PA	0.33	0.32	0.31	0.34	0.	0.32
Bucknell University Lewisburg, PA	0.34	0.33	0.32	0.32	0.	0.33
Butler University Indianapolis, IN	0.48	0.46	0.45	0.47	0.	0.48

DEPARTMENTS OF GRADUATE EDUCATION
Not On The Approved List of The Gourman Report (Continued)

RATING CATEGORIES	Numerical Range
Very Strong	4.51-4.99
Strong	4.01-4.49
Good	3.61-3.99
Acceptable Plus	3.01-3.59
Adequate	2.51-2.99
Marginal	2.01-2.49
Not Sufficient for Graduate Programs	0.

Department of Graduate Education INSTITUTION	Gourman Overall Academic Score (Combined Areas/Fields)	Administration (Attitude and Policy) (Quality of Leadership at All Levels of Administration)	Curriculum (Attractiveness of Program)	Faculty Effectiveness	Faculty (Quality of Research/ Scholarship)	Library Resources
California Lutheran College ..... Thousand Oaks, CA	0.46	0.44	0.43	0.45	0.	0.47
California Polytechnic State University, San Luis Obispo ...... San Luis Obispo, CA	0.49	0.51	0.49	0.47	0.	0.49
California State University, Bakersfield Bakersfield, CA	0.45	0.46	0.48	0.49	0.	0.29
California State Polytechnic University, Pomona .... Pomona, CA	0.46	0.48	0.47	0.48	0.	0.41
California State University, Chico Chico, CA	0.48	0.49	0.48	0.47	0.	0.48
California State University, Dominguez Hills .... Carson, CA	0.49	0.46	0.47	0.45	0.	0.47
California State University, Fresno Fresno, CA	0.52	0.49	0.49	0.48	0.	0.48
California State University, Fullerton Fullerton, CA	0.51	0.48	0.48	0.46	0.	0.38
California State University, Hayward Hayward, CA	0.47	0.46	0.45	0.46	0.	0.42
California State University, Long Beach .... Long Beach, CA	0.50	0.48	0.49	0.47	0.	0.50
California State University, Los Angeles .... Los Angeles, CA	0.50	0.46	0.47	0.48	0.	0.49
California State University, Northridge .... Northridge, CA	0.50	0.43	0.46	0.44	0.	0.43
California State University, Sacramento .... Sacramento, CA	0.48	0.49	0.47	0.48	0.	0.45
California State University, San Bernardino .... San Bernardino, CA	0.49	0.50	0.50	0.47	0.	0.46

Department of Graduate Education INSTITUTION	Gourman Overall Academic Score (Combined Areas/Fields)	Administration (Attitude and Policy) (Quality of Leadership at All Levels of Administration)	Curriculum (Attractiveness of Program)	Faculty Effectiveness	Faculty (Quality of Research/ Scholarship)	Library Resources
California State University, Stanislaus . . . . Turlock, CA	0.45	0.46	0.42	0.44	0.	0.37
California University of Pennsylvania California, PA	0.38	0.36	0.35	0.34	0.	0.35
Canisius College . . . . Buffalo, NY	0.36	0.35	0.33	0.32	0.	0.37
Catholic University of America . . . Washington, D.C.	0.54	0.49	0.47	0.50	0.	0.52
Central Connecticut State University New Britain, CT	0.46	0.43	0.42	0.44	0.	0.41
Central Michigan University . . . . . Mount Pleasant, MI	0.47	0.46	0.43	0.40	0.	0.38
Central Missouri State University . Warrensburg, MO	0.45	0.42	0.40	0.41	0.	0.39
Central State University . . . . Edmond, OK	0.32	0.28	0.26	0.27	0.	0.26
Central Washington University . . Ellensburg, WA	0.43	0.39	0.35	0.38	0.	0.37
Chapman College . . . . Orange, CA	0.41	0.39	0.38	0.40	0.	0.35
Cheyney University of Pennsylvania Cheyney, PA	0.37	0.35	0.33	0.36	0.	0.34
Chicago State University . . . . Chicago, IL	0.38	0.40	0.39	0.39	0.	0.38
City University of New York, Bernard M. Baruch College . . . . . New York, NY	0.34	0.33	0.31	0.34	0.	0.32
City University of New York, Brooklyn College . . . . Brooklyn, NY	0.49	0.45	0.44	0.46	0.	0.48
City University of New York, City College . . . . New York, NY	0.52	0.46	0.48	0.49	0.	0.46
City University of New York, College of Staten Island . . . . Staten Island, NY	0.32	0.31	0.30	0.32	0.	0.31
City University of New York, Herbert H. Lehman College . . . . . Bronx, NY	0.34	0.33	0.31	0.33	0.	0.32
City University of New York, Hunter College . . . . New York, NY	0.51	0.47	0.46	0.49	0.	0.48
City University of New York, Queens College . . . . Flushing, NY	0.51	0.46	0.45	0.48	0.	0.49
Claremont Graduate School . . . . Claremont, CA	0.48	0.46	0.44	0.48	0.	0.36

DEPARTMENTS OF GRADUATE EDUCATION
Not On The Approved List of The Gourman Report (Continued)

RATING CATEGORIES	Numerical Range
Very Strong	4.51-4.99
Strong	4.01-4.49
Good	3.61-3.99
Acceptable Plus	3.01-3.59
Adequate	2.51-2.99
Marginal	2.01-2.49

Not Sufficient for Graduate Programs   0.

Department of Graduate Education INSTITUTION	Gourman Overall Academic Score (Combined Areas/Fields)	Administration (Attitude and Policy) (Quality of Leadership at All Levels of Administration)	Curriculum (Attractiveness of Program)	Faculty Effectiveness	Faculty (Quality of Research/ Scholarship)	Library Resources
Clarion University of Pennsylvania Clarion, PA	0.36	0.35	0.34	0.35	0.	0.34
Clark University .... Worcester, MA	0.46	0.45	0.42	0.46	0.	0.41
Clemson University .... Clemson, SC	0.49	0.44	0.41	0.45	0.	0.47
Cleveland State University ...... Cleveland, OH	0.44	0.43	0.42	0.43	0.	0.45
College of William and Mary .... Williamsburg, VA	0.43	0.44	0.40	0.44	0.	0.43
Colorado State University ...... Fort Collins, CO	0.50	0.46	0.44	0.47	0.	0.48
Connecticut College .... New London, CT	0.39	0.40	0.38	0.40	0.	0.40
Cornell University .... Ithaca, NY	0.88	0.83	0.79	0.81	0.	0.81
Corpus Christi State University .. Corpus Christi, TX	0.32	0.33	0.31	0.34	0.	0.32
Creighton University .... Omaha, NE	0.41	0.39	0.36	0.38	0.	0.37
Delta State University .... Cleveland, MS	0.27	0.26	0.23	0.26	0.	0.22
De Paul University .... Chicago, IL	0.49	0.46	0.42	0.47	0.	0.48
Drake University .... Des Moines, IA	0.47	0.45	0.41	0.46	0.	0.48
Drury College .... Springfield, MO	0.27	0.28	0.25	0.27	0.	0.28
Duquesne University .... Pittsburgh, PA	0.45	0.43	0.40	0.44	0.	0.41
East Carolina University .... Greenville, NC	0.43	0.42	0.39	0.41	0.	0.42
East Central University .... Ada, OK	0.42	0.40	0.38	0.40	0.	0.31

Department of Graduate Education INSTITUTION	Gourman Overall Academic Score (Combined Areas/Fields)	Administration (Attitude and Policy) (Quality of Leadership at All Levels of Administration)	Curriculum (Attractiveness of Program)	Faculty Effectiveness	Faculty (Quality of Research/ Scholarship)	Library Resources
Eastern Connecticut State University Willimantic, CT	0.41	0.39	0.36	0.40	0.	0.38
Eastern Illinois University . . . . Charleston, IL	0.43	0.41	0.40	0.42	0.	0.39
Eastern Kentucky University . . . . Richmond, KY	0.44	0.38	0.37	0.39	0.	0.38
Eastern Michigan University . . . . Ypsilanti, MI	0.45	0.43	0.40	0.44	0.	0.41
Eastern New Mexico University . . Portales, NM	0.43	0.38	0.37	0.39	0.	0.39
Eastern Washington University . . Cheney, WA	0.47	0.43	0.42	0.44	0.	0.41
East Stroudsburg University of Pennsylvania . . . . East Stroudsburg, PA	0.38	0.36	0.35	0.37	0.	0.38
East Tennessee State University . Johnson City, TN	0.39	0.38	0.33	0.38	0.	0.39
East Texas State University . . . . . Commerce, TX	0.37	0.36	0.32	0.37	0.	0.38
Edinboro University of Pennsylvania Edinboro, PA	0.35	0.34	0.33	0.34	0.	0.36
Emporia State University . . . . Emporia, KS	0.39	0.35	0.34	0.36	0.	0.37
Fairfield University . . . . Fairfield, CT	0.39	0.35	0.32	0.36	0.	0.38
Fairleigh Dickinson University, Teaneck-Hackensack Campus . . Teaneck, NJ	0.46	0.42	0.38	0.43	0.	0.40
Fayetteville State University . . . . Fayetteville, NC	0.36	0.33	0.32	0.34	0.	0.35
Florida Agricultural and Mechanical University . . . . Tallahassee, FL	0.31	0.30	0.29	0.30	0.	0.33
Florida Atlantic University . . . . . . Boca Raton, FL	0.32	0.31	0.30	0.31	0.	0.32
Florida International University . . Miami, FL	0.31	0.30	0.29	0.30	0.	0.31
Florida State University . . . . Tallahassee, FL	0.63	0.59	0.56	0.60	0.	0.60
Fordham University . . . . Bronx, NY	0.56	0.52	0.50	0.53	0.	0.53
Fort Hays University . . . . Hays, KS	0.38	0.36	0.35	0.36	0.	0.32
Framingham State College . . . . . Framingham, MA	0.39	0.35	0.33	0.36	0.	0.34
Frostburg State University . . . . . . Frostburg, MD	0.28	0.25	0.23	0.24	0.	0.26

DEPARTMENTS OF GRADUATE EDUCATION
Not On The Approved List of The Gourman Report (Continued)

RATING CATEGORIES	Numerical Range
Very Strong	4.51-4.99
Strong	4.01-4.49
Good	3.61-3.99
Acceptable Plus	3.01-3.59
Adequate	2.51-2.99
Marginal	2.01-2.49

Not Sufficient for Graduate Programs   0.

Department of Graduate Education INSTITUTION	Gourman Overall Academic Score (Combined Areas/Fields)	Administration (Attitude and Policy) (Quality of Leadership at All Levels of Administration)	Curriculum (Attractiveness of Program)	Faculty Effectiveness	Faculty (Quality of Research/ Scholarship)	Library Resources
Gannon University .... Erie, PA	0.29	0.28	0.25	0.27	0.	0.28
George Mason University ...... Fairfax, VA	0.32	0.33	0.30	0.34	0.	0.34
George Washington University .. Washington D.C.	0.68	0.64	0.61	0.65	0.	0.62
Georgia College .... Milledgeville, GA	0.30	0.27	0.24	0.26	0.	0.29
Georgia Southern University .... Statesboro, GA	0.30	0.26	0.23	0.25	0.	0.28
Georgia State University .... Atlanta, GA	0.41	0.35	0.32	0.34	0.	0.36
Gonzaga University .... Spokane, WA	0.48	0.47	0.45	0.48	0.	0.47
Governors State University ..... Park Forest South, IL	0.38	0.39	0.36	0.38	0.	0.39
Grand Valley State University ... Allendale, MI	0.37	0.36	0.35	0.37	0.	0.37
Hampton University .... Hampton, VA	0.28	0.26	0.25	0.23	0.	0.22
Hardin-Simmons University ..... Abilene, TX	0.36	0.34	0.32	0.33	0.	0.34
Harvard University .... Cambridge, MA	0.93	0.94	0.88	0.84	0.	0.90
Henderson State University ..... Arkadelphia, AR	0.30	0.29	0.25	0.22	0.	0.28
Hofstra University .... Hempstead, NY	0.51	0.46	0.43	0.47	0.	0.49
Howard University .... Washington D.C.	0.35	0.33	0.31	0.34	0.	0.34
Humboldt State University ...... Arcata, CA	0.36	0.35	0.32	0.33	0.	0.33
Idaho State University .... Pocatello, ID	0.37	0.34	0.33	0.34	0.	0.36

Department of Graduate Education INSTITUTION	Gourman Overall Academic Score (Combined Areas/Fields)	Administration (Attitude and Policy) (Quality of Leadership at All Levels of Administration)	Curriculum (Attractiveness of Program)	Faculty Effectiveness	Faculty (Quality of Research/ Scholarship)	Library Resources
Illinois State University Normal, IL	0.49	0.45	0.42	0.46	0.	0.46
Indiana State University at Terre Haute Terre Haute, IN	0.48	0.44	0.43	0.45	0.	0.47
Indiana University at South Bend South Bend, IN	0.40	0.41	0.40	0.42	0.	0.45
Indiana University, Bloomington Bloomington, IN	0.86	0.85	0.80	0.84	0.	0.91
Indiana University of Pennsylvania Indiana, PA	0.38	0.35	0.32	0.36	0.	0.35
Indiana University – Purdue University at Fort Wayne Fort Wayne, IN	0.49	0.45	0.42	0.46	0.	0.39
Indiana University – Purdue University at Indianapolis Indianapolis, IN	0.50	0.49	0.47	0.49	0.	0.48
Iowa State University Ames, IA	0.58	0.57	0.50	0.58	0.	0.59
Jackson State University Jackson, MS	0.29	0.25	0.21	0.22	0.	0.18
Jacksonville State University Jacksonville, AL	0.30	0.24	0.20	0.21	0.	0.19
Jacksonville University Jacksonville, FL	0.39	0.35	0.31	0.33	0.	0.30
James Madison University Harrisonburg, VA	0.36	0.32	0.29	0.33	0.	0.35
Jersey City State College Jersey City, NJ	0.37	0.36	0.32	0.35	0.	0.36
John Carroll University University Heights, OH	0.30	0.31	0.26	0.31	0.	0.30
Johns Hopkins University Baltimore, MD	0.71	0.68	0.72	0.64	0.	0.70
Kansas State University Manhattan, KS	0.58	0.57	0.52	0.58	0.	0.56
Kean College of New Jersey Union, NJ	0.39	0.36	0.34	0.37	0.	0.34
Keene State College Keene, NH	0.27	0.25	0.20	0.22	0.	0.20
Kent State University Kent, OH	0.52	0.51	0.47	0.52	0.	0.50
Kutztown University of Pennsylvania Kutztown, PA	0.36	0.33	0.30	0.32	0.	0.31
Lamar University Beaumont, TX	0.37	0.34	0.32	0.30	0.	0.33

RATING CATEGORIES	Numerical Range
Very Strong	4.51-4.99
Strong	4.01-4.49
Good	3.61-3.99
Acceptable Plus	3.01-3.59
Adequate	2.51-2.99
Marginal	2.01-2.49

Not Sufficient for Graduate Programs   0.

Department of Graduate Education INSTITUTION	Gourman Overall Academic Score (Combined Areas/Fields)	Administration (Attitude and Policy) (Quality of Leadership at All Levels of Administration)	Curriculum (Attractiveness of Program)	Faculty Effectiveness	Faculty (Quality of Research/ Scholarship)	Library Resources
Laredo State University .... Laredo, TX	0.32	0.30	0.30	0.27	0.	0.29
Lehigh University .... Bethlehem, PA	0.40	0.42	0.39	0.43	0.	0.41
Loma Linda University .... Loma Linda, CA	0.36	0.35	0.31	0.34	0.	0.35
Long Island University, Brooklyn Center .... Brooklyn, NY	0.35	0.36	0.35	0.30	0.	0.30
Long Island University, C.W. Post Campus .... Greenvale, NY	0.43	0.41	0.36	0.40	0.	0.41
Louisiana State University and Agricultural and Mechanical College Baton Rouge, LA	0.57	0.55	0.51	0.56	0.	0.58
Louisiana State University in Shreveport .... Shreveport, LA	0.31	0.32	0.29	0.31	0.	0.29
Louisiana Tech University ...... Ruston, LA	0.32	0.33	0.31	0.32	0.	0.30
Loyola College .... Baltimore, MD	0.29	0.28	0.25	0.27	0.	0.26
Loyola Marymount University ... Los Angeles, CA	0.40	0.39	0.33	0.37	0.	0.36
Loyola University, New Orleans .. New Orleans, LA	0.39	0.38	0.32	0.36	0.	0.35
Loyola University of Chicago .... Chicago, IL	0.42	0.40	0.38	0.41	0.	0.41
Lynchburg College .... Lynchburg, VA	0.31	0.28	0.25	0.28	0.	0.30
Mankato State University .... Mankato, MN	0.32	0.29	0.24	0.29	0.	0.29
Mansfield University of Pennsylvania Mansfield, PA	0.36	0.35	0.30	0.34	0.	0.37
Marquette University .... Milwaukee, WI	0.51	0.50	0.46	0.49	0.	0.47

Department of Graduate Education INSTITUTION	Gourman Overall Academic Score (Combined Areas/Fields)	Administration (Attitude and Policy) (Quality of Leadership at All Levels of Administration)	Curriculum (Attractiveness of Program)	Faculty Effectiveness	Faculty (Quality of Research/ Scholarship)	Library Resources
Marshall University Huntington, WV	0.38	0.36	0.32	0.37	0.	0.35
Memphis State University Memphis, TN	0.49	0.48	0.45	0.49	0.	0.47
Mercer University Macon, GA	0.28	0.26	0.25	0.24	0.	0.26
Mercer University in Atlanta Atlanta, GA	0.25	0.25	0.22	0.22	0.	0.23
Miami University Oxford, OH	0.41	0.38	0.35	0.39	0.	0.37
Michigan State University East Lansing, MI	0.78	0.75	0.72	0.76	0.	0.79
Middle Tennessee State University Murfreesboro, TN	0.46	0.43	0.40	0.44	0.	0.45
Midwestern State University Wichita Falls, TX	0.40	0.38	0.36	0.35	0.	0.39
Millersville University of Pennsylvania Millersville, PA	0.36	0.35	0.32	0.35	0.	0.33
Mississippi State University Mississippi State, MS	0.46	0.44	0.41	0.45	0.	0.41
Montana State University Bozeman, MT	0.43	0.42	0.40	0.43	0.	0.40
Montclair State College Upper Monclair, NJ	0.39	0.38	0.36	0.39	0.	0.37
Moorhead State University Moorhead, MN	0.39	0.35	0.32	0.36	0.	0.34
Morehead State University Morehead, KY	0.31	0.30	0.29	0.30	0.	0.30
Morgan State University Baltimore, MD	0.28	0.26	0.20	0.21	0.	0.21
Murray State University Murray, KY	0.31	0.30	0.29	0.30	0.	0.29
National Louis University Evanston, IL	0.40	0.38	0.35	0.39	0.	0.41
New Mexico Highlands University Las Vegas, NM	0.26	0.27	0.22	0.25	0.	0.25
New Mexico State University Las Cruces, NM	0.43	0.42	0.39	0.43	0.	0.41
New York University New York, NY	0.80	0.78	0.75	0.82	0.	0.83
Niagara University Niagara University, NY	0.30	0.29	0.24	0.23	0.	0.25
Nicholls State University Thibodaux, LA	0.31	0.30	0.26	0.29	0.	0.27
Norfolk State University Norfolk, VA	0.29	0.28	0.21	0.27	0.	0.20
North Adams State College North Adams, MA	0.30	0.30	0.23	0.30	0.	0.29

DEPARTMENTS OF GRADUATE EDUCATION
Not On The Approved List of The Gourman Report (Continued)

RATING CATEGORIES	Numerical Range
Very Strong	4.51-4.99
Strong	4.01-4.49
Good	3.61-3.99
Acceptable Plus	3.01-3.59
Adequate	2.51-2.99
Marginal	2.01-2.49

Not Sufficient for Graduate Programs   0.

Department of Graduate Education INSTITUTION	Gourman Overall Academic Score (Combined Areas/Fields)	Administration (Attitude and Policy) (Quality of Leadership at All Levels of Administration)	Curriculum (Attractiveness of Program)	Faculty Effectiveness	Faculty (Quality of Research/ Scholarship)	Library Resources
North Carolina Agricultural and Technical State University ...... Greensboro, NC	0.25	0.26	0.19	0.25	0.	0.21
North Carolina Central University Durham, NC	0.26	0.27	0.18	0.24	0.	0.20
North Carolina State University at Raleigh .... Raleigh, NC	0.49	0.48	0.43	0.49	0.	0.48
North Dakota State University ... Fargo, ND	0.38	0.39	0.32	0.38	0.	0.36
Northeastern Illinois University .. Chicago, IL	0.43	0.42	0.41	0.43	0.	0.43
Northeastern State University ... Tahlequah, OK	0.30	0.30	0.26	0.28	0.	0.29
Northeastern University .... Boston, MA	0.46	0.43	0.39	0.42	0.	0.45
Northeast Louisiana University .. Monroe, LA	0.38	0.37	0.36	0.36	0.	0.36
Northeast Missouri State University Kirksville, MO	0.32	0.31	0.29	0.32	0.	0.31
Northern Arizona University ..... Flagstaff, AZ	0.35	0.36	0.33	0.37	0.	0.35
Northern Illinois University ...... DeKalb, IL	0.43	0.42	0.40	0.43	0.	0.41
Northern Kentucky University ... Highland Heights, KY	0.30	0.31	0.26	0.30	0.	0.29
Northern Michigan University .... Marquette, MI	0.39	0.40	0.38	0.41	0.	0.39
Northern State University .... Aberdeen, SD	0.28	0.26	0.20	0.22	0.	0.21
Northwestern Oklahoma State University .... Alva, OK	0.29	0.31	0.26	0.30	0.	0.28

DEPARTMENTS OF GRADUATE EDUCATION
Not On The Approved List of The Gourman Report (Continued)

Department of Graduate Education INSTITUTION	Gourman Overall Academic Score (Combined Areas/Fields)	Administration (Attitude and Policy) (Quality of Leadership at All Levels of Administration)	Curriculum (Attractiveness of Program)	Faculty Effectiveness	Faculty (Quality of Research/ Scholarship)	Library Resources
Northwestern State University of Louisiana . . . . Natchitoches, LA	0.31	0.32	0.27	0.31	0.	0.29
Northwestern University . . . . Evanston, IL	0.79	0.82	0.80	0.84	0.	0.83
Northwest Missouri State University Maryville, MO	0.36	0.34	0.30	0.35	0.	0.32
Norwich University . . . . Northfield, VT	0.28	0.26	0.22	0.23	0.	0.27
Nova University . . . . Fort Lauderdale, FL	0.32	0.30	0.30	0.28	0.	0.31
Oakland University . . . . Rochester, MI	0.29	0.30	0.26	0.25	0.	0.23
Ohio State University . . . . Columbus, OH	0.79	0.81	0.79	0.82	0.	0.80
Ohio University . . . . Athens, OH	0.57	0.58	0.53	0.59	0.	0.56
Oklahoma State University . . . . . Stillwater, OK	0.41	0.43	0.41	0.38	0.	0.44
Old Dominion University . . . . Norfolk, VA	0.43	0.42	0.40	0.43	0.	0.42
Oral Roberts University . . . . Tulsa, OK	0.25	0.23	0.20	0.21	0.	0.18
Oregon State University . . . . Corvallis, OR	0.59	0.58	0.54	0.59	0.	0.57
Pace University . . . . New York, NY	0.43	0.41	0.40	0.37	0.	0.42
Pacific Lutheran University . . . . . Tacoma, WA	0.31	0.32	0.29	0.31	0.	0.30
Pacific University . . . . Forest Grove, OR	0.30	0.31	0.28	0.29	0.	0.29
Pennsylvania State University – Capitol Campus . . . . Middletown, PA	0.22	0.21	0.20	0.18	0.	0.19
Pennsylvania State University – University Park Campus . . . . University Park, PA	0.62	0.63	0.61	0.62	0.	0.64
Pepperdine University . . . . Malibu, CA	0.38	0.34	0.30	0.29	0.	0.31
Pittsburg State University . . . . . . Pittsburg, KS	0.32	0.32	0.29	0.30	0.	0.28
Portland State University . . . . Portland, OR	0.34	0.35	0.31	0.34	0.	0.33
Prairie View A&M University . . . . Prairie View, TX	0.26	0.22	0.18	0.19	0.	0.20
Purdue University . . . . West Lafayette, IN	0.70	0.72	0.73	0.68	0.	0.74

DEPARTMENTS OF GRADUATE EDUCATION
Not On The Approved List of The Gourman Report (Continued)

RATING CATEGORIES	Numerical Range
Very Strong	4.51-4.99
Strong	4.01-4.49
Good	3.61-3.99
Acceptable Plus	3.01-3.59
Adequate	2.51-2.99
Marginal	2.01-2.49

Not Sufficient for Graduate Programs   0.

Department of Graduate Education INSTITUTION	Gourman Overall Academic Score (Combined Areas/Fields)	Administration (Attitude and Policy) (Quality of Leadership at All Levels of Administration)	Curriculum (Attractiveness of Program)	Faculty Effectiveness	Faculty (Quality of Research/ Scholarship)	Library Resources
Purdue University – Calumet .... Hammond, IN	0.31	0.32	0.28	0.26	0.	0.25
Radford University .... Radford, VA	0.33	0.34	0.30	0.29	0.	0.28
Roosevelt University .... Chicago, IL	0.49	0.51	0.47	0.52	0.	0.50
Rutgers University, New Brunswick New Brunswick, NJ	0.65	0.68	0.65	0.69	0.	0.67
St. Bonaventure University ..... St. Bonaventure, NY	0.30	0.31	0.29	0.30	0.	0.30
St. Cloud State University ...... St. Cloud, MN	0.31	0.33	0.30	0.34	0.	0.32
St. John's University .... Jamaica, NY	0.44	0.43	0.40	0.38	0.	0.41
Saint Louis University .... St. Louis, MO	0.47	0.49	0.43	0.48	0.	0.47
Samford University .... Birmingham, AL	0.30	0.31	0.28	0.30	0.	0.29
Sam Houston State University ... Huntsville, TX	0.32	0.32	0.29	0.31	0.	0.31
San Diego State University ...... San Diego, CA	0.45	0.44	0.43	0.40	0.	0.41
San Francisco State University .. San Francisco, CA	0.46	0.46	0.44	0.41	0.	0.45
Sangamon State University ..... Springfield, IL	0.32	0.31	0.29	0.30	0.	0.31
San Jose State University ...... San Jose, CA	0.44	0.43	0.42	0.39	0.	0.44
Seattle University .... Seattle, WA	0.40	0.41	0.39	0.40	0.	0.41
Seton Hall University .... South Orange, NJ	0.39	0.43	0.40	0.44	0.	0.42
Shippensburg University of Pennsylvania .... Shippensburg, PA	0.35	0.34	0.32	0.33	0.	0.31

Department of Graduate Education INSTITUTION	Gourman Overall Academic Score (Combined Areas/Fields)	Administration (Attitude and Policy) (Quality of Leadership at All Levels of Administration)	Curriculum (Attractiveness of Program)	Faculty Effectiveness	Faculty (Quality of Research/ Scholarship)	Library Resources
Simmons College .... Boston, MA	0.36	0.37	0.33	0.38	0.	0.35
Slippery Rock University of Pennsylvania .... Slippery Rock, PA	0.32	0.33	0.31	0.33	0.	0.32
Smith College .... Northampton, MA	0.33	0.34	0.30	0.32	0.	0.33
Sonoma State University .... Rohnert Park, CA	0.36	0.35	0.31	0.29	0.	0.34
South Dakota State University ... Brookings, SD	0.37	0.36	0.32	0.31	0.	0.33
Southeastern Louisiana University Hammond, LA	0.32	0.29	0.28	0.30	0.	0.30
Southeastern Massachusetts University .... North Dartmouth, MA	0.38	0.37	0.35	0.38	0.	0.37
Southeast Missouri State University Cape Girardeau, MO	0.30	0.35	0.33	0.36	0.	0.31
Southern Connecticut State University New Haven, CT	0.32	0.36	0.30	0.37	0.	0.34
Southern Illinois University at Carbondale .... Carbondale, IL	0.61	0.65	0.60	0.66	0.	0.66
Southern Illinois University at Edwardsville .... Edwardsville, IL	0.51	0.60	0.58	0.53	0.	0.52
Southern University and Agricultural and Mechanical College .... Baton Rouge, LA	0.28	0.27	0.20	0.25	0.	0.28
Southwestern Oklahoma State University .... Weatherford, OK	0.31	0.30	0.24	0.29	0.	0.28
Southwest Missouri State University Springfield, MO	0.30	0.29	0.26	0.28	0.	0.27
Southwest Texas State University San Marcos, TX	0.32	0.31	0.27	0.30	0.	0.30
Stanford University .... Stanford, CA	0.92	0.92	0.87	0.91	0.	0.89
State University of New York at Albany Albany, NY	0.53	0.54	0.50	0.55	0.	0.52
State University of New York at Binghamton .... Binghamton, NY	0.54	0.55	0.51	0.56	0.	0.54
State University of New York at Buffalo Buffalo, NY	0.66	0.67	0.65	0.64	0.	0.68
State University of New York College at Brockport .... Brockport, NY	0.30	0.31	0.26	0.30	0.	0.29

RATING CATEGORIES	Numerical Range
Very Strong	4.51-4.99
Strong	4.01-4.49
Good	3.61-3.99
Acceptable Plus	3.01-3.59
Adequate	2.51-2.99
Marginal	2.01-2.49

Not Sufficient for Graduate Programs   0.

Department of Graduate Education INSTITUTION	Gourman Overall Academic Score (Combined Areas/Fields)	Administration (Attitude and Policy) (Quality of Leadership at All Levels of Administration)	Curriculum (Attractiveness of Program)	Faculty Effectiveness	Faculty (Quality of Research/ Scholarship)	Library Resources
State University of New York College at Buffalo Buffalo, NY	0.31	0.32	0.27	0.31	0.	0.30
State University of New York College at Cortland Cortland, NY	0.29	0.31	0.30	0.31	0.	0.31
State University of New York College at Fredonia Fredonia, NY	0.34	0.33	0.30	0.32	0.	0.32
State University of New York College at Geneseo Geneseo, NY	0.35	0.34	0.31	0.33	0.	0.33
State University of New York College at New Paltz New Paltz, NY	0.36	0.35	0.32	0.34	0.	0.34
State University of New York College at Oneonta Oneonta, NY	0.33	0.30	0.30	0.30	0.	0.32
State University of New York College at Oswego Oswego, NY	0.34	0.29	0.28	0.31	0.	0.33
State University of New York College at Plattsburgh Plattsburgh, NY	0.30	0.31	0.30	0.31	0.	0.32
State University of New York College at Potsdam Potsdam, NY	0.35	0.33	0.32	0.34	0.	0.35
Stephen F. Austin State University Nacogdoches, TX	0.37	0.35	0.33	0.34	0.	0.32
Stetson University Deland, FL	0.30	0.29	0.26	0.29	0.	0.30
Suffolk University Boston, MA	0.35	0.31	0.30	0.30	0.	0.34
Sul Ross State University Alpine, TX	0.30	0.29	0.28	0.29	0.	0.30

Department of Graduate Education INSTITUTION	Gourman Overall Academic Score (Combined Areas/Fields)	Administration (Attitude and Policy) (Quality of Leadership at All Levels of Administration)	Curriculum (Attractiveness of Program)	Faculty Effectiveness	Faculty (Quality of Research/ Scholarship)	Library Resources
Syracuse University Syracuse, NY	0.71	0.74	0.72	0.75	0.	0.76
Tarleton State University Stephenville, TX	0.41	0.46	0.40	0.47	0.	0.45
Teachers College, Columbia University New York, NY	0.79	0.75	0.71	0.76	0.	0.80
Temple University Philadelphia, PA	0.73	0.76	0.74	0.77	0.	0.79
Tennessee State University Nashville, TN	0.30	0.28	0.25	0.27	0.	0.26
Tennessee Technological University Cookeville, TN	0.29	0.30	0.26	0.25	0.	0.24
Texas A&I University at Kingsville Kingsville, TX	0.28	0.29	0.21	0.28	0.	0.23
Texas A&M University College Station, TX	0.61	0.63	0.60	0.65	0.	0.62
Texas Christian University Fort Worth, TX	0.30	0.33	0.30	0.30	0.	0.33
Texas Southern University Houston, TX	0.27	0.25	0.20	0.19	0.	0.20
Texas Tech University Lubbock, TX	0.49	0.46	0.41	0.47	0.	0.48
Texas Woman's University Denton, TX	0.33	0.35	0.30	0.36	0.	0.31
Towson State University Baltimore, MD	0.28	0.27	0.20	0.21	0.	0.23
Trenton State College Trenton, NJ	0.34	0.34	0.30	0.34	0.	0.31
Trinity University San Antonio, TX	0.30	0.31	0.29	0.29	0.	0.28
Troy State University Troy, AL	0.33	0.32	0.31	0.28	0.	0.29
Tufts University Medford, MA	0.49	0.53	0.48	0.46	0.	0.47
Tulane University New Orleans, LA	0.50	0.54	0.49	0.48	0.	0.50
Tuskegee University Tuskegee, AL	0.21	0.22	0.17	0.20	0.	0.16
United States International University San Diego, CA	0.30	0.26	0.25	0.27	0.	0.24
University of Akron Akron, OH	0.31	0.27	0.23	0.27	0.	0.29
University of Alabama University, AL	0.52	0.49	0.48	0.50	0.	0.48
University of Alabama in Birmingham Birmingham, AL	0.30	0.32	0.31	0.29	0.	0.32

RATING CATEGORIES	Numerical Range
Very Strong	4.51-4.99
Strong	4.01-4.49
Good	3.61-3.99
Acceptable Plus	3.01-3.59
Adequate	2.51-2.99
Marginal	2.01-2.49

Not Sufficient for Graduate Programs   0.

Department of Graduate Education INSTITUTION	Gourman Overall Academic Score (Combined Areas/Fields)	Administration (Attitude and Policy) (Quality of Leadership at All Levels of Administration)	Curriculum (Attractiveness of Program)	Faculty Effectiveness	Faculty (Quality of Research/ Scholarship)	Library Resources
University of Alaska, Anchorage . Anchorage, AK	0.26	0.23	0.19	0.18	0.	0.17
University of Alaska, Fairbanks .. Fairbanks, AK	0.31	0.32	0.29	0.30	0.	0.28
University of Arizona .... Tucson, AZ	0.63	0.62	0.60	0.61	0.	0.61
University of Arkansas .... Fayetteville, AR	0.52	0.50	0.48	0.47	0.	0.52
University of Arkansas at Little Rock Little Rock, AR	0.30	0.29	0.28	0.26	0.	0.29
University of Bridgeport .... Bridgeport, CT	0.34	0.33	0.32	0.34	0.	0.32
University of California, Berkeley . Berkeley, CA	0.91	0.92	0.86	0.85	0.	0.91
University of California, Davis ... Davis, CA	0.63	0.64	0.60	0.63	0.	0.64
University of California, Los Angeles Los Angeles, CA	0.85	0.87	0.81	0.84	0.	0.85
University of California, Riverside Riverside, CA	0.51	0.50	0.48	0.49	0.	0.50
University of California, Santa Barbara Santa Barbara, CA	0.70	0.68	0.66	0.63	0.	0.71
University of California, Santa Cruz Santa Cruz, CA	0.41	0.42	0.40	0.39	0.	0.40
University of Central Arkansas .. Conway, AR	0.29	0.28	0.20	0.26	0.	0.27
University of Central Florida .... Orlando, FL	0.30	0.27	0.21	0.19	0.	0.20
University of Chicago .... Chicago, IL	0.94	0.93	0.90	0.94	0.	0.91
University of Cincinnati .... Cincinnati, OH	0.63	0.64	0.60	0.61	0.	0.63
University of Colorado at Boulder Boulder, CO	0.65	0.66	0.63	0.64	0.	0.65

DEPARTMENTS OF GRADUATE EDUCATION
Not On The Approved List of The Gourman Report (Continued)

Department of Graduate Education INSTITUTION	Gourman Overall Academic Score (Combined Areas/Fields)	Administration (Attitude and Policy) (Quality of Leadership at All Levels of Administration)	Curriculum (Attractiveness of Program)	Faculty Effectiveness	Faculty (Quality of Research/ Scholarship)	Library Resources
University of Colorado at Colorado Springs Colorado Springs, CO	0.31	0.29	0.21	0.24	0.	0.22
University of Colorado at Denver Denver, CO	0.41	0.40	0.35	0.38	0.	0.36
University of Connecticut Storrs, CT	0.66	0.65	0.64	0.66	0.	0.64
University of Dallas Irving, TX	0.31	0.29	0.24	0.22	0.	0.27
University of Dayton Dayton, OH	0.32	0.35	0.31	0.30	0.	0.31
University of Delaware Newark, DE	0.50	0.47	0.43	0.46	0.	0.45
University of Denver Denver, CO	0.53	0.51	0.49	0.50	0.	0.50
University of Detroit Mercy Detroit, MI	0.36	0.37	0.34	0.36	0.	0.36
University of Evansville Evansville, IN	0.34	0.36	0.33	0.32	0.	0.35
University of Florida Gainesville, FL	0.61	0.60	0.58	0.60	0.	0.58
University of Georgia Athens, GA	0.62	0.61	0.59	0.61	0.	0.62
University of Guam Mangilao, GU	0.27	0.24	0.19	0.20	0.	0.21
University of Hartford West Hartford, CT	0.31	0.28	0.26	0.28	0.	0.29
University of Hawaii at Manoa Honolulu, HI	0.36	0.35	0.34	0.33	0.	0.33
University of Houston – Clear Lake Houston, TX	0.27	0.28	0.22	0.23	0.	0.26
University of Houston – University Park Houston, TX	0.49	0.50	0.46	0.48	0.	0.49
University of Idaho Moscow, ID	0.41	0.43	0.41	0.40	0.	0.43
University of Illinois at Chicago Chicago, IL	0.76	0.72	0.69	0.71	0.	0.75
University of Illinois at Urbana-Champaign Urbana, IL	0.82	0.84	0.81	0.85	0.	0.84
University of Iowa Iowa City, IA	0.77	0.79	0.77	0.80	0.	0.80
University of Kansas Lawrence, KS	0.62	0.63	0.61	0.64	0.	0.64
University of Kentucky Lexington, KY	0.49	0.48	0.46	0.47	0.	0.48

DEPARTMENTS OF GRADUATE EDUCATION
Not On The Approved List of The Gourman Report (Continued)

RATING CATEGORIES	Numerical Range
Very Strong	4.51-4.99
Strong	4.01-4.49
Good	3.61-3.99
Acceptable Plus	3.01-3.59
Adequate	2.51-2.99
Marginal	2.01-2.49
Not Sufficient for Graduate Programs	0.

Department of Graduate Education INSTITUTION	Gourman Overall Academic Score (Combined Areas/Fields)	Administration (Attitude and Policy) (Quality of Leadership at All Levels of Administration)	Curriculum (Attractiveness of Program)	Faculty Effectiveness	Faculty (Quality of Research/ Scholarship)	Library Resources
University of Louisville .... Louisville, KY	0.43	0.42	0.40	0.42	0.	0.41
University of Lowell .... Lowell, MA	0.30	0.28	0.26	0.27	0.	0.29
University of Maine at Orono .... Orono, ME	0.33	0.34	0.31	0.34	0.	0.34
University of Maryland at College Park College Park, MD	0.58	0.61	0.60	0.61	0.	0.63
University of Maryland, Baltimore County .... Catonsville, MD	0.27	0.25	0.20	0.19	0.	0.19
University of Massachusetts at Amherst .... Amherst, MA	0.48	0.49	0.46	0.41	0.	0.50
University of Massachusetts at Boston Boston, MA	0.30	0.29	0.26	0.27	0.	0.25
University of Miami .... Coral Gables, FL	0.33	0.34	0.30	0.31	0.	0.33
University of Michigan .... Ann Arbor, MI	0.92	0.91	0.89	0.92	0.	0.90
University of Minnesota, Duluth .. Duluth, MN	0.28	0.29	0.22	0.26	0.	0.25
University of Minnesota, Twin Cities Minneapolis, MN	0.82	0.86	0.83	0.86	0.	0.84
University of Mississippi .... University, MS	0.41	0.44	0.40	0.43	0.	0.44
University of Missouri – Columbia Columbia, MO	0.59	0.61	0.60	0.61	0.	0.61
University of Missouri – Kansas City Kansas City, MO	0.49	0.50	0.49	0.50	0.	0.48
University of Missouri – St. Louis . St. Louis, MO	0.26	0.27	0.25	0.26	0.	0.27
University of Montana .... Missoula, MT	0.31	0.33	0.31	0.32	0.	0.33
University of Montevallo .... Montevallo, AL	0.28	0.24	0.20	0.21	0.	0.21

DEPARTMENTS OF GRADUATE EDUCATION
Not On The Approved List of The Gourman Report (Continued)

Department of Graduate Education INSTITUTION	Gourman Overall Academic Score (Combined Areas/Fields)	Administration (Attitude and Policy) (Quality of Leadership at All Levels of Administration)	Curriculum (Attractiveness of Program)	Faculty Effectiveness	Faculty (Quality of Research/ Scholarship)	Library Resources
University of Nebraska at Omaha Omaha, NE	0.30	0.29	0.21	0.26	0.	0.25
University of Nebraska – Lincoln . Lincoln, NE	0.55	0.58	0.57	0.58	0.	0.57
University of Nevada – Las Vegas Las Vegas, NV	0.33	0.34	0.29	0.33	0.	0.32
University of Nevada – Reno . . . . Reno, NV	0.31	0.33	0.28	0.32	0.	0.31
University of New Hampshire . . . Durham, NH	0.46	0.45	0.44	0.43	0.	0.42
University of New Mexico . . . . . . Albuquerque, NM	0.49	0.50	0.46	0.48	0.	0.49
University of New Orleans . . . . . . New Orleans, LA	0.30	0.31	0.28	0.30	0.	0.29
University of North Alabama . . . . Florence, AL	0.29	0.32	0.29	0.30	0.	0.28
University of North Carolina at Chapel Hill . . . . Chapel Hill, NC	0.65	0.66	0.65	0.66	0.	0.66
University of North Carolina at Charlotte . . . . Charlotte, NC	0.32	0.33	0.31	0.32	0.	0.35
University of North Carolina at Greensboro . . . . Greensboro, NC	0.41	0.42	0.39	0.41	0.	0.40
University of North Carolina at Wilmington . . . . Wilmington, NC	0.20	0.19	0.18	0.16	0.	0.15
University of North Dakota . . . . . . Grand Forks, ND	0.35	0.34	0.31	0.32	0.	0.30
University of Northern Colorado . Greeley, CO	0.38	0.39	0.36	0.37	0.	0.34
University of Northern Iowa . . . . . Cedar Falls, IA	0.33	0.34	0.30	0.33	0.	0.32
University of North Florida . . . . . . Jacksonville, FL	0.31	0.32	0.29	0.31	0.	0.31
University of North Texas . . . . . . Denton, TX	0.43	0.42	0.39	0.41	0.	0.40
University of Oklahoma . . . . Norman, OK	0.58	0.59	0.56	0.59	0.	0.58
University of Oregon . . . . Eugene, OR	0.60	0.64	0.60	0.64	0.	0.63
University of Pennsylvania . . . . . . Philadelphia, PA	0.74	0.66	0.71	0.61	0.	0.70
University of Pittsburgh . . . . Pittsburgh, PA	0.72	0.73	0.70	0.72	0.	0.71
University of Portland . . . . Portland, OR	0.36	0.31	0.29	0.28	0.	0.30

DEPARTMENTS OF GRADUATE EDUCATION
Not On The Approved List of The Gourman Report (Continued)

RATING CATEGORIES	Numerical Range
Very Strong	4.51-4.99
Strong	4.01-4.49
Good	3.61-3.99
Acceptable Plus	3.01-3.59
Adequate	2.51-2.99
Marginal	2.01-2.49
Not Sufficient for Graduate Programs	0.

Department of Graduate Education INSTITUTION	Gourman Overall Academic Score (Combined Areas/Fields)	Administration (Attitude and Policy) (Quality of Leadership at All Levels of Administration)	Curriculum (Attractiveness of Program)	Faculty Effectiveness	Faculty (Quality of Research/ Scholarship)	Library Resources
University of Puget Sound ...... Tacoma, WA	0.32	0.33	0.30	0.31	0.	0.31
University of Redlands .... Redlands, CA	0.31	0.32	0.29	0.28	0.	0.29
University of Rhode Island ...... Kingston, RI	0.36	0.34	0.33	0.34	0.	0.33
University of Richmond .... Richmond, VA	0.34	0.33	0.28	0.31	0.	0.30
University of Rochester .... Rochester, NY	0.62	0.66	0.61	0.66	0.	0.66
University of San Diego .... San Diego, CA	0.31	0.30	0.24	0.30	0.	0.29
University of San Francisco ..... San Francisco, CA	0.39	0.38	0.35	0.36	0.	0.37
University of Santa Clara .... Santa Clara, CA	0.29	0.26	0.23	0.24	0.	0.26
University of Scranton .... Scranton, PA	0.32	0.31	0.29	0.30	0.	0.26
University of South Alabama .... Mobile, AL	0.34	0.32	0.30	0.29	0.	0.31
University of South Carolina .... Columbia, SC	0.47	0.46	0.45	0.46	0.	0.45
University of South Dakota ..... Vermillion, SD	0.34	0.31	0.30	0.30	0.	0.32
University of Southern California . Los Angeles, CA	0.67	0.68	0.64	0.61	0.	0.65
University of Southern Mississippi Hattiesburg, MS	0.33	0.33	0.29	0.29	0.	0.30
University of South Florida ...... Tampa, FL	0.32	0.34	0.30	0.31	0.	0.32
University of Southwestern Louisiana Lafayette, LA	0.34	0.32	0.29	0.30	0.	0.31
University of Tennessee at Chattanooga .... Chattanooga, TN	0.31	0.30	0.22	0.23	0.	0.26

DEPARTMENTS OF GRADUATE EDUCATION
Not On The Approved List of The Gourman Report (Continued)

Department of Graduate Education INSTITUTION	Gourman Overall Academic Score (Combined Areas/Fields)	Administration (Attitude and Policy) (Quality of Leadership at All Levels of Administration)	Curriculum (Attractiveness of Program)	Faculty Effectiveness	Faculty (Quality of Research/ Scholarship)	Library Resources
University of Tennessee at Martin Martin, TN	0.29	0.29	0.21	0.21	0.	0.22
University of Tennessee .... Knoxville, TN	0.48	0.49	0.45	0.46	0.	0.47
University of Texas at Austin .... Austin, TX	0.65	0.61	0.64	0.62	0.	0.66
University of Texas at Dallas .... Richardson, TX	0.32	0.33	0.31	0.30	0.	0.31
University of Texas at El Paso ... El Paso, TX	0.30	0.25	0.21	0.23	0.	0.24
University of Texas at San Antonio San Antonio, TX	0.28	0.27	0.23	0.22	0.	0.20
University of the District of Columbia Washington, D.C.	0.20	0.21	0.20	0.18	0.	0.16
University of the Pacific .... Stockton, CA	0.47	0.46	0.43	0.45	0.	0.43
University of Toledo .... Toledo, OH	0.34	0.35	0.31	0.34	0.	0.33
University of Tulsa .... Tulsa, OK	0.33	0.36	0.32	0.33	0.	0.34
University of Utah .... Salt Lake City, UT	0.61	0.60	0.58	0.60	0.	0.61
University of Vermont .... Burlington, VT	0.41	0.42	0.40	0.41	0.	0.42
University of Virginia .... Charlottesville, VA	0.51	0.53	0.55	0.53	0.	0.58
University of Washington .... Seattle, WA	0.69	0.72	0.71	0.68	0.	0.72
University of West Florida ...... Pensacola, FL	0.29	0.30	0.26	0.29	0.	0.30
University of Wisconsin – Eau Claire Eau Claire, WI	0.29	0.29	0.25	0.24	0.	0.25
University of Wisconsin – La Crosse La Crosse, WI	0.27	0.26	0.24	0.22	0.	0.22
University of Wisconsin – Madison Madison, WI	0.74	0.77	0.76	0.73	0.	0.84
University of Wisconsin – Milwaukee Milwaukee, WI	0.51	0.52	0.54	0.53	0.	0.59
University of Wisconsin – Oshkosh Oshkosh, WI	0.26	0.27	0.25	0.24	0.	0.24
University of Wisconsin – Platteville Platteville, WI	0.28	0.26	0.23	0.25	0.	0.23
University of Wisconsin – River Falls River Falls, WI	0.25	0.24	0.20	0.22	0.	0.22
University of Wisconsin – Stevens Point .... Stevens Point, WI	0.24	0.23	0.22	0.18	0.	0.21

DEPARTMENTS OF GRADUATE EDUCATION
Not On The Approved List of The Gourman Report (Continued)

RATING CATEGORIES	Numerical Range
Very Strong	4.51-4.99
Strong	4.01-4.49
Good	3.61-3.99
Acceptable Plus	3.01-3.59
Adequate	2.51-2.99
Marginal	2.01-2.49

Not Sufficient for Graduate Programs   0.

Department of Graduate Education INSTITUTION	Gourman Overall Academic Score (Combined Areas/Fields)	Administration (Attitude and Policy) (Quality of Leadership at All Levels of Administration)	Curriculum (Attractiveness of Program)	Faculty Effectiveness	Faculty (Quality of Research/ Scholarship)	Library Resources
University of Wisconsin – Stout .. Menomonie, WI	0.21	0.22	0.20	0.19	0.	0.19
University of Wisconsin – Superior Superior, WI	0.23	0.21	0.19	0.21	0.	0.20
University of Wisconsin – Whitewater Whitewater, WI	0.26	0.24	0.20	0.22	0.	0.21
University of Wyoming .... Laramie, WY	0.36	0.37	0.35	0.36	0.	0.35
Utah State University .... Logan, UT	0.37	0.38	0.36	0.37	0.	0.34
Valdosta State College .... Valdosta, GA	0.27	0.26	0.24	0.25	0.	0.24
Vanderbilt University .... Nashville, TN	0.52	0.50	0.49	0.50	0.	0.50
Villanova University .... Villanova, PA	0.30	0.31	0.26	0.29	0.	0.28
Virginia Commonwealth University Richmond, VA	0.48	0.47	0.44	0.46	0.	0.47
Virginia Polytechnic Institute and State University .... Blackburg, VA	0.49	0.50	0.48	0.42	0.	0.49
Virginia State University .... Petersburg, VA	0.20	0.21	0.16	0.15	0.	0.15
Wake Forest University .... Winston-Salem, NC	0.30	0.31	0.29	0.28	0.	0.30
Washburn University of Topeka .. Topeka, KS	0.27	0.25	0.23	0.20	0.	0.24
Washington State University .... Pullman, WA	0.58	0.59	0.56	0.51	0.	0.59
Washington University .... St. Louis, MO	0.62	0.66	0.64	0.66	0.	0.65
Wayne State University .... Detroit, MI	0.68	0.70	0.67	0.66	0.	0.70
Westchester University of Pennsylvania .... Westchester, PA	0.36	0.33	0.30	0.31	0.	0.30

DEPARTMENTS OF GRADUATE EDUCATION
Not On The Approved List of The Gourman Report (Continued)

Department of Graduate Education INSTITUTION	Gourman Overall Academic Score (Combined Areas/Fields)	Administration (Attitude and Policy) (Quality of Leadership at All Levels of Administration)	Curriculum (Attractiveness of Program)	Faculty Effectiveness	Faculty (Quality of Research/ Scholarship)	Library Resources
Western Carolina University . . . . Cullowhee, NC	0.37	0.38	0.36	0.34	0.	0.36
Western Illinois University . . . . . . Macomb, IL	0.44	0.45	0.43	0.41	0.	0.42
Western Kentucky University . . . . Bowling Green, KY	0.40	0.41	0.40	0.40	0.	0.41
Western Michigan University . . . . Kalamazoo, MI	0.45	0.46	0.45	0.44	0.	0.46
Western Washington University . . Bellingham, WA	0.41	0.42	0.41	0.42	0.	0.42
West Texas State University . . . . Canyon, TX	0.38	0.39	0.36	0.35	0.	0.35
West Virginia University . . . . Morgantown, WV	0.48	0.47	0.46	0.41	0.	0.47
Wichita State University . . . . Wichita, KS	0.27	0.30	0.26	0.25	0.	0.24
Widener University . . . . Chester, PA	0.30	0.31	0.28	0.29	0.	0.27
William Patterson College of New Jersey . . . . Wayne, NJ	0.31	0.32	0.29	0.30	0.	0.28
Winona State University . . . . Winona, MN	0.32	0.30	0.27	0.28	0.	0.29
Wright State University . . . . Dayton, OH	0.33	0.34	0.29	0.33	0.	0.31
Xavier University . . . . Cincinnati, OH	0.30	0.29	0.26	0.27	0.	0.25
Yeshiva University . . . . New York, NY	0.58	0.59	0.56	0.49	0.	0.56
Youngstown State University . . . . Youngstown, OH	0.27	0.28	0.25	0.26	0.	0.26

The GOURMAN REPORT
PART XV

A RATING OF THE TOP 50 GRADUATE SCHOOLS
IN THE UNITED STATES

A RATING OF GRADUATE QUALITY INSTITUTIONS

U.S.A. UNIVERSITIES
Leading Institutions

Fifty institutions with scores in the 4.21-4.99 range, in rank order

INSTITUTION	Rank	Score
HARVARD	1	4.95
CALIFORNIA, BERKELEY	2	4.94
MICHIGAN (Ann Arbor)	3	4.93
YALE	4	4.92
STANFORD	5	4.91
CHICAGO	6	4.90
PRINCETON	7	4.89
M.I.T.	8	4.88
WISCONSIN (Madison)	9	4.85
UCLA	10	4.82
CORNELL (N.Y.)	11	4.81
CAL TECH	12	4.80
COLUMBIA (N.Y.)	13	4.79
MINNESOTA (Minneapolis)	14	4.78
PENNSYLVANIA	15	4.77
NORTHWESTERN (Illinois)	16	4.76
ILLINOIS (Urbana)	17	4.75
TEXAS (Austin)	18	4.73
CALIFORNIA, SAN DIEGO	19	4.72
WASHINGTON (Seattle)	20	4.71
DUKE	21	4.70
BROWN	22	4.68
INDIANA (Bloomington)	23	4.67
IOWA (Iowa City)	24	4.65
NORTH CAROLINA (Chapel Hill)	25	4.63
N.Y.U.	26	4.61
PURDUE (Lafayette)	27	4.60
OHIO STATE (Columbus)	28	4.57
JOHNS HOPKINS	29	4.56
SUNY (Buffalo)	30	4.54
VIRGINIA (Charlottesville)	31	4.53
MICHIGAN STATE	32	4.51
CALIFORNIA, DAVIS	33	4.50
WASHINGTON (St. Louis)	34	4.49
PENN STATE (University Park)	35	4.46
CARNEGIE-MELLON	36	4.43
PITTSBURGH (Pittsburgh)	37	4.42
RICE	38	4.41
VANDERBILT	39	4.39
NOTRE DAME	40	4.37
CALIFORNIA, IRVINE	41	4.36
KANSAS (Lawrence)	42	4.33
ROCHESTER (N.Y.)	43	4.32
RENSSELAER (N.Y.)	44	4.28
UTAH	45	4.27
GEORGIA TECH	46	4.26
RUTGERS (New Brunswick)	47	4.23
TULANE	48	4.21
CASE WESTERN RESERVE	49	4.16
BRANDEIS	50	4.14

NOTE: *Departments of Education excluded from the overall ratings of graduate schools. (See Part XVI.)*

The GOURMAN REPORT
PART XVI

A RATING OF GRADUATE SCHOOLS
IN THE UNITED STATES

A Rating of United States Graduate Schools: Academic and Selective

RATING CATEGORIES	Numerical Range
Very Strong	4.51-4.99
Strong	4.01-4.49
Good	3.61-3.99
Acceptable Plus	3.01-3.59
Adequate	2.51-2.99
Marginal	2.01-2.49

Not Sufficient for Graduate Programs   0.

INSTITUTION	Gourman Overall Academic Rating
Abilene Christian University ...... Abilene, TX	0.
Adams State College .... Alamosa, CO	0.
Adelphi University .... Garden City, NY	2.29
Air Force Institute of Technology .. Wright-Patterson AFB, OH	2.79
Alabama Agricultural and Mechanical University .... Normal, AL	0.
Alabama State University .... Montgomery, AL	0.
Alaska Pacific University .... Anchorage, AK	0.
Albany State College .... Albany, GA	0.
Alcorn State University .... Lorman, MS	0.
Alfred University .... Alfred, NY	3.06
American International College .... Springfield, MA	0.
American University .... Washington, D.C.	3.17
Andrews University .... Berrien Springs, MI	0.
Angelo State University .... San Angelo, TX	0.
Appalachian State University ..... Boone, NC	0.
Arizona State University .... Tempe, AZ	3.64

INSTITUTION	Gourman Overall Academic Rating
Arkansas State University .... State University, AR	0.
Arkansas Tech University .... Russellville, AR	0.
Auburn University .... Auburn, AL	2.99
Auburn University at Montgomery .. Montgomery, AL	0.
Austin Peay State University ...... Clarksville, TN	0.
Azusa Pacific University .... Azusa, CA	0.
Ball State University .... Muncie, IN	2.77
Barry University .... Miami Shores, FL	0.
Baylor University .... Waco, TX	2.98
Bemidji State University .... Bemidji, MN	0.
Biola University .... La Mirada, CA	0.
Bloomsburg University of Pennsylvania Bloomsburg, PA	0.
Boise State University .... Boise, ID	0.
Boston College .... Chestnut Hill, MA	2.58
Boston University .... Boston, MA	3.90
Bowie State University .... Bowie, MD	0.

NOTE: See Part II, III and IV for ratings on
Law, Dental, Medicine, Nursing, Optometry, Pharmacy and Public Health.

INSTITUTION	Gourman Overall Academic Rating
Bowling Green State University . . . . Bowling Green, OH	2.89
Bradley University . . . . Peoria, IL	2.39
Brandeis University . . . . Waltham, MA	4.14
Bridgewater State College . . . . Bridgewater, MA	0.
Brigham Young University . . . . Provo, UT	2.67
Brown University . . . . Providence, RI	4.68
Bryn Mawr College . . . . Bryn Mawr, PA	3.29
Bucknell University . . . . Lewisburg, PA	2.45
Butler University . . . . Indianapolis, IN	2.41
California Institute of Technology . . Pasadena, CA	4.80
California Lutheran College . . . . Thousand Oaks, CA	0.
California Polytechnic State University, San Luis Obispo . . . . San Luis Obispo, CA	2.54
California State University, Bakersfield Bakersfield, CA	0.
California State Polytechnic University, Pomona . . . . Pomona, CA	2.04
California State University, Chico . . Chico, CA	2.02
California State University, Dominguez Hills . . . . Carson, CA	2.08
California State University, Fresno . Fresno, CA	2.55
California State University, Fullerton Fullerton, CA	2.62
California State University, Hayward Hayward, CA	2.03
California State University, Long Beach Long Beach, CA	2.63

INSTITUTION	Gourman Overall Academic Rating
California State University, Los Angeles Los Angeles, CA	2.59
California State University, Northridge . Northridge, CA	2.64
California State University, Sacramento Sacramento, CA	2.56
California State University, San Bernardino . . . . San Bernardino, CA	2.07
California State University, Stanislaus Turlock, CA	0.
California University of Pennsylvania California, PA	0.
Canisius College . . . . Buffalo, NY	0.
Carnegie-Mellon University . . . . Pittsburgh, PA	4.43
Case Western Reserve University . Cleveland, OH	4.16
Catholic University of America . . . . Washington, D.C.	3.07
Central Connecticut State University New Britain, CT	2.48
Central Michigan University . . . . Mount Pleasant, MI	2.40
Central Missouri State University . . Warrensburg, MO	2.10
Central State University . . . . Edmond, OK	0.
Central Washington University . . . . Ellensburg, WA	0.
Chapman College . . . . Orange, CA	0.
Cheyney University of Pennsylvania Cheyney, PA	0.
Chicago State University . . . . Chicago, IL	0.
City University of New York, Bernard M. Baruch College . . . . New York, NY	2.69
City University of New York, Brooklyn College	3.09

RATING CATEGORIES	Numerical Range
Very Strong	4.51-4.99
Strong	4.01-4.49
Good	3.61-3.99
Acceptable Plus	3.01-3.59
Adequate	2.51-2.99
Marginal	2.01-2.49
Not Sufficient for Graduate Programs	0.

INSTITUTION	Gourman Overall Academic Rating
City University of New York, City College .... New York, NY	3.29
City University of New York, College of Staten Island .... Staten Island, NY	0.
City University of New York, Graduate School & University Center New York, NY	3.87
City University of New York, Herbert H. Lehman College .... Bronx, NY	2.67
City University of New York, Hunter College .... New York, NY	3.12
City University of New York, Queens College .... Flushing, NY	3.10
Claremont Graduate School ...... Claremont, CA	3.51
Clarion University of Pennsylvania . Clarion, PA	0.
Clarkson University .... Potsdam, NY	2.76
Clark University .... Worcester, MA	3.55
Clemson University .... Clemson, SC	3.10
Cleveland State University .... Cleveland, OH	2.50
College of William & Mary .... Williamsburg, VA	2.51
Colorado School of Mines .... Golden, CO	3.82

INSTITUTION	Gourman Overall Academic Rating
Colorado State University .... Fort Collins, CO	2.91
Columbia University .... New York, NY	4.79
Connecticut College .... New London, CT	2.05
Cooper Union for the Advancement of Science and Art .... New York, NY	2.58
Cornell University .... Ithaca, NY	4.81
Corpus Christi State University .... Corpus Christi, TX	0.
Creighton University .... Omaha, NE	2.74
Dartmouth College .... Hanover, NH	4.08
Delta State University .... Cleveland, MS	0.
De Paul University .... Chicago, IL	2.88
Drake University .... Des Moines, IA	2.90
Drew University .... Madison, NJ	2.63
Drexel University .... Philadelphia, PA	3.62
Duke University .... Durham, NC	4.70
Duquesne University .... Pittsburgh, PA	2.69
East Carolina University .... Greenville, NC	2.53
East Central University .... Ada, OK	0.

INSTITUTION	Gourman Overall Academic Rating	INSTITUTION	Gourman Overall Academic Rating
Eastern Illinois University Charleston, IL	2.41	Florida State University Tallahassee, FL	3.51
Eastern Kentucky University Richmond, KY	2.31	Fordham University Bronx, NY	3.06
Eastern Michigan University Ypsilanti, MI	2.80	Fort Hays State University Hays, KS	0.
Eastern New Mexico University Portales, NM	2.21	Framingham State College Framingham, MA	0.
Eastern Washington University Cheney, WA	0.	Frostburg State University Frostburg, MD	0.
East Stroudsburg University of Pennsylvania East Stroudsburg, PA	0.	Gallaudet University Washington, D.C.	2.45
East Tennessee State University Johnson City, TN	2.19	Gannon University Erie, PA	0.
East Texas State University Commerce, TX	0.	George Mason University Fairfax, VA	2.11
Edinboro University of Pennsylvania Edinboro, PA	0.	Georgetown University Washington, D.C.	4.03
Emory University Atlanta, GA	3.79	George Washington University Washington, D.C.	3.67
Emporia State University Emporia, KS	2.18	Georgia College Milledgeville, GA	0.
Fairfield University Fairfield, CT	0.	Georgia Institute of Technology Atlanta, GA	4.26
Fairleigh Dickinson University, Florham-Madison Campus Madison, NJ	0.	Georgia Southern University Statesboro, GA	0.
Fairleigh Dickinson University, Rutherford Campus Rutherford, NJ	0.	Georgia State University Atlanta, GA	2.27
Fairleigh Dickinson University, Teaneck-Hackensack Campus Teaneck, NJ	3.03	Golden Gate University San Francisco, CA	2.25
Fayetteville State University Fayetteville, NC	0.	Gonzaga University Spokane, WA	2.94
Florida Agricultural and Mechanical University Tallahassee, FL	2.02	Governors State University Park Forest South, IL	0.
Florida Atlantic University Boca Raton, FL	2.04	Grand Valley State University Allendale, MI	0.
Florida Institute of Technology Melbourne, FL	2.05	Hamline University St. Paul, MN	2.20
Florida International University Miami, FL	2.06	Hampton University Hampton, VA	0.
		Hardin-Simmons University Abilene, TX	0.
		Harvard University Cambridge, MA	4.95

RATING CATEGORIES	Numerical Range
Very Strong	4.51-4.99
Strong	4.01-4.49
Good	3.61-3.99
Acceptable Plus	3.01-3.59
Adequate	2.51-2.99
Marginal	2.01-2.49
Not Sufficient for Graduate Programs	0.

INSTITUTION	Gourman Overall Academic Rating
Henderson State University . . . . Arkadelphia, AR	0.
Hofstra University . . . . Hempstead, NY	2.88
Howard University . . . . Washington D.C.	2.68
Humboldt State University . . . . Arcata, CA	2.01
Idaho State University . . . . Pocatello, ID	2.28
Illinois Institute of Technology . . . . . Chicago, IL	2.54
Illinois State University . . . . Normal, IL	2.45
Indiana State University at Terre Haute Terre Haute, IN	2.01
Indiana University at South Bend . . South Bend, IN	0.
Indiana University at Bloomington . . Bloomington, IN	4.67
Indiana University of Pennsylvania . Indiana, PA	0.
Indiana University–Purdue University Fort Wayne . . . . Fort Wayne, IN	0.
Indiana University–Purdue University Indianapolis . . . . Indianapolis, IN	3.42

INSTITUTION	Gourman Overall Academic Rating
Iowa State University . . . . Ames, IA	3.60
Ithaca College . . . . Ithaca, NY	2.15
Jackson State University . . . . Jackson, MS	0.
Jacksonville State University . . . . . . Jacksonville, AL	0.
Jacksonville University . . . . Jacksonville, FL	0.
James Madison University . . . . Harrisonburg, VA	2.31
Jersey City State College . . . . Jersey City, NJ	0.
John Carroll University . . . . University Heights, OH	0.
Johns Hopkins University . . . . Baltimore, MD	4.56
Kansas State University . . . . Manhattan, KS	3.48
Kean College of New Jersey . . . . . . Union, NJ	2.26
Keene State College . . . . Keene, NH	0.
Kent State University . . . . Kent, OH	2.70
Kutztown University of Pennsylvania Kutztown, PA	0.
Lamar University . . . . Beaumont, TX	0.

INSTITUTION	Gourman Overall Academic Rating	INSTITUTION	Gourman Overall Academic Rating
Laredo State University Laredo, TX	0.	Mercer University in Atlanta Atlanta, GA	0.
Lehigh University Bethlehem, PA	3.78	Miami University Oxford, OH	2.94
Loma Linda University Loma Linda, CA	2.67	Michigan State University East Lansing, MI	4.51
Long Island University, Brooklyn Center Brooklyn, NY	3.20	Michigan Technological University Houghton, MI	2.92
Long Island University, C.W. Post Campus Greenvale, NY	2.98	Middlebury College Middlebury, VT	2.70
Louisiana State University and Agricultural and Mechanical College Baton Rouge, LA	3.67	Middle Tennessee State University Murfreesboro, TN	2.16
Louisiana State University in Shreveport Shreveport, LA	0.	Midwestern State University Wichita Falls, TX	0.
Louisiana Tech University Ruston, LA	2.02	Millersville University of Pennsylvania Millersville, PA	0.
Loyola College Baltimore, MD	0.	Milwaukee School of Engineering Milwaukee, WI	2.62
Loyola Marymount University Los Angeles, CA	2.51	Mississippi State University Mississippi State, MS	2.67
Loyola University, New Orleans New Orleans, LA	2.30	Montana College of Mineral Science and Technology Butte, MT	2.96
Loyola University of Chicago Chicago, IL	3.09	Montana State University Bozeman, MT	2.50
Lynchburg College Lynchburg, VA	0.	Montclair State College Upper Montclair, NJ	2.77
Manhattan College Riverdale, NY	0.	Moorhead State University Moorhead, MN	2.11
Mankato State University Mankato, MN	0.	Morehead State University Morehead, KY	2.08
Mansfield University of Pennsylvania Mansfield, PA	0.	Morgan State University Baltimore, MD	0.
Marquette University Milwaukee, WI	3.36	Mount Holyoke College South Hadley, MA	2.38
Marshall University Huntington, WV	2.33	Murray State University Murray, KY	2.02
Massachusetts Institute of Technology Cambridge, MA	4.88	Naval Postgraduate School Monterey, CA	2.84
Memphis State University Memphis, TN	3.02	New Jersey Institute of Technology Newark, NJ	2.87
Mercer University Macon, GA	2.44	New Mexico Highlands University Las Vegas, NM	0.

A Rating of United States Graduate Schools: Academic and Selective (Continued)

RATING CATEGORIES	Numerical Range
Very Strong	4.51-4.99
Strong	4.01-4.49
Good	3.61-3.99
Acceptable Plus	3.01-3.59
Adequate	2.51-2.99
Marginal	2.01-2.49

Not Sufficient for Graduate Programs   0.

INSTITUTION	Gourman Overall Academic Rating
New Mexico Institute of Mining and Technology .... Socorro, NM	2.94
New Mexico State University ...... Las Cruces, NM	2.37
New School for Social Research ... New York, NY	3.58
New York Institute of Technology, Old Westbury Campus .... Old Westbury, NY	2.32
New York University .... New York, NY	4.61
Niagara University .... Niagara University, NY	0.
Nicholls State University .... Thibodaux, LA	0.
Norfolk State University .... Norfolk, VA	0.
North Adams State College .... North Adams, MA	0.
North Carolina Agricultural and Technical State University .... Greensboro, NC	0.
North Carolina Central University .. Durham, NC	0.
North Carolina State University at Raleigh .... Raleigh, NC	3.41
North Dakota State University ..... Fargo, ND	2.98
Northeastern Illinois University .... Chicago, IL	2.19
Northeastern State University ..... Tahlequah, OK	0.

INSTITUTION	Gourman Overall Academic Rating
Northeastern University .... Boston, MA	3.29
Northeast Louisiana University .... Monroe, LA	0.
Northeast Missouri State University Kirksville, MO	0.
Northern Arizona University ...... Flagstaff, AZ	2.03
Northern Illinois University .... DeKalb, IL	3.08
Northern Kentucky University ..... Highland Heights, KY	0.
Northern Michigan University ..... Marquette, MI	2.31
Northern State University .... Aberdeen, SD	0.
Northwestern Oklahoma State University .... Alva, OK	0.
Northwestern State University of Louisiana .... Natchitoches, LA	0.
Northwestern University .... Evanston, IL	4.76
Northwest Missouri State University Maryville, MO	0.
Norwich, University .... Northfield, VT	0.
Nova University .... Fort Lauderdale, FL	0.
Oakland University .... Rochester, MI	3.22
Ohio State University .... Columbus, OH	4.57

INSTITUTION	Gourman Overall Academic Rating	INSTITUTION	Gourman Overall Academic Rating
Ohio University Athens, OH	3.25	Rice University Houston, TX	4.41
Oklahoma State University Stillwater, OK	2.71	Rochester Institute of Technology Rochester, NY	2.83
Old Dominion University Norfolk, VA	2.75	Rockefeller University New York, NY	4.01
Oral Roberts University Tulsa, OK	0.	Roosevelt University Chicago, IL	2.70
Oregon State University Corvallis, OR	3.56	Rose-Hulman Institute of Technology Terre Haute, IN	2.49
Pace University New York, NY	2.49	Rutgers University, Newark Newark, NJ	2.73
Pacific Lutheran University Tacoma, WA	2.02	Rutgers University, New Brunswick New Brunswick, NJ	4.23
Pacific University Forest Grove, OR	2.01	St. Bonaventure University St. Bonaventure, NY	0.
Pennsylvania State University – University Park Campus University Park, PA	4.46	St. Cloud State University St. Cloud, MN	0.
Pepperdine University Malibu, CA	0.	St. John's University Jamaica, NY	2.49
Pittsburg State University Pittsburg, KS	0.	Saint Louis University St. Louis, MO	3.07
Polytechnic University, Brooklyn Campus Brooklyn, NY	3.11	St. Mary's University of San Antonio San Antonio, TX	0.
Portland State University Portland, OR	2.01	Samford University Birmingham, AL	0.
Prairie View A&M University Prairie View, TX	0.	Sam Houston State University Huntsville, TX	0.
Pratt Institute Brooklyn, NY	2.58	San Diego State University San Diego, CA	2.71
Princeton University Princeton, NJ	4.89	San Francisco State University San Francisco, CA	2.69
Purdue University West Lafayette, IN	4.60	Sangamon State University Springfield, IL	0.
Purdue University – Calumet Hammond, IN	0.	San Jose State University San Jose, CA	2.65
Radford University Radford, VA	2.51	Seattle University Seattle, WA	2.51
Rensselaer Polytechnic Institute Troy, NY	4.28	Seton Hall University South Orange, NJ	2.53
		Shippensburg University of Pennsylvania Shippensburg, PA	0.

RATING CATEGORIES	Numerical Range
Very Strong	4.51-4.99
Strong	4.01-4.49
Good	3.61-3.99
Acceptable Plus	3.01-3.59
Adequate	2.51-2.99
Marginal	2.01-2.49

Not Sufficient for Graduate Programs   0.

INSTITUTION	Gourman Overall Academic Rating
Simmons College Boston, MA	2.39
Slippery Rock University of Pennsylvania Slippery Rock, PA	0.
Smith College Northhampton, MA	2.66
Sonoma State University Rohnert Park, CA	0.
South Dakota School of Mines and Technology Rapid City, SD	2.91
South Dakota State University Brookings, SD	2.48
Southeastern Louisiana University Hammond, LA	0.
Southeastern Massachusetts University North Dartmouth, MA	2.10
Southeast Missouri State University Cape Giradeau, MO	2.01
Southern Connecticut State University New Haven, CT	2.04
Southern Illinois University at Carbondale Carbondale, IL	3.33
Southern Illinois University at Edwardsville Edwardsville, IL	2.17
Southern Methodist University Dallas, TX	2.92
Southern University and Agricultural and Mechanical College Baton Rouge, LA	0.

INSTITUTION	Gourman Overall Academic Rating
Southwestern Oklahoma State University Weatherford, OK	0.
Southwest Missouri State University Springfield, MO	0.
Southwest Texas State University San Marcos, TX	0.
Stanford University Stanford, CA	4.91
State University of New York at Albany Albany, NY	3.92
State University of New York at Binghamton Binghamton, NY	3.98
State University of New York at Buffalo Buffalo, NY	4.54
State University of New York at Stony Brook Stony Brook, NY	4.13
State University of New York College at Brockport Brockport, NY	0.
State University of New York College at Buffalo Buffalo, NY	0.
State University of New York College at Cortland Cortland, NY	0.
State University of New York College at Fredonia Fredonia, NY	0.
State University of New York College at Geneseo Geneseo, NY	0.

INSTITUTION	Gourman Overall Academic Rating	INSTITUTION	Gourman Overall Academic Rating
State University of New York College at New Paltz .... New Paltz, NY	0.	Texas Christian University .... Fort Worth, TX	2.51
State University of New York College at Oneonta .... Oneonta, NY	0.	Texas Southern University .... Houston, TX	0.
State University of New York College at Oswego .... Oswego, NY	0.	Texas Tech University .... Lubbock, TX	2.91
State University of New York College at Plattsburgh .... Plattsburgh, NY	0.	Texas Woman's University .... Denton, TX	2.59
State University of New York College at Potsdam .... Potsdam, NY	0.	Towson State University .... Baltimore, MD	0.
State University of New York College of Environmental Science & Forestry Syracuse, NY	3.79	Trenton State College .... Trenton, NJ	2.08
Stephen F. Austin State University . Nacogdoches, TX	0.	Trinity University .... San Antonio, TX	2.04
Stetson University .... Deland, FL	0.	Troy State University .... Troy, AL	0.
Stevens Institute of Technology ... Hoboken, NJ	3.30	Tufts University .... Medford, MA	4.05
Suffolk University .... Boston, MA	2.12	Tulane University .... New Orleans, LA	4.21
Sul Ross State University .... Alpine, TX	0.	Tuskegee University .... Tuskegee Institute, AL	2.40
Syracuse University .... Syracuse, NY	3.77	Union College .... Schenectady, NY	2.87
Tarleton State University .... Stephenville, TX	0.	United States International University San Diego, CA	0.
Teachers College, Columbia University New York, NY	3.31	University of Akron .... Akron, OH	2.34
Temple University .... Philadelphia, PA	3.65	University of Alabama .... University, AL	3.04
Tennessee State University ...... Nashville, TN	0.	University of Alabama in Birmingham Birmingham, AL	3.35
Tennessee Technological University Cookeville, TN	0.	University of Alabama in Huntsville . Huntsville, AL	2.76
Texas A&I University at Kingsville .. Kingsville, TX	0.	University of Alaska, Anchorage ... Anchorage, AK	0.
Texas A&M University .... College Station, TX	3.58	University of Alaska, Fairbanks .... Fairbanks, AK	2.58
		University of Alaska, Juneau ...... Juneau, AK	0.
		University of Arizona .... Tucson, AZ	3.70
		University of Arkansas .... Fayetteville, AR	3.03

RATING CATEGORIES	Numerical Range
Very Strong	4.51-4.99
Strong	4.01-4.49
Good	3.61-3.99
Acceptable Plus	3.01-3.59
Adequate	2.51-2.99
Marginal	2.01-2.49

Not Sufficient for Graduate Programs   0.

INSTITUTION	Gourman Overall Academic Rating
University of Arkansas at Little Rock Little Rock, AR	2.19
University of Baltimore .... Baltimore, MD	2.25
University of Bridgeport .... Bridgeport, CT	2.22
University of California, Berkeley .. Berkeley, CA	4.94
University of California, Davis ..... Davis, CA	4.50
University of California, Irvine ..... Irvine, CA	4.36
University of California, Los Angeles Los Angeles, CA	4.82
University of California, Riverside .. Riverside, CA	3.81
University of California, San Diego . La Jolla, CA	4.73
University of California, San Francisco San Francisco, CA	4.11
University of California, Santa Barbara Santa Barbara, CA	3.96
University of California, Santa Cruz Santa Cruz, CA	3.49
University of Central Arkansas .... Conway, AR	0.
University of Central Florida ...... Orlando, FL	2.01
University of Chicago .... Chicago, IL	4.90
University of Cincinnati .... Cincinnati, OH	3.61
University of Colorado at Boulder .. Boulder, CO	3.72

INSTITUTION	Gourman Overall Academic Rating
University of Colorado at Colorado Springs .... Colorado Springs, CO	0.
University of Colorado at Denver .. Denver, CO	3.05
University of Connecticut .... Storrs, CT	3.65
University of Dallas .... Irving, TX	2.12
University of Dayton .... Dayton, OH	2.49
University of Delaware .... Newark, DE	3.27
University of Denver .... Denver, CO	3.48
University of Detroit Mercy .... Detroit, MI	2.89
University of Evansville .... Evansville, IN	2.07
University of Florida .... Gainesville, FL	3.56
University of Georgia .... Athens, GA	3.35
University of Guam .... Mangilao, GU	0.
University of Hartford .... West Hartford, CT	2.69
University of Hawaii at Manoa ..... Honolulu, HI	3.31
University of Houston – Clear Lake . Houston, TX	0.
University of Houston – University Park Houston, TX	3.46
University of Idaho .... Moscow, ID	2.97

INSTITUTION	Gourman Overall Academic Rating
University of Illinois at Chicago .... Chicago, IL	3.76
University of Illinois at Urbana-Champaign .... Urbana, IL	4.75
University of Indianapolis .... Indianapolis, IN	2.45
University of Iowa .... Iowa City, IA	4.65
University of Kansas .... Lawrence, KS	4.33
University of Kentucky .... Lexington, KY	3.23
University of Louisville .... Louisville, KY	3.20
University of Lowell .... Lowell, MA	3.25
University of Maine at Orono ...... Orono, ME	3.15
University of Maryland at Baltimore . Baltimore, MD	0.
University of Maryland at College Park College Park, MD	3.74
University of Maryland Baltimore County .... Catonsville, MD	0.
University of Massachusetts at Amherst Amherst, MA	3.86
University of Massachusetts at Boston Boston, MA	2.20
University of Miami .... Coral Gables, FL	2.98
University of Michigan .... Ann Arbor, MI	4.93
University of Michigan – Dearborn . Dearborn, MI	2.40
University of Minnesota, Duluth .... Duluth, MN	2.60
University of Minnesota, Twin Cities Minneapolis, MN	4.78
University of Mississippi .... University, MS	2.92
University of Missouri – Columbia .. Columbia, MO	3.78

INSTITUTION	Gourman Overall Academic Rating
University of Missouri – Kansas City Kansas City, MO	3.18
University of Missouri – Rolla ..... Rolla, MO	3.31
University of Missouri – St. Louis .. St. Louis, MO	2.90
University of Montana .... Missoula, MT	2.96
University of Montevallo .... Montevallo, AL	0.
University of Nebraska at Omaha .. Omaha, NE	2.37
University of Nebraska – Lincoln ... Lincoln, NE	3.28
University of Nevada – Las Vegas . Las Vegas, NV	2.45
University of Nevada – Reno ...... Reno, NV	2.57
University of New Hampshire ..... Durham, NH	2.97
University of New Haven .... West Haven, CT	2.54
University of New Mexico .... Albuquerque, NM	3.22
University of New Orleans .... New Orleans, LA	2.49
University of North Alabama ...... Florence, AL	0.
University of North Carolina at Chapel Hill .... Chapel Hill, NC	4.63
University of North Carolina at Charlotte .... Charlotte, NC	2.34
University of North Carolina at Greensboro .... Greensboro, NC	2.32
University of North Carolina at Wilmington .... Wilmington, AL	2.30
University of North Dakota .... Grand Forks, ND	2.99
University of Northern Colorado ... Greeley, CO	0.

A Rating of United States Graduate Schools: Academic and Selective (Continued)

RATING CATEGORIES	Numerical Range
Very Strong	4.51-4.99
Strong	4.01-4.49
Good	3.61-3.99
Acceptable Plus	3.01-3.59
Adequate	2.51-2.99
Marginal	2.01-2.49

Not Sufficient for Graduate Programs   0.

INSTITUTION	Gourman Overall Academic Rating
University of Northern Iowa .... Cedar Falls, IA	2.03
University of North Florida .... Jacksonville, FL	0.
University of North Texas .... Denton, TX	2.83
University of Notre Dame .... Notre Dame, IN	4.37
University of Oklahoma .... Norman, OK	3.22
University of Oregon .... Eugene, OR	3.78
University of Pennsylvania .... Philadelphia, PA	4.76
University of Pittsburgh .... Pittsburgh, PA	4.42
University of Portland .... Portland, OR	2.01
University of Puget Sound .... Tacoma, WA	2.25
University of Redlands .... Redlands, CA	0.
University of Rhode Island .... Kingston, RI	2.86
University of Richmond .... Richmond, VA	2.51
University of Rochester .... Rochester, NY	4.32
University of San Diego .... San Diego, CA	0.
University of San Francisco .... San Francisco, CA	2.10
University of Santa Clara .... Santa Clara, CA	2.46

INSTITUTION	Gourman Overall Academic Rating
University of Scranton .... Scranton, PA	0.
University of South Alabama ...... Mobile, AL	2.37
University of South Carolina ...... Columbia, SC	3.06
University of South Dakota .... Vermillion, SD	2.95
University of Southern California ... Los Angeles, CA	3.83
University of Southern Mississippi . Hattiesburg, MS	2.35
University of South Florida .... Tampa, FL	3.05
University of Southwestern Louisiana Lafayette, LA	2.20
University of Tennessee at Chattanooga .... Chattanooga, TN	0.
University of Tennessee .... Knoxville, TN	3.50
University of Tennessee at Martin .. Martin, TN	0.
University of Texas at Arlington .... Arlington, TX	2.18
University of Texas at Austin ...... Austin, TX	4.72
University of Texas at Dallas ...... Richardson, TX	2.92
University of Texas at El Paso .... El Paso, TX	2.04
University of Texas at San Antonio . San Antonio, TX	2.14
University of the District of Columbia Washington, D.C.	0.

INSTITUTION	Gourman Overall Academic Rating
University of the Pacific .... Stockton, CA	2.80
University of Toledo .... Toledo, OH	2.55
University of Tulsa .... Tulsa, OK	2.61
University of Utah .... Salt Lake City, UT	4.27
University of Vermont .... Burlington, VT	2.96
University of Virginia .... Charlottesville, VA	4.53
University of Washington .... Seattle, WA	4.71
University of West Florida .... Pensacola, FL	0.
University of Wisconsin – Eau Claire Eau Claire, WI	0.
University of Wisconsin – Green Bay Green Bay, WI	0.
University of Wisconsin – La Crosse La Crosse, WI	0.
University of Wisconsin – Madison . Madison, WI	4.85
University of Wisconsin – Milwaukee Milwaukee, WI	3.43
University of Wisconsin – Oshkosh . Oshkosh, WI	0.
University of Wisconsin – Parkside . Kenosha, WI	0.
University of Wisconsin – Platteville Platteville, WI	0.
University of Wisconsin – River Falls River Falls, WI	0.
University of Wisconsin – Stevens Point Stevens Point, WI	0.
University of Wisconsin – Stout .... Menomonie, WI	0.
University of Wisconsin – Superior . Superior, WI	0.
University of Wisconsin – Whitewater Whitewater, WI	0.
University of Wyoming .... Laramie, WY	3.06

INSTITUTION	Gourman Overall Academic Rating
Utah State University .... Logan, UT	2.94
Valdosta State College .... Valdosta, GA	0.
Vanderbilt University .... Nashville, TN	4.39
Villanova University .... Villanova, PA	0.
Virginia Commonwealth University . Richmond, VA	3.10
Virginia Polytechnic Institute and State University .... Blacksburg, VA	3.74
Virginia State University .... Petersburg, VA	0.
Wake Forest University .... Winston-Salem, NC	2.82
Washburn University of Topeka ... Topeka, KS	0.
Washington State University ...... Pullman, WA	3.38
Washington University .... St. Louis, MO	4.49
Wayne State University .... Detroit, MI	3.36
Wesleyan University .... Middletown, CT	2.35
Westchester University of Pennsylvania Westchester, PA	0.
Western Carolina University ...... Cullowhee, NC	0.
Western Illinois University .... Macomb, IL	2.08
Western Kentucky University ..... Bowling Green, KY	2.15
Western Michigan University ...... Kalamazoo, MI	2.52
Western Washington University ... Bellingham, WA	0.
West Texas State University ...... Canyon, TX	0.
West Virginia University .... Morganville, WV	3.16
Wichita State University .... Wichita, KS	2.70

RATING CATEGORIES	Numerical Range
Very Strong	4.51-4.99
Strong	4.01-4.49
Good	3.61-3.99
Acceptable Plus	3.01-3.59
Adequate	2.51-2.99
Marginal	2.01-2.49

Not Sufficient for Graduate Programs   0.

INSTITUTION	Gourman Overall Academic Rating
Widener University .... Chester, PA	2.17
William Patterson College of New Jersey .... Wayne, NJ	2.01
Winona State University .... Winona, MN	0.
Worcester Polytechnic Institute .... Worcester, MA	2.94
Wright State University .... Dayton, OH	2.90
Xavier University .... Cincinnati, OH	0.
Yale University .... New Haven, CT	4.92
Yeshiva University .... New York, NY	3.78
Youngstown State University ..... Youngstown, OH	0.

The GOURMAN REPORT
PART XVII

APPENDIXES – INCLUDED IN THE 6TH EDITION

Appendix A
List of Tables

Appendix B
International Law Schools

Appendix C
Law Schools in Canada

Appendix D
United States Law Schools

Appendix E
Dental Schools in Canada

Appendix F
United States Dental Schools

Appendix G
Medical Schools in Canada

Appendix H
International Medical Schools

Appendix I
United States Medical Schools

Appendix J
United States Veterinary Schools

Appendix K
United States Nursing Schools

Appendix L
United States Optometry Schools

Appendix M
Pharmacy Schools in Canada

Appendix N
United States Pharmacy Schools

Appendix O
United States Public Health Schools

TABLE 1
A Rating of Graduate Programs in the United States

FIELD OF STUDY	Selected Number of Institutions Granting Degree	Total Number of Programs (Curriculum) Evaluated	Total Number of Areas of Study Evaluated	Total Number of Faculty Areas Evaluated	Quality Institutions Listed in the Gourman Report
Accounting	540	540	3,679	810	88
Aerospace Engineering	39	39	878	368	32
African Studies	12	12	210	41	6
Agricultural Economics	50	50	667	158	34
Agricultural Engineering	42	42	664	211	33
Agricultural Sciences	71	71	5,414	970	32
Analytical Chemistry	56	56	992	73	10
Anthropology	160	160	1,119	714	47
Applied Mathematics	71	71	043	340	24
Applied Physics	35	35	333	60	11
Architecture	61	61	980	431	30
Art History	90	90	1,223	452	30
Asian Languages	30	30	463	82	10
Asian Studies	57	57	933	212	11
Astronomy	55	55	1,165	462	33
Biochemistry	214	214	3,180	589	51
Bioengineering/Biomedical Engineering	55	55	1,490	320	24
Botany	120	120	1,878	319	40
Business Administration (EMBA)[1]	See Table 14.				
Business Administration (MBA)[2]	See Table 15.				
Business Administration (Ph.D./DBA)[3]	See Table 16.				
Cellular/Molecular Biology	80	80	2,151	521	42
Ceramic Sciences/Engineering	12	12	606	220	9
Chemical Engineering	140	140	3,220	631	50
Chemistry	570	570	8,777	1,043	52
City/Regional Planning	51	51	944	90	16
Civil Engineering	161	161	5,980	823	50
Classics	85	85	927	190	30
Clinical Psychology	156	156	2,753	540	30
Clothing and Textiles	36	36	778	62	12
Communication	328	328	945	64	12
Comparative Literature	80	80	710	270	25
Computer Science	260	260	3,993	574	40
Consumer Economics	24	24	315	50	11
Demography/Population Studies	31	31	480	73	10
Developmental Psychology	54	54	912	59	11
Drama/Theatre	270	270	3,900	495	32
East European/Soviet Studies	30	30	704	62	8
Economics	390	390	6,150	705	43
Electrical Engineering	208	208	4,429	464	50

TABLE 1
A Rating of Graduate Programs in the United States (Continued)

FIELD OF STUDY	Selected Number of Institutions Granting Degree	Total Number of Programs (Curriculum) Evaluated	Total Number of Areas of Study Evaluated	Total Number of Faculty Areas Evaluated	Quality Institutions Listed in the Gourman Report
English	566	566	5,493	896	53
Entomology	50	50	1,155	557	31
Environmental Design	17	17	209	40	5
Environmental Engineering	26	26	124	38	10
Environmental Policy/Resource Management	87	87	704	84	15
Experimental Psychology (General)	152	152	2,714	583	19
Finance	431	431	2,222	761	88
Forestry	40	40	768	246	33
French	202	202	3,227	460	36
Geochemistry	31	31	409	58	12
Geography	150	150	985	488	29
Geoscience	110	110	4,628	455	41
German	135	135	2,813	438	35
Graphic Design	64	64	788	72	11
History	460	460	8,799	990	44
Industrial Design	20	20	406	49	10
Industrial Engineering	98	98	2,112	314	39
Industrial Labor Relations	50	50	319	51	6
Industrial/Organizational Psychology	138	138	941	95	23
Information Sciences	70	70	964	80	14
Inorganic Chemistry	60	60	988	72	16
Italian	42	42	308	52	12
International Relations	80	80	912	81	8
Journalism	66	66	800	307	22
Landscape Architecture	16	16	334	90	27
Library Science	66	66	1,600	371	18
Linguistics	81	81	978	570	30
Management/Organizational Behavior	460	460	2,093	496	88
Marketing	533	533	3,637	507	88
Mass Communication/Theory	158	158	3,888	509	18
Mass/Organizational Communication	50	50	900	78	10
Materials Science	56	56	754	349	38
Mathematics	361	361	5,914	955	50
Mechanical Engineering	183	183	3,406	437	50
Metallurgical Engineering	25	25	995	112	15
Metallurgy	16	16	765	101	10
Meteorology/Atmospheric Sciences	40	40	975	89	15

TABLE 1
A Rating of Graduate Programs in the United States (Continued)

FIELD OF STUDY	Selected Number of Institutions Granting Degree	Total Number of Programs (Curriculum) Evaluated	Total Number of Areas of Study Evaluated	Total Number of Faculty Areas Evaluated	Quality Institutions Listed in the Gourman Report
Microbiology	130	130	4,576	551	52
Music	412	412	4,760	541	38
Near/Middle Eastern Languages	15	15	297	63	10
Near/Middle Eastern Studies	37	37	820	72	10
Nuclear Engineering	34	34	989	410	26
Occupational Therapy	16	16	984	219	15
Operations Research	97	97	981	284	25
Organic Chemistry	66	66	994	174	16
Petroleum Engineering	16	16	938	136	14
Philosophy	207	207	4,891	712	45
Physical Chemistry	75	75	991	84	16
Physical Therapy	16	16	973	317	16
Physics	288	288	5,520	450	51
Physiology	80	80	2,017	428	35
Planetary Sciences	14	14	390	42	10
Plasma Physics	12	12	113	40	8
Political Science	336	336	3,442	680	36
Polymer Sciences/Plastics Engineering	30	30	600	42	9
Psychology	458	458	10,001	1,116	48
Psychology/Neuropsychology	29	29	233	56	13
Psychology/Neuroscience	32	32	228	50	23
Public Administration	212	212	1,017	319	20
Radio/TV/Film	110	110	988	119	10
Russian	30	30	164	47	10
Slavic Languages	34	34	446	57	16
Social Psychology	91	91	1,001	238	11
Social Welfare/Social Work	110	110	1,002	483	31
Sociology	341	341	8,722	666	43
Spanish	220	220	5,965	573	40
Statistics	140	140	2,461	432	27
Urban Design	14	14	280	54	8
Zoology	70	70	2,238	315	38

TABLE 2
A Rating of Law Schools: Canada

	Canadian Law Schools
Selected Number of Law Schools Evaluated	14
Quality Law Schools Listed in the Gourman Report	14
Total Number of Law Programs Evaluated	14
Total Number of Faculty Areas Evaluated	214
Total Number of Administrative Areas Evaluated	283
Total Number of Curriculum Areas Evaluated	251

TABLE 3
A Rating of Law Schools: International and the United States

	International Law Schools	U.S.A. Law Schools
Selected Number of Law Schools Evaluated	543	175
Quality Law Schools Listed in the Gourman Report	53	175*
Total Number of Law Programs Evaluated	543	175
Total Number of Faculty Areas Evaluated	2,116	981
Total Number of Administrative Areas Evaluated	3,264	1,862
Total Number of Curriculum Areas Evaluated	5,690	2,856

*U.S.A. SCHOOLS OF LAW

Rating Categories	Numerical Range	Number of Institutions
Very Strong	4.6-5.0	20
Strong	4.0-4.5	23
Good	3.6-3.9	31
Acceptable Plus	3.0-3.5	43
Adequate	2.1-2.9	58
	TOTAL	175

TABLE 4
A Rating of Dental Schools in Canada

	Canadian Dental Schools
Selected Number of Dental Schools Evaluated	10
Quality Dental Schools Listed in the Gourman Report	10
Total Number of Dental Programs Evaluated	10
Total Number of Curriculum Areas Evaluated	1,111
Total Number of Faculty Areas Evaluated	645
Total Number of Administrative Areas Evaluated	932

TABLE 5
A Rating of Dental Schools in the United States

	U.S.A. Dental Schools
Selected Number of Dental Schools Evaluated	54
Quality Dental Schools Listed in the Gourman Report	54
Total Number of Dental Programs Evaluated	54
Total Number of Curriculum Areas Evaluated	3,245
Total Number of Faculty Areas Evaluated	781
Total Number of Administrative Areas Evaluated	1,352

TABLE 6
A Rating of Medical Schools in Canada

	Canadian Medical Schools
Selected Number of Medical Schools Evaluated	16
Quality Medical Schools Listed in the Gourman Report	16
Total Number of Medical Programs Evaluated	16
Total Number of Faculty Areas Evaluated	347
Total Number of Administrative Areas Evaluated	799
Total Number of Curriculum Areas Evaluated	1,054

TABLE 7
A Rating of Medical Schools: International and the United States

	International Medical Schools	U.S.A. Medical Schools
Selected Number of Medical Schools Evaluated	712	125
Quality Medical Schools Listed in the Gourman Report	55	125*
Total Number of Medical Programs Evaluated	712	125
Total Number of Faculty Areas Evaluated	1,647	888
Total Number of Administrative Areas Evaluated	2,228	1,064
Total Number of Curriculum Areas Evaluated	5,894	4,671

*U.S.A. SCHOOLS OF MEDICINE

Rating Categories	Numerical Range	Number of Institutions
Very Strong	4.6-5.0	19
Strong	4.0-4.5	32
Good	3.6-3.9	29
Acceptable Plus	3.0-3.5	45
	TOTAL	125

TABLE 8
A Rating of United States Veterinary Schools

	U.S.A. Veterinary Schools
Selected Number of Veterinary Schools Evaluated	27
Quality Veterinary Schools Listed in the Gourman Report	26
Total Number of Veterinary Programs Evaluated	27
Total Number of Curriculum Areas Evaluated	2,834
Total Number of Faculty Areas Evaluated	721
Total Number of Administrative Areas Evaluated	908

TABLE 9
A Rating of United States Nursing Schools

	U.S.A Nursing Schools
Selected Number of Nursing Schools Evaluated	73
Quality Nursing Schools Listed in the Gourman Report	73
Total Number of Nursing Programs Evaluated	73
Total Number of Curriculum Areas Evaluated	1,982
Total Number of Faculty Areas Evaluated	723
Total Number of Administrative Areas Evaluated	951

TABLE 10
A Rating of United States Optometry Schools

	U.S.A. Optometry Schools
Selected Number of Optometry Schools Evaluated	16
Quality Optometry Schools Listed in the Gourman Report	16
Total Number of Optometry Programs Evaluated	16
Total Number of Curriculum Areas Evaluated	909
Total Number of Faculty Areas Evaluated	163
Total Number of Administrative Areas Evaluated	512

TABLE 11
A Rating of Pharmacy Schools in Canada

	Canadian Pharmacy Schools
Selected Number of Pharmacy Schools Evaluated	8
Quality Pharmacy Schools Listed in the Gourman Report	8
Total Number of Pharmacy Programs Evaluated	8
Total Number of Curriculum Areas Evaluated	714
Total Number of Faculty Areas Evaluated	166
Total Number of Administrative Areas Evaluated	347

TABLE 12
A Rating of United States Pharmacy Schools

	U.S.A Pharmacy Schools
Selected Number of Pharmacy Schools Evaluated	73
Quality Pharmacy Schools Listed in the Gourman Report	73
Total Number of Pharmacy Programs Evaluated	73
Total Number of Curriculum Areas Evaluated	5,861
Total Number of Faculty Areas Evaluated	879
Total Number of Administrative Areas Evaluated	997

TABLE 13
A Rating of United States Public Health Schools

	U.S.A. Public Health Schools
Selected Number of Public Health Schools Evaluated	22
Quality Public Health Schools Listed in the Gourman Report	22
Total Number of Public Health Programs Evaluated	22
Total Number of Curriculum Areas Evaluated	1,231
Total Number of Faculty Areas Evaluated	386
Total Number of Administrative Areas Evaluated	681

TABLE 14
A Rating of United States EMBA/Management Schools

	U.S.A. EMBA/Management Schools
Number of Schools Evaluated	30
Number of Schools Listed in the Gourman Report	13
Total Number of Administrative Areas Evaluated	63
Total Number of Curriculum Areas Evaluated	320
Total Number of Faculty Areas Evaluated	78

TABLE 15
A Rating of United States MBA/Management Schools

	U.S.A MBA/Management Schools
Number of Schools Evaluated	528
Number of Schools Listed in the Gourman Report	100
Total Number of Administrative Areas Evaluated	4,915
Total Number of Curriculum Areas Evaluated	7,956
Total Number of Faculty Areas Evaluated	978

TABLE 16
A Rating of United States Doctoral Business/Management Schools

	U.S.A. Doctoral/ Bus. Managemnt Schools
Number of Schools Evaluated	110
Number of Schools Listed in the Gourman Report	88
Total Number of Administrative Areas Evaluated	1,506
Total Number of Curriculum Areas Evaluated	2,010
Total Number of Faculty Areas Evaluated	854

TABLE 17
A Rating of United States Engineering Schools

	U.S.A. Engineering Schools
Number of Schools Evaluated	230
Number of Schools Listed in the Gourman Report	139
Total Number of Administrative Areas Evaluated	1,057
Total Number of Curriculum Areas Evaluated	4,231
Total Number of Faculty Areas Evaluated	881

APPENDIX B
International Institutions of Law Included in the 6th Edition

COUNTRY AND LAW SCHOOL

AUSTRIA
University of Innsbruck
University of Vienna

BELGIUM
Free University of Brussels

DENMARK
University of Copenhagen

FRANCE
University of Aix-Marseilles II
University of Besancon
University of Bordeaux I
University of Caen
University of Clermont
University of Dijon
University of Social Sciences (Grenoble II)
University of Law and Health Sciences
(Lille II)
University of Limoges
University of Lyon III (Jean Moulin)
University of Montpellier I
University of Nancy I
University of Nantes
University of Nice
University of Orleans
University of Paris (Pantheon-Sorbonne)
University of Law, Economics, and
Social Sciences (Paris II)
University of Paris-Nanterre (Paris X)
University of Paris XII
University of Paris-Nord (Paris XIII)
University of Poitiers
University of Reims
University of Rennes I
University of Rouen
University of Saint-Etienne
University of Social Sciences (Toulouse I)

FEDERAL REPUBLIC OF GERMANY
Rhemish Friedrich-Wilhelm University of
Bonn
University of Cologne
Friedrich Alexander University of
Erlangen-Nuremberg

FEDERAL REPUBLIC OF GERMANY
Albert Ludwig University of Freiburg
Georg August University of Göttingen
Rupert Charles University of Heidelberg
Christian Albrecht University of Kiel
Johannes Gutenberg University of Mainz
Philipps University of Marburg
Ludwig Maximilian University of Munich
University of Munster
Eberhard Karl University of Tubingen
University of Würzburg

GREECE
National and Capodistrian University
of Athens

IRELAND
University of Dublin, Trinity College

ISRAEL
The Hebrew University of Jerusalem

ITALY
University of Rome

JAPAN
The University of Tokyo

NETHERLANDS
University of Amsterdam

SPAIN
University of Madrid

SWEDEN
University of Stockholm

SWITZERLAND
University of Fribourg
University of Geneva

UNITED KINGDOM
University of Cambridge
University of Edinburgh
University of London
University of Oxford

APPENDIX C
Law Schools in Canada Included in the 6th Edition

PROVINCE AND LAW SCHOOL

ALBERTA

University of Alberta
Faculty of Law
Edmonton, Alberta

University of Calgary
Faculty of Law
Calgary, Alberta

BRITISH COLUMBIA

University of British Columbia
Faculty of Law
Vancouver, British Columbia

University of Victoria
Faculty of Law
Victoria, British Columbia

MANITOBA

University of Manitoba
Faculty of Law
Winnipeg, Manitoba

NOVA SCOTIA

Dalhousie University
Faculty of Law
Halifax, Nova Scotia

ONTARIO

University of Ottawa
Common Law Section
Ottawa, Ontario

Queen's University
Faculty of Law
Kingston, Ontario

University of Toronto
Faculty of Law
Toronto, Ontario

University of Western Ontario
Faculty of Law
London, Ontario

University of Windsor
Faculty of Law
Windsor, Ontario

York University
Osgoode Hall Law School
Downsview, Ontario

QUEBEC

McGill University
Faculty of Law
Montreal, Quebec

SASKATCHEWAN

University of Saskatchewan
College of Law
Saskatoon, Saskatchewan

APPENDIX D
United States Institutions of Law Included in the 6th Edition

STATE AND LAW SCHOOL

ALABAMA
University of Alabama
Samford University

ARIZONA
University of Arizona
Arizona State University

ARKANSAS
University of Arkansas, Fayetteville
University of Arkansas at Little Rock

CALIFORNIA
University of California, Berkeley
University of California, Davis
University of California, Los Angeles
University of California, San Francisco
California Western School of Law
Golden Gate University
Loyola Law School
McGeorge School of Law
Pepperdine University
University of San Diego
University of San Francisco
University of Santa Clara
University of Southern California
Southwestern University
Stanford University
Whittier College

COLORADO
University of Colorado
University of Denver

CONNECTICUT
Bridgeport School of Law
   at Quinnipac College
University of Connecticut
Yale University

DELAWARE
Delaware Law School of Widener University

DISTRICT OF COLUMBIA
American University
Catholic University of America
District of Columbia School of Law
Georgetown University
George Washington University
Howard University

FLORIDA
University of Florida
Florida State University
University of Miami
Nova University
Stetson University

GEORGIA
Emory University
Georgia State University
University of Georgia
Mercer University

HAWAII
University of Hawaii at Manoa

IDAHO
University of Idaho

ILLINOIS
University of Chicago
De Paul University
University of Illinois
Illinois Institute of Technology
John Marshall Law School
Loyola University
Northern Illinois University
Northwestern University
Southern Illinois University

INDIANA
Indiana University, Bloomington
Indiana University, Indianapolis
University of Notre Dame
Valparaiso University

IOWA
Drake University
University of Iowa

KANSAS
University of Kansas
Washburn University of Topeka

KENTUCKY
University of Kentucky
University of Louisville
Northern Kentucky University

STATE AND LAW SCHOOL

LOUISIANA
Louisiana State University
Loyola University
Southern University
Tulane University

MAINE
University of Maine

MARYLAND
University of Baltimore
University of Maryland

MASSACHUSETTS
Boston College
Boston University
Harvard University
New England School of Law
Northeastern University
Suffolk University
Western New England College

MICHIGAN
University of Detroit Mercy School of Law
Detroit College of Law
University of Michigan
Thomas M. Cooley Law School
Wayne State University

MINNESOTA
Hamline University
University of Minnesota
William Mitchell College of Law

MISSISSIPPI
University of Mississippi
Mississippi College School of Law

MISSOURI
University of Missouri, Columbia
University of Missouri, Kansas City
Saint Louis University
Washington University

MONTANA
University of Montana

NEBRASKA
Creighton University
University of Nebraska

NEW HAMPSHIRE
Franklin Pierce Law Center

NEW JERSEY
Rutgers, State University, Camden
Rutgers, State University, Newark
Seton Hall University

NEW MEXICO
University of New Mexico

NEW YORK
Albany Law School
Brooklyn Law School
Cardozo School of Law (Yeshiva University)
Columbia University
Cornell University
Fordham University
Hofstra University School of Law
City University of New York Law School
    at Queens College
State University of New York at Buffalo
New York Law School
New York University
Pace University
St. John's University
Syracuse University
Touro College

NORTH CAROLINA
Campbell University
Duke University
University of North Carolina
North Carolina Central University
Wake Forest University

NORTH DAKOTA
University of North Dakota

STATE AND LAW SCHOOL

OHIO
University of Akron
Capital University
Case Western Reserve University
University of Cincinnati
Cleveland State University
University of Dayton
Ohio Northern University
Ohio State University
University of Toledo

OKLAHOMA
University of Oklahoma
Oklahoma City University
University of Tulsa

OREGON
Lewis and Clark Law School
University of Oregon
Williamette University

PENNSYLVANIA
Dickinson School of Law
Duquesne University
University of Pennsylvania
University of Pittsburgh
Temple University
Villanova University
Widener University at Harrisburg

SOUTH CAROLINA
University of South Carolina

SOUTH DAKOTA
University of South Dakota

TENNESSEE
Memphis State University
University of Tennessee
Vanderbilt University

TEXAS
Baylor University

TEXAS (Continued)
University of Houston
St. Mary's University of San Antonio
Southern Methodist University
South Texas College of Law
University of Texas
Texas Southern University
Texas Tech University

UTAH
Brigham Young University
University of Utah

VERMONT
Vermont Law School

VIRGINIA
George Mason University
University of Richmond
University of Virginia
Washington and Lee University
College of William and Mary

WASHINGTON
Gonzaga University
University of Puget Sound
University of Washington

WEST VIRGINIA
West Virginia University

WISCONSIN
Marquette University
University of Wisconsin

WYOMING
University of Wyoming

COMMONWEALTH OF PUERTO RICO
Catholic University of Puerto Rico
Inter American University of Puerto Rico
University of Puerto Rico

PROVINCE AND DENTISTRY SCHOOL

ALBERTA
University of Alberta
Faculty of Dentistry

BRITISH COLUMBIA
University of British Columbia
Faculty of Dentistry

MANITOBA
University of Manitoba
Faculty of Dentistry

NOVA SCOTIA
Dalhousie University
Faculty of Dentistry

ONTARIO
University of Toronto
Faculty of Dentistry
University of Western Ontario
Faculty of Dentistry

QUEBEC
Université Laval,
Ecole de Médecine Dentaire
McGill University
Faculty of Dentistry
Université de Montréal,
Faculté de Médecine Dentaire

SASKATCHEWAN
University of Saskatchewan
College of Dentistry

APPENDIX F
United States Institutions of Dentistry Included in the 6th Edition

STATE AND DENTAL SCHOOL

ALABAMA
University of Alabama
School of Dentistry

CALIFORNIA
University of California, Los Angeles
School of Dentistry
University of California, San Francisco
School of Dentistry
Loma Linda University
School of Dentistry
University of the Pacific
School of Dentistry
University of Southern California
School of Dentistry

COLORADO
University of Colorado
School of Dentistry

CONNECTICUT
University of Connecticut
School of Dental Medicine

DISTRICT OF COLUMBIA
Howard University
College of Dentistry

FLORIDA
University of Florida
College of Dentistry

GEORGIA
Medical College of Georgia
School of Dentistry

ILLINOIS
University of Illinois at the Medical Center,
Chicago College of Dentistry
Northwestern University
Dental School
Southern Illinois University at Edwardsville
School of Dental Medicine

INDIANA
Indiana University
School of Dentistry

IOWA
The University of Iowa
College of Dentistry

KENTUCKY
University of Kentucky
College of Dentistry
University of Louisville
School of Dentistry

LOUISIANA
Louisiana State University
School of Dentistry

MARYLAND
University of Maryland at Baltimore
Baltimore College of Dental Surgery
Dental School

MASSACHUSETTS
Boston University
Henry M. Goldman School of
Graduate Dentistry
Harvard School of Dental Medicine
Tufts University
School of Dental Medicine

MICHIGAN
University of Detroit Mercy
School of Dentistry
The University of Michigan
School of Dentistry

MINNESOTA
University of Minnesota
School of Dentistry

MISSISSIPPI
University of Mississippi
School of Dentistry

MISSOURI
University of Missouri
Kansas City School of Dentistry
Washington University
School of Dental Medicine

STATE AND DENTAL SCHOOL

NEBRASKA
Creighton University
Boyne School of Dental Science
University of Nebraska Medical Center
Lincoln College of Dentistry

NEW JERSEY
New Jersey Dental School
University of Medicine and Dentistry
of New Jersey

NEW YORK
Columbia University
School of Dental and Oral Surgery
New York University
College of Dentistry
State University of New York at Buffalo
School of Dentistry
State University of New York at Stony Brook
School of Dental Medicine

NORTH CAROLINA
University of North Carolina
School of Dentistry

OHIO
Case Western Reserve University
School of Dentistry
The Ohio State University
College of Dentistry

OKLAHOMA
University of Oklahoma
College of Dentistry

OREGON
University of Oregon Health Sciences Center
School of Dentistry

PENNSYLVANIA
University of Pennsylvania
School of Dental Medicine
University of Pittsburgh
School of Dental Medicine
Temple University
School of Dentistry

SOUTH CAROLINA
Medical University of South Carolina
College of Dental Medicine

TENNESSEE
Meharry Medical College
School of Dentistry
University of Tennessee
College of Dentistry

TEXAS
Baylor College of Dentistry
University of Texas Health Sciences Center
at Houston, Dental Branch
University of Texas Dental School
at San Antonio

VIRGINIA
Virginia Commonwealth University
Medical College of Virginia
School of Dentistry

WASHINGTON
University of Washington
School of Dentistry

WEST VIRGINIA
West Virginia University
School of Dentistry

WISCONSIN
Marquette University
School of Dentistry

PUERTO RICO
University of Puerto Rico
School of Dentistry

PROVINCE AND MEDICAL SCHOOL

ALBERTA
University of Alberta
Faculty of Medicine
University of Calgary
Faculty of Medicine

BRITISH COLUMBIA
University of British Columbia
Faculty of Medicine

MANITOBA
University of Manitoba
Faculty of Medicine

NEWFOUNDLAND
Memorial University of Newfoundland
School of Medicine

NOVA SCOTIA
Dalhousie University
Faculty of Medicine

ONTARIO
McMaster University
School of Medicine
University of Ottawa
School of Medicine
Queen's University
Faculty of Medicine
University of Toronto
Faculty of Medicine
University of Western Ontario
Faculty of Medicine

QUEBEC
Laval University
Faculty of Medicine
McGill University
Faculty of Medicine
University of Montreal
Faculty of Medicine
University of Sherbrooke
Faculty of Medicine

SASKATCHEWAN
University of Saskatchewan
College of Medicine

APPENDIX H
International Medical Institutions Included in the 6th Edition

COUNTRY AND MEDICAL SCHOOL

AUSTRIA
University of Vienna

BELGIUM
Free University of Brussels
Catholic University of Louvain

FRANCE
University of Aix-Marseilles II
University of Picardie (Amiens)
University of Angers
University of Besancon
University of Bordeaux II
University of Caen
University of Clermont-Ferrand
University of Dijon
Scientific and Medical University
(University of Grenoble I)
Catholic Faculties of Lille
(Faculte Libre de Medecine)
University of Law and Health Sciences
(Lille II)
University of Limoges
University Claude-Bernard (Lyons I)
University of Montpellier I
University of Nancy I
University of Nantes
University of Nice
Paris (University Medical and Academic
Departments)
U. of Paris V, VI, VII, XI, XII, XIII
University of Poitiers
University of Reims
University of Rennes I
University of Rouen
University of Saint-Etienne
Louis Pasteur University (Strasbourg I)
University Paul-Sabatier (Toulouse III)
University of Tours

FEDERAL REPUBLIC OF GERMANY
Rhemish Friedrich-Wilhelm University of
Bonn
Friedrich Alexander University of
Erlangen-Nuremberg
Johann Wolfgang Goethe University
of Frankfurt
Albert Ludwig University of Freiburg
Georg August University of Göttingen
University of Hamburg

FEDERAL REPUBLIC OF GERMANY
Rupert Charles University of Heidelberg
Johannes Gutenberg University of Mainz
Philipps University of Marburg
Ludwig Maximilian University of Munich
University of Munster
Eberhard Karl University of Tubingen
University of Würzburg

IRELAND
Royal College of Surgeons in Ireland

ISRAEL
The Hebrew University of Jerusalem

ITALY
University of Rome

JAPAN
Keio University
Tokyo Medical and Dental University

NETHERLANDS
University of Amsterdam
Leiden State University

SWEDEN
University of Stockholm

SWITZERLAND
University of Geneva
University of Zurich

UNITED KINGDOM
University of Cambridge
University of Edinburgh
University of London
Charing Cross Hospital Medical School
Guy's Hospital Medical School
King's College Hospital Medical School
London Hospital Medical College
The Middlesex Hospital Medical School
Royal Free Hospital School of Medicine
St. Bartholomew's Hospital Medical College
St. George's Hospital Medical School
St. Mary's Hospital Medical School
St. Thomas's Hospital Medical School
University College Hospital Medical School
Westminster Medical School
University of Oxford

APPENDIX I
United States Institutions of Medicine Included in the 6th Edition

STATE AND MEDICAL SCHOOL

ALABAMA
University of Alabama
School of Medicine
University of South Alabama
College of Medicine

ARIZONA
The University of Arizona
College of Medicine

ARKANSAS
The University of Arkansas
School of Medicine

CALIFORNIA
Loma Linda University
School of Medicine
Stanford University
School of Medicine
University of California, Davis
School of Medicine
University of California, Irvine
California College of Medicine
University of California, Los Angeles
School of Medicine
University of California, San Diego
School of Medicine
University of California, San Francisco
School of Medicine
University of Southern California
School of Medicine

COLORADO
University of Colorado
School of Medicine

CONNECTICUT
University of Connecticut
School of Medicine
Yale University
School of Medicine

DISTRICT OF COLUMBIA
Georgetown University
School of Medicine
The George Washington University
School of Medicine and Health Sciences
Howard University
College of Medicine

FLORIDA
University of Florida
College of Medicine
University of Miami
School of Medicine
University of South Florida
College of Medicine

GEORGIA
Emory University
School of Medicine
Medical College of Georgia
School of Medicine
Mercer University
School of Medicine
Morehouse College
School of Medicine

HAWAII
University of Hawaii
School of Medicine

ILLINOIS
Loyola University of Chicago
Stritch School of Medicine
Northwestern University
Medical School
University of Health Sciences
The Chicago Medical School
University of Illinois
College of Medicine
Rush Medical College of Rush University,
Rush-Presbyterian-St. Luke's
Medical Center
Southern Illinois University
School of Medicine
The University of Chicago
Pritzker School of Medicine

STATE AND MEDICAL SCHOOL

INDIANA
Indiana University
School of Medicine

IOWA
The University of Iowa
College of Medicine

KANSAS
University of Kansas
Medical Center College of Health Sciences
and Hospital School of Medicine

KENTUCKY
University of Kentucky
College of Medicine
University of Louisville
School of Medicine-Health Sciences Center

LOUISIANA
Louisiana State University
Medical Center School of Medicine
in New Orleans
Louisiana State University
Medical Center School of Medicine
in Shreveport
Tulane University
School of Medicine

MARYLAND
The Johns Hopkins University
School of Medicine
University of Maryland
School of Medicine
Uniformed Services University
of the Health Sciences

MASSACHUSETTS
Boston University
School of Medicine
Harvard Medical School
Tufts University
School of Medicine
The University of Massachusetts
Medical School

MICHIGAN
Michigan State University
College of Human Medicine
The University of Michigan
Medical School
Wayne State University
School of Medicine

MINNESOTA
Mayo Medical School
University of Minnesota
Medical School – Minneapolis

MISSISSIPPI
University of Mississippi
School of Medicine

MISSOURI
St. Louis University
School of Medicine
The University of Missouri
Columbia School of Medicine
The University of Missouri
Kansas City School of Medicine
Washington University
School of Medicine

NEBRASKA
Creighton University
School of Medicine
The University of Nebraska
College of Medicine

NEVADA
The University of Nevada
Reno School of Medical Sciences

NEW HAMPSHIRE
Dartmouth Medical School

NEW JERSEY
University of Medicine and Dentistry of
New Jersey, New Jersey Medical School
University of Medicine and Dentistry of
New Jersey, Rutgers Medical School

STATE AND MEDICAL SCHOOL

NEW MEXICO
The University of New Mexico
School of Medicine

NEW YORK
The Albany Medical College
Albert Einstein College of Medicine of
Yeshiva University
Columbia University
College of Physicians and Surgeons
Cornell University
Medical College
Mount Sinai School of Medicine of the
City University of New York
New York Medical College
New York University
School of Medicine
State University of New York at Buffalo
School of Medicine
State University of New York,
Downstate Medical Center
College of Medicine
State University of New York at Stony Brook
Health Sciences Center
School of Medicine
State University of New York,
Upstate Medical Center
College of Medicine
University of Rochester
School of Medicine and Dentistry

NORTH CAROLINA
The Bowman Gray School of Medicine
of Wake Forest University
Duke University
School of Medicine
The University of North Carolina
School of Medicine
East Carolina University
School of Medicine

NORTH DAKOTA
University of North Dakota
School of Medicine

OHIO
Case Western Reserve University
School of Medicine
Medical College of Ohio at Toledo
The Ohio State University
College of Medicine
Northeastern Ohio Universities
College of Medicine
University of Cincinnati
College of Medicine
Wright State University
School of Medicine

OKLAHOMA
University of Oklahoma
College of Medicine

OREGON
University of Oregon
Medical School

PENNSYLVANIA
The Hahnemann University
School of Medicine, Philadelphia
Jefferson Medical College
of Thomas Jefferson University
The Medical College of Pennsylvania
The Pennsylvania State University
College of Medicine
The Milton S. Hershey Medical Center
Temple University of the Commonwealth
System of Higher Education
School of Medicine
University of Pennsylvania
School of Medicine
The University of Pittsburgh
School of Medicine

PUERTO RICO
Universidad Central del Caribe
School of Medicine
Ponce School of Medicine
The University of Puerto Rico
Medical Sciences Campus
School of Medicine

STATE AND MEDICAL SCHOOL

RHODE ISLAND
Brown University
Program in Medicine

SOUTH CAROLINA
Medical University of South Carolina
College of Medicine
University of South Carolina
School of Medicine

SOUTH DAKOTA
The University of South Dakota
School of Medicine

TENNESSEE
East Tennessee State University
College of Medicine
Meharry Medical College
School of Medicine
The University of Tennessee
Center for the Health Sciences
College of Medicine
Vanderbilt University
School of Medicine

TEXAS
Baylor College of Medicine
Texas Tech University
School of Medicine
The University of Texas
Medical Branch at Galveston
School of Medicine
The University of Texas
Health Science Center at San Antonio
Medical School
The University of Texas
Health Science Center at Dallas
Southwestern Medical School
Texas A&M University
College of Medicine
The University of Texas
Medical School at Houston

UTAH
University of Utah
College of Medicine

VERMONT
University of Vermont
College of Medicine

VIRGINIA
Eastern Virginia Medical School
Medical College of Virginia
School of Medicine
of Virginia Commonwealth University
University of Virginia
School of Medicine

WASHINGTON
University of Washington
School of Medicine

WEST VIRGINIA
West Virginia University
School of Medicine
Marshall University
School of Medicine

WISCONSIN
The Medical College of Wisconsin
University of Wisconsin
Medical School

APPENDIX J
United States Institutions of Veterinary Medicine Included in the 6th Edition

ALABAMA
Auburn University, Auburn
School of Veterinary Medicine

Tuskegee University, Tuskegee
School of Veterinary Medicine

CALIFORNIA
University of California, Davis
School of Veterinary Medicine

COLORADO
Colorado State University, Fort Collins
College of Veterinary Medicine and
Biomedical Sciences

FLORIDA
University of Florida, Gainesville
College of Veterinary Medicine

GEORGIA
University of Georgia, Athens
College of Veterinary Medicine

ILLINOIS
University of Illinois, Urbana
College of Veterinary Medicine

INDIANA
Purdue University, Lafayette
School of Veterinary Science and Medicine

IOWA
Iowa State University of Science and
Technology, Ames
College of Veterinary Medicine

KANSAS
Kansas State University, Manhattan
College of Veterinary Medicine

LOUISIANA
Louisiana State University, Baton Rouge
College of Veterinary Medicine

MASSACHUSETTS
Tufts University, Boston
School of Veterinary Medicine

MICHIGAN
Michigan State University, East Lansing
College of Veterinary Medicine

MINNESOTA
University of Minnesota, St. Paul
College of Veterinary Medicine

MISSISSIPPI
Mississippi State University, Mississippi State
College of Veterinary Medicine

MISSOURI
University of Missouri, Columbia
College of Veterinary Medicine

NEW YORK
New York State Veterinary College
at Cornell University, Ithaca

NORTH CAROLINA
North Carolina State University, Raleigh
School of Veterinary Medicine

OKLAHOMA
Oklahoma State University, Stillwater
College of Veterinary Medicine

OHIO
The Ohio State University, Columbus
College of Veterinary Medicine

PENNSYLVANIA
University of Pennsylvania, Philadelphia
School of Veterinary Medicine

TENNESSEE
University of Tennessee, Knoxville
College of Veterinary Medicine

TEXAS
Texas A&M University, College Station
College of Veterinary Medicine

VIRGINIA
Virginia Polytechnic Institute and State U.
Blackburg Virginia-Maryland Regional
College of Veterinary Medicine

WASHINGTON
Washington State University, Pullman
College of Veterinary Medicine

WISCONSIN
University of Wisconsin, Madison
School of Veterinary Medicine

APPENDIX K
United States Institutions of Nursing Included in the 6th Edition

STATE AND NURSING SCHOOL

ALABAMA
University of Alabama in Birmingham

ARIZONA
Arizona State University
University of Arizona

ARKANSAS
University of Arkansas, Little Rock

CALIFORNIA
California State University, Fresno
California State University, Los Angeles
Loma Linda University
University of California, Los Angeles
University of California, San Francisco

COLORADO
University of Colorado, Denver

CONNECTICUT
University of Connecticut (Storrs)
Yale University

DELAWARE
University of Delaware, Newark

DISTRICT OF COLUMBIA
Catholic University of America

FLORIDA
University of Florida

GEORGIA
Emory University
Medical College of Georgia

ILLINOIS
De Paul University
Loyola University of Chicago
Northern Illinois University
Rush University
University of Illinois, Chicago

INDIANA
Indiana University, Indianapolis

IOWA
University of Iowa

KANSAS
University of Kansas, Kansas City

KENTUCKY
University of Kentucky

LOUISIANA
Louisiana State University, New Orleans

MARYLAND
University of Maryland, Baltimore

MASSACHUSETTS
Boston College

MICHIGAN
University of Michigan, Ann Arbor
Wayne State University

MINNESOTA
University of Minnesota, Minneapolis

MISSISSIPPI
University of Southern Mississippi

MISSOURI
St. Louis University
University of Missouri, Columbia

NEBRASKA
University of Nebraska, Omaha

NEW JERSEY
Rutgers University, The State University
of New Jersey

STATE AND NURSING SCHOOL

NEW YORK
Adelphi University
Columbia University
Columbia University, Teachers College
Hunter College of the City University
    of New York
New York University
The Sage Colleges
State University of New York (Binghamton)
State University of New York at Buffalo
Syracuse University
University of Rochester

NORTH CAROLINA
University of North Carolina, Chapel Hill
    School of Nursing
University of North Carolina, Chapel Hill
    School of Public Health

OHIO
Case Western Reserve University
Ohio State University (Columbus)
University of Cincinnati

OKLAHOMA
University of Oklahoma, Oklahoma City

OREGON
The Oregon Health Sciences University
    (Portland)

PENNSYLVANIA
The Pennsylvania State University
    (University Park)
University of Pennsylvania
University of Pittsburgh (Pittsburgh)

PUERTO RICO
University of Puerto Rico, San Juan

SOUTH CAROLINA
University of South Carolina

TENNESSEE
University of Tennessee, Memphis
Vanderbilt University

TEXAS
Texas Woman's University
University of Texas at Austin
University of Texas Health Science Center
    at Houston
University of Texas, San Antonio

UTAH
Brigham Young University
University of Utah

VIRGINIA
Virginia Commonwealth University, Richmond
University of Virginia

WASHINGTON
University of Washington

WISCONSIN
Marquette University
University of Wisconsin, Madison
University of Wisconsin, Milwaukee

APPENDIX L
United States Institutions of Optometry Included in the 6th Edition

STATE AND OPTOMETRY SCHOOL

ALABAMA
University of Alabama in Birmingham
School of Optometry/The Medical Center

CALIFORNIA
Southern California College of Optometry
University of California, Berkeley
School of Optometry

ILLINOIS
Illinois College of Optometry

INDIANA
Indiana University
School of Optometry

MASSACHUSETTS
New England College of Optometry

MICHIGAN
Ferris State College
College of Optometry

MISSOURI
University of Missouri, St. Louis
School of Optometry

NEW YORK
State University of New York State
College of Optometry

OHIO
The Ohio State University
College of Optometry

OKLAHOMA
Northeastern State University
College of Optometry

OREGON
Pacific University
College of Optometry

PENNSYLVANIA
Pennsylvania College of Optometry

PUERTO RICO
Inter American University of Puerto Rico

TENNESSEE
Southern College of Optometry

TEXAS
University of Houston
College of Optometry

APPENDIX M
Canadian Institutions of Pharmacy Included in the 6th Edition

PROVINCE AND PHARMACY SCHOOL

ALBERTA
Faculty of Pharmacy & Pharmaceutical
Sciences
University of Alberta
Edmonton, Alberta

BRITISH COLUMBIA
Faculty of Pharmaceutical Sciences
University of British Columbia
Vancouver, British Columbia

MANITOBA
Faculty of Pharmacy
University of Manitoba
Winnipeg, Manitoba

NOVA SCOTIA
College of Pharmacy
Dalhousie University
Halifax, Nova Scotia

ONTARIO
Faculty of Pharmacy
University of Toronto
Toronto, Ontario

QUEBEC
Ecole de Pharmacie
Université Laval
Quebec, Quebec
Faculte de Pharmacie
Université de Montréal
Montreal, Quebec

SASKATCHEWAN
College of Pharmacy
University of Saskatchewan
Saskatoon, Saskatchewan

STATE AND PHARMACY SCHOOL

ALABAMA
Auburn University
School of Pharmacy
Samford University
School of Pharmacy

ARIZONA
University of Arizona
School of Pharmacy

ARKANSAS
University of Arkansas for Medical Sciences
College of Pharmacy

CALIFORNIA
University of California, San Francisco
School of Pharmacy
University of the Pacific
School of Pharmacy
University of Southern California
School of Pharmacy

COLORADO
University of Colorado
School of Pharmacy

CONNECTICUT
University of Connecticut
School of Pharmacy

DISTRICT OF COLUMBIA
Howard University
College of Pharmacy and
Pharmacal Sciences

FLORIDA
Florida Agricultural and Mechanical University
School of Pharmacy
University of Florida
College of Pharmacy
J. Hillis Miller Health Center

GEORGIA
Mercer University Southern
School of Pharmacy
University of Georgia
School of Pharmacy

IDAHO
Idaho State University
College of Pharmacy

ILLINOIS
University of Illinois at the Medical Center,
Chicago College of Pharmacy

INDIANA
Butler University
College of Pharmacy
Purdue University
School of Pharmacy and
Pharmacal Sciences

IOWA
Drake University
College of Pharmacy
The University of Iowa
College of Pharmacy

KANSAS
University of Kansas
School of Pharmacy

KENTUCKY
University of Kentucky
College of Pharmacy

LOUISIANA
Northeast Louisiana University
School of Pharmacy
Xavier University of Louisiana
College of Pharmacy

MARYLAND
University of Maryland
School of Pharmacy

MASSACHUSETTS
Massachusetts College of Pharmacy
Northeastern University
College of Pharmacy and Allied Health
Professions

MICHIGAN
Ferris State College
School of Pharmacy
University of Michigan
College of Pharmacy
Wayne State University
College of Pharmacy and Allied Health
Professions

STATE AND PHARMACY SCHOOL

MINNESOTA
University of Minnesota
College of Pharmacy

MISSISSIPPI
University of Mississippi
School of Pharmacy

MISSOURI
St. Louis College of Pharmacy
University of Missouri, Kansas City
School of Pharmacy

MONTANA
University of Montana
School of Pharmacy

NEBRASKA
Creighton University
School of Pharmacy
University of Nebraska
College of Pharmacy

NEW JERSEY
Rutgers, The State University of New Jersey
College of Pharmacy

NEW MEXICO
University of New Mexico
College of Pharmacy

NEW YORK
Long Island University
Arnold and Marie Schwartz
College of Pharmacy and Health Sciences
St. John's University
College of Pharmacy and Allied Health
Professions
State University of New York at Buffalo
School of Pharmacy
Union University
Albany College of Pharmacy

NORTH CAROLINA
Campbell University
School of Pharmacy
The University of North Carolina at Chapel Hill
School of Pharmacy

NORTH DAKOTA
North Dakota State University
College of Pharmacy

OHIO
Ohio Northern University
College of Pharmacy
Ohio State University
College of Pharmacy
University of Cincinnati
College of Pharmacy
University of Toledo
College of Pharmacy

OKLAHOMA
Southwestern Oklahoma State University
School of Pharmacy
University of Oklahoma
College of Pharmacy

OREGON
Oregon State University
School of Pharmacy

PENNSYLVANIA
Duquesne University
School of Pharmacy
Philadelphia College of Pharmacy
and Science
Temple University
School of Pharmacy
University of Pittsburgh
School of Pharmacy

PUERTO RICO
University of Puerto Rico
College of Pharmacy

RHODE ISLAND
University of Rhode Island
College of Pharmacy

SOUTH CAROLINA
Medical University of South Carolina
College of Pharmacy
University of South Carolina
College of Pharmacy

STATE AND PHARMACY SCHOOL

SOUTH DAKOTA
South Dakota State University
College of Pharmacy

TENNESSEE
University of Tennessee
Center for the Health Sciences
College of Pharmacy

TEXAS
Texas Southern University
School of Pharmacy
University of Houston
College of Pharmacy
The University of Texas at Austin
College of Pharmacy

UTAH
University of Utah
College of Pharmacy

VIRGINIA
Virginia Commonwealth University
School of Pharmacy Medical College
of Virginia

WASHINGTON
University of Washington
School of Pharmacy
Washington State University
College of Pharmacy

WEST VIRGINIA
West Virginia University
School of Pharmacy Medical Center

WISCONSIN
University of Wisconsin, Madison
School of Pharmacy

WYOMING
University of Wyoming
School of Pharmacy

APPENDIX O
United States Institutions of Public Health Included in the 6th Edition

STATE AND PUBLIC HEALTH SCHOOL

ALABAMA
University of Alabama in Birmingham

CALIFORNIA
Loma Linda University
University of California, Berkeley
University of California, Los Angeles

CONNECTICUT
Yale University

HAWAII
University of Hawaii

ILLINOIS
University of Illinois, Chicago

LOUISIANA
Tulane University

MARYLAND
The Johns Hopkins University

MASSACHUSETTS
Boston University
Harvard University
University of Massachusetts, Amherst

MICHIGAN
University of Michigan, Ann Arbor

MINNESOTA
University of Minnesota, Minneapolis

NEW YORK
Columbia University

NORTH CAROLINA
University of North Carolina, Chapel Hill

OKLAHOMA
University of Oklahoma, Oklahoma City

PENNSYLVANIA
University of Pittsburgh

PUERTO RICO
University of Puerto Rico, San Juan

SOUTH CAROLINA
University of South Carolina

TEXAS
University of Texas, Houston

WASHINGTON
University of Washington